Classroom Discourse Analysis

Open Linguistics Series

Series Editor
Robin Fawcett, Cardiff University

The series is 'open' in two related ways. First, it is not confined to works associated with any one school of linguistics. For almost two decades the series has played a significant role in establishing and maintaining the present climate of 'openness' in linguistics, and we intend to maintain this tradition. However, we particularly welcome works which explore the nature and use of language through modelling its potential for use in social contexts, or through a cognitive model of language – or indeed a combination of the two.

The series is also 'open' in the sense that it welcomes works that open out 'core' linguistics in various ways: to give a central place to the description of natural texts and the use of corpora; to encompass discourse 'above the sentence'; to relate language to other semiotic systems; to apply linguistics in fields such as education, language pathology and law; and to explore the areas that lie between linguistics and its neighbouring disciplines such as semiotics, psychology, sociology, philosophy, and cultural and literary studies.

Continuum also publishes a series that offers a forum for primarily functional descriptions of languages or parts of languages – *Functional Descriptions of Language*, Relations between linguistics and computing are covered in the *Communication in Artificial Intelligence* series, two series, *Advances in Applied Linguistics* and *Communication in Public Life*, publish books in applied linguistics and the series *Modern Pragmatics in Theory and Practice* publishes both social and cognitive perspectives on the making of meaning in language use. We also publish a range of introductory textbooks on topics in linguistics, semiotics and deaf studies.

Recent titles in this series

Construing Experience through Meaning: A Language-based Approach to Cognition,
   M. A. K. Halliday and Christian M. I. M. Matthiessen
Culturally Speaking: Managing Rapport through Talk across Cultures, Helen Spencer-Oatey (ed.)
Educating Eve: The 'Language Instinct' Debate, Geoffrey Sampson
Empirical Linguistics, Geoffrey Sampson
Genre and Institutions: Social Processes in the Workplace and School, Frances Christie and
   J. R. Martin (eds)
The Intonation Systems of English, Paul Tench
Language Policy in Britain and France: The Processes of Policy, Dennis Ager
*Language Relations across Bering Strait: Reappraising the Archaeological and Linguistic
   Evidence*, Michael Fortescue
Learning through Language in Early Childhood, Clare Painter
Pedagogy and the Shaping of Consciousness: Linguistic and Social Processes, Frances Christie (ed.)
Register Analysis: Theory and Practice, Mohsen Ghadessy (ed.)
Relations and Functions within and around Language, Peter II. Fries, Michael Cummings,
   David Lockwood and William Spruiell (eds)
Researching Language in Schools and Communities: Functional Linguistic Perspectives,
   Len Unsworth (ed.)
Summary Justice: Judges Address Juries, Paul Robertshaw
Syntactic Analysis and Description: A Constructional Approach, David G. Lockwood
Thematic Developments in English Texts, Mohsen Ghadessy (ed.)
Ways of Saying: Ways of Meaning. Selected Papers of Ruqaiya Hasan. Carmen Cloran,
   David Butt and Geoffrey Williams (eds)
Words, Meaning and Vocabulary: An Introduction to Modern English Lexicology, Howard
   Jackson and Etienne Zé Amvela
Working with Discourse: Meaning beyond the Clause, J. R. Martin and David Rose

Classroom Discourse Analysis

A Functional Perspective

Frances Christie

continuum
LONDON • NEW YORK

Continuum
The Tower Building, 11 York Road, London, SE1 7NX
15 East 26th Street, New York, NY 10010

First published 2002
This paperback edition published 2005

© Frances Christie 2002

British Library Cataloguing-in-Publication Data
A catalogue record for this book is available from the British Library.

Hb ISBN 0–8264–5373–2
Pb ISBN 0–8264–7605–8

Library of Congress Cataloging-in-Publication Data
Christie, Frances.
    Classroom discourse analysis: a functional perspective / Frances Christie.
        p. cm. — (Open linguistics series)
    Includes bibliographical references (p.) and index.
    ISBN 0–8264–5373–2
    1. Communication in education. 2. Interaction analysis in education. 3. Discourse
analysis. I. Title. II. Series.

    LB1033.5 .C45 2002
    371.102′2—dc21

                                                                    2002071645

Typeset by BookEns Ltd.
Printed and bound in Great Britain by MPG, Bodmin, Cornwall

Contents

List of figures

List of tables

Preface

In writing this book I am indebted to a number of people from whom I have learned a great deal over the years. Among these I would number first Michael Halliday and Jim Martin, who originally taught me systemic functional theory, and from both of whom I have continued to learn. My debt to Basil Bernstein is also considerable, and it is a source of regret to me that he did not live to see the book completed. He was, however, aware that I was writing it and, while I was in London during the last months of his life, he was encouraging to me in my efforts. I am also indebted to others in London, where I spent some study leave while I started the book. First of all those in London, I must mention Janet White, who generously gave me a home to stay in, and who was always available with stimulating company and conversation. Thanks too are due to Euan Reid and his colleagues in the Culture, Communication and Society Group at the Institute of Education, University of London, where I spent three months. Among other things, they gave me access to an office and a library, and were available to talk, while generously leaving me to my own pursuits. Ralph Adendorff, Bill Tyler and Parlo Singh, among others, read some chapters in draft, and I was grateful for their comments.

The book itself emerges from many years of collecting and analysing classroom language across all school years, across many school subjects and in three different Australian cities. What I present here is thus a very small sample drawn from a considerable body of data. While the various schools, teachers and students must remain anonymous, I must record my warm thanks to the many people who have willingly allowed me access to so many classrooms. It is a great privilege to go into other people's classrooms and record and study what goes on in them.

Finally, my thanks go to Chris Ulbrick, who helped with the preparation of some of the figures in the book, and who was always a patient source of assistance and advice over many matters.

Frances Christie

Acknowledgements

Some of the classroom texts used in this book have been used elsewhere. Sometimes they appeared in extended length in another source, and sometimes different extracts from the classroom texts were used.

Texts used in Chapter 4 appeared in:

F. Christie (1997), 'Curriculum macrogenres as forms of initiation into a culture', in F. Christie and J. R. Martin (eds), *Genre and Institutions: Social Processes in the Workplace and School*. London and Washington, DC: Cassell, 134–60.

F. Christie (1998), 'Science and apprenticeship: the pedagogic discourse', in J. R. Martin and R. Veel (eds), *The Language of Science*. London: Routledge, 152–77.

The text in Chapter 5 was used in:

F. Christie (2000), 'The language of classroom interaction and learning', in L. Unsworth (ed.), *Researching Language in Schools and Communities: Functional Linguistic Perspectives*. London and Washington, DC: Cassell Academic, 184–203.

1 A theoretical framework

Introduction

Classroom discourse analysis has been a major theme in much research – linguistic, applied linguistic and educational – for some years now. Sinclair and Coulthard (1975: 15) suggested that an interest in classroom language studies dated from the 1940s. Since the 1960s and early 1970s on, a great deal of research into many areas of discourse, including classroom discourse, has been undertaken in the English-speaking world. This development paralleled the upsurge of scholarly interest in linguistics and applied linguistics in the same period, while the invention of the tape recorder, later augmented by the emergence of cheap video recording facilities, rendered much more accessible than hitherto the whole enterprise of recording talk and analysing it. Very various are the models of classroom discourse that have emerged, some drawing on one or more of several traditions of linguistics, others on ethnographic approaches, others on various psychological approaches. Others still have been reasonably eclectic in their methodologies, pursuing, with whatever tools seemed appropriate, what have been seen as the goals of educational and/or pedagogical research of various kinds.

Just as the approaches and methodologies in classroom language analysis have been various, so too have been the justifications offered for such research. Sinclair and Couthard's (1975: 6) study made clear that their interest was primarily to take an identified field of discourse and subject it to study in order to understand more about the nature of discourse. In other words, theirs was not a piece of educational research, in that there was no intention to improve the nature of educational practices, for their focus, as linguists, was rather different. (They did, however, conclude the report of their work with a section reflecting on some of the possible applications of their findings, including educational applications. In addition, Sinclair and Brazil in 1982, wrote a book exploring *Teacher Talk* in some detail.) The work of Flanders (1970) and that of Bellack (Bellack *et al.*, 1966) predated by a few years that of Sinclair and Coulthard, and it was quite deliberately focused on the nature of classroom activity with a view to understanding and ultimately improving classroom work. Barnes (Barnes *et al.*, 1971; Barnes and Todd, 1977) was also concerned to understand the nature of classroom talk, as well as the possibilities of small group talk in class settings, and his studies were intended to lead to improvements in practice. Mehan (1979), as influential in his way as all the other researchers just mentioned, developed an important ethnographic study, in which he explored how classroom teaching and learning were structured.

Since the 1970s many other studies, linguistic, applied linguistic, ethnographic, ethnomethodological and what I shall term 'loosely educational' in character, have proliferated. Very useful reviews of research into classroom discourse have been offered, among others, by Cazden (1988), Edwards and Westgate (1994), Hicks (1995) and Lemke (1998). Over the years, what constitute the concerns of discourse analysis generally, and those of classroom discourse in particular, have changed. This has been partly because of changed perceptions about what the purposes should be of such analysis. It has also partly been because new methods of discourse analysis, more generally, have been forged to meet the challenges of articulating what might be seen as an adequate account of language in the social construction of experience. Gee (1999) offers such an account of discourse analysis, stating that, if asked to propose a primary function of human language, he would offer not one, but two: 'to scaffold the performance of social activities (whether play or work or both) and to scaffold human affiliation within cultures and social groups and institutions' (Gee, 1999: 1). Basing his discussion on this general position, he goes on to develop an account of discourse analysis whose major preoccupation is with discourse as an instrument for the social construction of experience – a general principle that applies whether he is examining classroom discourse or any other kind.

The account of classroom discourse analysis I shall offer, while differing in some ways from earlier studies, owes a great deal to many of the earlier researchers who have worked in the broad area, helping to give definition and direction to what has become a major area of inquiry. It must be held a major area of inquiry if for no other reason than that so much significance now attaches to children spending years in schools. In all developed societies most children now spend significant periods of their lives in school, while in the developing world, where patterns of school attendance are often less regular, there is at least an official aspiration that children will attend school, and indeed many children do so. In all contemporary societies, developed and developing, educational provision rates a sizeable share of the national budget. So significant an institution as schooling requires some serious reflection and discussion, the better to understand and interpret it as a social phenomenon, and the better to provide for enhanced educational practices in the future. Furthermore, since I share at least some of the general stance adopted by Gee alluded to above, I would add that, unless we are willing to engage seriously with the discourse patterns particular to the institution of schooling, then we fail genuinely to understand it. It is in language, after all, that the business of schooling is still primarily accomplished, whether that be spoken or written and, even though language is necessarily to be understood not as some discretely independent entity, but rather as part of complex sets of interconnecting forms of human semiosis.

The purpose of this chapter is to indicate the nature of the theoretical framework adopted here, owing most to systemic functional (SF) linguistic theory (e.g., Halliday, 1994; Martin, 1992; Halliday and Matthiessen, 1999), but also making use of aspects of the sociological theories of Bernstein (e.g., 1990, 2000). I shall begin the discussion by proceeding in the next section to consider at least some of the other research that has been done into classroom discourse analysis. I shall indicate in what ways this study is informed by reference to such work, in particular its significance for a view of classroom activity as *structured experience,* and associated notions of classroom work as *social practice.* I will go on in a later section to provide a brief introduction to SF theory. A subsequent section will outline the model of classroom discourse analysis adopted, drawing on both genre theory in the SF tradition (e.g., Martin, 1992; Christie and Martin, 1997) and on Bernstein's theoretical work on pedagogic discourse (e.g., Bernstein, 1990, 2000). Adapting Bernstein's theory in order to inform the linguistic analysis undertaken, I shall suggest that pedagogic discourse can be thought of as creating *curriculum genres* and sometimes larger unities referred to as *curriculum macrogenres.* These, I shall argue, are to be analysed and understood in terms of the operation of two registers, a *first order or regulative register,* to do with the overall goals, directions, pacing and sequencing of classroom activity, and a *second order or instructional register,* to do with the particular 'content' being taught and learned. As an instance of classroom activity unfolds, I shall suggest, the two registers work in patterned ways to bring the pedagogic activity into being, to establish goals, to introduce and sequence the teaching and learning of the field of knowledge at issue, and to evaluate the success with which the knowledge is learned.

I shall conclude the chapter by offering a brief overview of the later chapters, indicating some major themes that should emerge from the overall discussion of classroom discourse analysis throughout the book. These include a concern for the nature of the pedagogic subject as apprentice, and an associated concern for the values and nature of knowledge as that is negotiated and constructed in classroom activity.

Classroom work as structured activity

One fundamental theme that runs through virtually all the work in classroom discourse analysis is the recognition it gives to behaviour, including language behaviour, as *structured experience.* The point may seem self-evident. However, such a notion is not always recognized, mainly because in the give-and-take of everyday life a great deal of the structured, even routinized, aspects of our behaviour ceases to be noticeable as we get on with the business of working and of living. Such an observation is by no means unique to classroom discourse. Casual conversation, for example, in the family or workplace, or among friends (e.g., Eggins and Slade, 1997), is also structured, as persons take up particular relationships vis-à-vis each other and negotiate some kind of experiential information, although participants in the discourse are not necessarily aware that the talk they jointly construct is so structured.

[Among those who early began to conceive classroom talk in terms of structure was Flanders (1970), who, though not a linguist, studied what he termed 'interaction analysis', the better to understand the nature of teacher interactions with students.]Flanders, and also Bellack and his colleagues, categorized patterns of interaction or talk in different ways. Flanders (1970), for instance, focused in particular on teacher talk and its consequences for students' achievements, using terms such as *Asking Questions, Giving Directions, Accepting Feeling*, and so on. These were rather general terms and often difficult to apply with certainty to different utterances. Bellack and his colleagues (1966), pursuing issues of the structured nature of classroom work rather more fully, began to conceive any lesson in more ordered and hierarchical terms. They recognized four units of analysis to which Bellack gave the names: *game, sub-game, cycle* and *move*. The *move*, though not described in linguistic terms, nonetheless had features a little like those eventually adopted by Sinclair and Coulthard, whose work was linguistic. A move could be one of four types: *Soliciting*, in which responses (verbal or non-verbal) were actively sought by the person doing the soliciting; *Responding*, involving some reciprocal relation to the Soliciting move; *Structuring*, in which pedagogical activity was set in train, either by initiating some course of action or by excluding others; and finally *Reacting*, where this was a move undertaken in reaction to any of the others.

Sinclair and Coulthard, borrowing from Halliday's theory of scale and category grammar as it was then conceived (e.g., Halliday, 1961), developed a model of classroom discourse involving a series of ranks and levels arranged in hierarchical order. Ranks at the discourse level, for example, were, in descending order: *Lesson, Transaction, Exchange, Move* and *Act*. While the whole structure was important to the overall model adopted, in practice Sinclair and Coulthard were to be remembered most for the particular character they gave to the structure of one of the Moves they identified: the so-called *Initiation, Response, Feedback* move, known as the *IRF*, or sometimes, following a similar description in Mehan's work (1979) as the *Initiation, Response, Evaluation* move, the *IRE*. The pattern, for anyone unfamiliar with it, may be represented by the following made-up example:

> T: What's the capital of France?
> Student: Paris.
> T: Correct.

The IRE pattern was to become the subject of extensive discussion for many years, causing many involved in educational research to criticize teaching practices that constrained students through use of the pattern. It also led to research into ways to generate what might be considered more open and exploratory patterns of talk, in which students would have greater opportunity to initiate and take the talk where they willed it. (See, for example, the discussion in Edwards and Westgate, 1994: 138–49, for some review of the criticisms of IRE, and some discussion of possible alternatives of classroom talk.)

More recently, some researchers (e.g., Wells, 1993, 1999; van Lier, 1996, 2000; and Mercer, 2000) have suggested the need to look more carefully at the total patterns of talk in which the IRE pattern occurs. The evidence suggests that rather than merely reject such a discourse pattern as the IRE as needlessly constraining of students, we should look at the total sequences of classroom talk (often over quite long periods of time), in order to make judgements about the relative values of these or any other patterns of discourse. What is the role of the IRE pattern in the overall structuring and negotiation of meanings in curriculum activity? Ironically, a great deal of classroom discourse analysis has had a lot to say about the structuring of talk in terms of the IRE and related moves, but it has often neglected to look at the nature of the meanings in construction, the relative roles and responsibilities of teachers and students at the time of constructing those meanings, and the placement of such patterns in the overall larger cycle of classroom work. As I have already suggested, I shall propose in this book that we think of larger units of curriculum activity as either curriculum genres or curriculum macrogenres. As I shall also argue in later chapters, a focus on the larger pedagogical unity that is the genre or the macrogenre will enable us to see how the patterns of classroom discourse emerge, develop, change and are modified over time, allowing negotiation and construction of meanings in many ways, and achieving a form of *logogenesis*, or growth and development in the text (Halliday in Halliday and Martin, 1993: 18). In the overall sequence that is the genre or macrogenre, the IRE – like many other instances of classroom discourse – often has an important, even an essential, role to play in pursuing the pedagogic goals of schooling.

Concerns with the nature of classroom talk as structured experience have been taken up by researchers other than linguists, including Mehan (1979) whose work has been already mentioned. Even the title of his book was significant – *Learning Lessons: Social Organization in the Classroom* – for it suggested the ethnographic interests he brought to bear in his study. These are interests of a kind shared by many others in the USA including, of course, Hymes (1977), famous for his work as an ethnographer of speech, Cazden (1988) with whom Mehan worked closely in preparing his book, as well as Green (e.g., Green and Kantor-Smith, 1988) and Heath (1983). Where linguists such as Sinclair and Coulthard, but also Stubbs (1976, 1986) had a concern for the language used in classrooms, ethnographers, though interested in language too, were also interested to study other aspects of behaviour in which students and teachers engaged, including for example: the routines and/or 'rules' which operated, often quite tacitly, and within which students and teachers structured their daily lives, the physical dispositions of persons in the classroom, the manner in which they moved and interacted during the school day. Mehan (1979: 126–71), for example, offered an early and very thorough account of the various modes and methods of activity required to achieve what he referred to as 'effective participation or membership in the classroom' (ibid: 127).

Ethnography overlaps with ethnomethodology, an area of work in which the concern has been to make close study of people communicating in familiar settings, including undertaking *conversational analysis,* and the object has been to bring to the surface all the many implicit conventions and understandings that must apply in order to make communication possible. Ethnomethodology (e.g., Gumperz and Hymes, 1972) has drawn attention to various kinds of 'speech events' like greetings and storytelling. In classrooms, it has examined such things as 'story time', or 'sharing time', and other classroom activities having well-defined routines, and distinct openings and closures (discussed, for example, in several chapters in Cazden, 1988). Under the influence of such figures as Goffman (1981) and Sacks (e.g., Sacks, 1992, edited by Jefferson), conversational analysis examined such things as *turn taking* and *adjacency pairs* (a term used to refer to utterances that are mutually dependent, such as a question and its answer) and, while these did not emerge from classroom discourse analysis, they have had some influence in classroom language studies. Thus, conversational analysts (reviewed by Edwards and Westgate, 1994: 115–16) have drawn attention among, other things, to the manner in which participants assume joint responsibility for the construction of conversation and, by implication at least, they have raised the possibility of other more 'open' patterns of classroom talk than are conventionally encountered in such settings.

Those who work in ethnography and/or ethnomethodology have sometimes questioned the claims of linguistic research, mainly because they suggest that a preoccupation with linguistic analysis can blind the researcher to other critically important dimensions of classroom behaviour, including the whole range of non-verbal behaviours – routines, rules and procedures for activity, physical dispositions of participants, arrangements of furniture in the classroom, uses of gesture among other things. Others, such as Barnes (1978), alluded to much earlier, was critical of what linguistic research had to offer to educational research, on the grounds that it had little of relevance to offer concerns with students learning in schools. One of the most influential of the English researchers into classrooms whose work dated from the late 1960s, Barnes (e.g., 1971) sought to record and discuss patterns of teacher interaction and also the patterns that could apply in small group talk among students (Barnes and Todd, 1977). His commentaries on the patterns of talk examined were often very perceptive, revealing for example, ways in which teachers' talk appeared to impact on students' learning, sometimes facilitating it, sometimes stifling it, while other work, most notably on students learning in small groups, also revealed a great deal of ways students could usefully learn together as they collectively build some understanding in talk. Barnes was, however, sometimes open to the charges both that the principles that lay behind his commentaries were not well motivated or explained, and that he made what appeared at times to be somewhat idiosyncratic selections from the classroom data available to him, when a more comprehensive treatment of the longer texts of which they were a part might well have led the reader to reach different conclusions. (Stubbs, 1986: 44–5, for example, wrote that there was 'no method or guiding principle' available in Barnes' work for those not as 'sensitive' in his observations about classrooms as was Barnes.) The issue of what text(s) should be selected for classroom discourse analysis, and of how best to motivate and justify the selection is in fact a very important one, both theoretically and practically, and I shall return to this below.

I earlier noted that with the passage of the years the concerns of discourse analysis generally and of classroom discourse analysis in particular have changed. The changes reflect shifts in the preoccupations of a great deal of linguistic and sociolinguistic research, all of them pointing to a greatly enhanced interest in the role of language in the social construction of experience. The influences at work in bringing about the changes have been various, drawing on several traditions of research in linguistics and sociolinguistics, social psychology, sociology, post-structuralist theories of discourse and critical discourse analysis, to name only a few. Here one can do no more than suggest some of the many influences at work. Some reflect the increasingly sophisticated accounts of linguistic theory offered in some traditions. We have already noted, for example, that Sinclair and Coulthard used a model of English grammar they took from Halliday (1961); the systemic theory to which that model was pointing was not available when Sinclair and Coulthard did their study. Over the intervening years, SF theory has been significantly extended, where this has involved development of much more comprehensive accounts of the grammar (e.g., Benson and Greaves, 1973; Fawcett, 1980; Halliday, 1994; Martin, 1992; Matthiessen, 1995; Halliday and Matthiessen, 1999) as well as developments in register theory and genre theory (e.g., Gregory and Carroll, 1978; Halliday and Hasan, 1985; Martin, 1985, 1992; Christie and Martin, 1997). Not all the SF theorists, incidentally, agree about the theoretical accounts they offer, either of the grammar or of genre and register theory. But collectively they have contributed to a significant body of theory about language as a social semiotic of a kind that was not available when the first studies of classroom discourse were undertaken.

As the linguistic theories of language and of semiosis more generally have gained in sophistication, so too has come a much enhanced sense not only of the enactment of social practices in language, but also of the construction of various ideological positionings in language. Language is never neutral, for it is necessarily involved in the realization of values and ideologies; just as it serves to realize such values and ideologies, it also serves to silence others. Such an observation has as much relevance for studies of classroom discourse as for any other discourse. Schools work with and construct ideological positionings for their pedagogic subjects. As we shall see in later chapters, various ideologies of childhood and of adolescence come into play, and these are realized differently in the discourse at different stages of schooling. They are always worthy of examination and sometimes of challenge, because they have consequences for a great deal of the ways in which pedagogic activities are enacted.

Other recent linguistic research that has contributed to the much enhanced contemporary understanding of language as a social phenomenon, and relatedly, to research into ideologies and power, includes that of Gee (1992; 1999) already alluded to, as well as that of Fairclough (1992; Chouliaraki and Fairclough, 1999), and Lemke (1995). Drawing on notions of discourse, in part as that was discussed by Foucault, in part on linguistic theories of the kind proposed by Halliday, and in part on Bernstein's sociology, Fairclough (1992: 63) defines 'discourse' as 'a mode of action, one form in which people may act upon the world and especially upon each other, as well as a mode of representation'. Importantly, for him, the definition adopted implies 'a dialectical relationship between discourse and social structure' (ibid: 64), and it enables him to go on to develop a discussion of the nature of discursive practices – practices that is, in which texts are produced, distributed and consumed in various ways (ibid: 78). Fairclough uses the theory he proposes to develop methods of discourse analysis that will allow analysis of power in social relations, and analysis of social change. In fact, Fairclough is probably best known for his work on 'critical discourse analysis', sometimes also referred to as 'critical language awareness' (Fairclough, 1992; Chouliaraki and Fairclough, 1999). A programme in 'critical discourse analysis' as Fairclough and Chouliaraki discuss it, provides tools for challenging and critiquing many contemporary social practices.

Gee (1999: 6–7), also drawing to some extent on Foucault's work, adopts the notion of 'discourse', distinguishing between what he terms discourses with a 'small and a large "D"'. A discourse with a 'little "d"' refers to the various stretches of language that constitute much of the give and take of daily life: these are those activities of language in use which interest the applied linguist, concerned to explore the 'on site' activities and enactments of identity in which language is significantly involved. The notion of a 'Discourse with a big "D"' by contrast, refers to the larger, pervasive and often invisible sets of values, beliefs and ideas with which we are positioned in various social settings. Adoption and use of such values, beliefs and ideas has consequences for many other aspects of our behaviour – our uses of gesture, habits of dress, bodily dispositions, and so on. All these operate to signify the various Discourse communities in which an individual operates and lives. The discourses in the two senses are integrally related. Gee would argue that the distinction between the two is a useful one, enabling those interested in language 'to study discourse in Discourses' (ibid: 7), and hence to understand how and in what ways the immediate use of language is itself an aspect of participation in the larger interactions, events and actions that constitute social practice. An important theme in Gee's work is his interest in what he terms 'situated identities', and relatedly, 'situated meanings'. The former refers to identities people 'enact and recognise in different settings' (ibid: 12), while the latter refers to the meanings associated with a particular setting and/or event, where such meanings are jointly constructed as part of participation in some sociocultural practice. Issues of identity as a social construct, then, are quite fundamental to Gee's approach to discourse and its analysis.

Like Gee, Lemke (e.g., 1995) has sought to develop models of analysis that focus on the nature of human behaviour as situated social practice. In his case, an early interest in classroom talk (e.g., Lemke, 1985) led Lemke to explore the ways in which humans interact, negotiate and jointly construct understandings and complex sets of social practices. His initial research into classroom talk led in time to more complex and comprehensive discussions, in which he argued a theory of the social construction of experience. While he draws (1995) extensively on social theories of the kind used by Fairclough and Gee, including for example, those of Bakhtin, Foucault, Bernstein and Halliday among others, he also makes extensive use of the biological theories of figures such as Bateson, to develop a theory of human behaviour as involving situated meanings in social activity.

The notion of 'situated meanings' is one found fairly widely in several traditions of contemporary discourse study, while it is also found in some traditions of psychology (e.g., Wertsch, 1985, 1991). Bruner (1986, 1990) uses related notions, drawing on Vygotsky in building his social theory of the mind. Wertsch in particular develops a theory of mind by drawing on both Bakhtin and Vygotsky, arguing for a model of psychology whose goal is 'to explicate how human action is situated in cultural, historical, and institutional settings' (Wertsch, 1991: 119). It says much for the influence of the Russian theorists such as Bakhtin in language studies that Hicks (1995), commissioned a few years ago to develop a review of contemporary work on 'Discourse, learning and teaching', should develop a major section of the paper (ibid: 51–62) around the notion of discourse, where she acknowledged the work of Bakhtin. Her discussion, making reference to the writing of Fairclough, Gee and Lemke, among others, made clear the central role now given to discourse as 'situated social practice'.

Making a quite overt attempt to bring together perspectives from both the social psychology of the Russian theorists and contemporary SF theory as developed by Halliday, Wells (1993, 1999) seeks to develop a model of discourse in social practice, and hence in learning. He also makes considerable use of the theories of Leont'ev, in particular the latter's notion of *activity*, though this was apparently developed from original suggestions from Vygotsky. Activity theory, as Wells (1999: 169–70) discusses it after Leont'ev, recognizes 'a tristratal account of activity in terms of activity, action and operation'. While the three might be understood hierarchically, Wells notes, Leont'ev saw them as more accurately providing three perspectives on the same event: 'those respectively of motives, goals and conditions'(ibid: 169). In the classroom for example (ibid: 232–3) the major *activity* is that of education, while any *action* is to be understood as referring to any event that is directed towards achieving the goals of the educational activity. The third stratum, that of *operation*, refers to the actual means used by participants to achieve the goals.

As Wells uses the notion of activity structure, he suggests that the stratum of 'action' is in fact very close to the notion of 'curriculum genre' as it will be used in this book (ibid: 238). He says this because, for reasons to be explored more fully later, the notion of a curriculum genre, like any other genre in the SF tradition used here, is a staged, purposeful, goal-driven activity in language: this appears to compare quite closely with Wells's stratum of 'operation'. However, for several reasons, Wells also takes issue with notions of genre theory of the kind to be adopted here, not least, he suggests, because the idea of activity structure encompasses more than language use, involving reference to the other semiotic tools apart from language used by participants in classrooms. I shall suggest, however, both that any analysis of classroom activity must always involve some selection of the potential data available for consideration, and that, while I acknowledge the significance of other meaning-making systems, in my view language remains the most funda-mental resource with which participants negotiate and construct their meanings in classrooms. Furthermore, while I find much to enjoy and agree with in Wells's account of his models of dialogic inquiry, the methodology he adopts does not permit the very fine linguistic analysis that the functional grammar makes possible.

Enough has been said, hopefully, in sketching in some of the major developments in discourse analysis over the last 30 to 40 years, to indicate something of the main themes that have appeared, especially as they relate to classroom work. At least two broad themes have emerged, both of which are accepted as basic to the discussions in this book, though they will necessarily be expressed in ways particular to the systemic theory that is used. Thus, the first of the themes involved the initial interest of the late 1960s and 1970s in studying language behaviour in the classroom. This led in time to a range of research methods, often conflicting and contesting, but all of them committed to a general view of classroom activity as *structured experience*. For all theorists, language has been seen to have a role in the structuring of experience, though it would be true to say that the status accorded language, as distinct from other forms of semiosis in the classroom, has differed, depending on the theoretical perspective adopted. The second broad theme, more recent in its expression, concerns the greatly extended scholarly interest in language as *social phenomenon*, involved in the negotiation and construction of meaning. This interest finds expression in many ways. For example, it is found in such notions as 'situated meanings and identities' as discussed by Gee and others, but as also originally developed among the Russian theorists such as Vygotsky, Bakhtin and Leont'ev, whose work has become better known in the west than in the recent past. It is also found in Halliday's (1978; Halliday and Hasan, 1985) notion of language as a 'social semiotic', centrally involved in the building of social experience, and fundamental to the building of identity. Others, such as Lemke (1995: 9), also interested in meaning-making in social activities including language-using activities, assert that meaning-making is not 'something done by minds', but that it is a *social practice* in a community' (his italics).

These observations about trends in classroom discourse analysis having been noted, I shall now turn in the next section to a brief account of the systemic theory to be used in this study, outlining those aspects of the theory most relevant to the model of classroom discourse to be developed in great detail in subsequent chapters.

Systemic functional theory and its relevance for a model of classroom discourse analysis

Systemic functional theory grew out of the earlier model of 'scale and category grammar', to which reference was made above. Discussion of aspects of the emergence of the theory may be found for example, in a collection of papers by Halliday edited by Kress (1976), in an interview with Halliday conducted by Parret (1974), in volumes by Halliday and Hasan (1985), and by Halliday (1985), as well as those edited by Hasan and Martin (1989) and Fries and Gregory (1995). Other publications include those by Hasan (1996), Matthiessen (1995), Martin (1992) and Halliday and Matthiessen (1999). While no attempt will be made to review the complete theory here, enough will be said in this discussion to indicate those aspects of the theory of most significance for the model of classroom discourse analysis to be outlined in later chapters. This discussion will draw on all the authorities cited.

Systemic functional linguistic theory is distinctive in at least three senses: firstly, in the claims it makes regarding the *metafunctional* organization of all natural languages; secondly, in the particular uses and significance it attaches to the notion of 'system'; and thirdly, in the particular claims it makes regarding the relationship of language – or 'text' – and context. The last takes us into discussion of related terms of 'register' and 'genre'.

The metafunctions

To take the first of these, one of the most interesting and innovative of the developments that led to the emergence of SF theory was the proposal that the grammatical organization of all natural languages reflects the functions for which language has evolved in the human species. Any language use serves simultaneously to construct some aspect of experience, to negotiate relationship and to organize the language successfully so that it realizes a satisfactory message. While the grammatical choices adopted to achieve these things must always be judged in the terms of the particular language identified for examination, any language will serve these broad functions, and the clusters of grammatical choices with respect to each will be capable of identification and analysis. Indeed, so pervasive are the functions in any natural language that Halliday and his colleagues came to identify and name them as *metafunctions*: functions that is, that extend across any pattern of language use. This account will necessarily be concerned only with the English language.

The *ideational metafunction*, as Halliday discusses it, refers to those aspects of the grammar which are most directly involved in representation of the world and its experiences, both those of the 'outer world' of action, and those of the 'inner world' of consciousness, reflection and imagination. The ideational metafunction actually consists of two metafunctions: *the experiential* and *the logical*. The resources of transitivity and of lexis are involved in representing experience, and these are indeed the resources most directly involved in realizing the experiential metafunction. The logical metafunction is of a rather different order, for it is involved, not directly in the building of the meanings within the clause, but rather in the matter of building connectedness between the meanings of clauses. Such a logical connectedness is realized in those resources in the grammar which are involved in two different sets of relationships: those to do with the interdependency or 'taxis' between clauses; and those to do with the logico-semantic relations between clauses brought about by either projection or expansion (see Halliday, 1994: 215–91, for a detailed discussion).

The *interpersonal metafunction* refers to those grammatical resources in which the relationship of interlocutors is realized, including those of mood, modality and person. Finally, the *textual metafunction* refers to those aspects of the grammar that assist in organizing language as a message, and here the resources of theme, information and cohesion are most fundamentally involved. A simple way to capture the metafunctions, demonstrating in particular the relationship of the experiential and logical metafunctions, has been suggested by Halliday (1979: 57) thus:

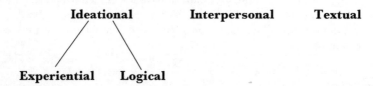

When one undertakes a grammatical analysis using such a metafunctional model of the English language, the object is to find the ways in which meanings – ideational, interpersonal and textual – are realized and tracked through the text. For the goal, while one always works with the meanings particular to the clause, is to interpret those meanings for their role in the overall organization of the text that the clauses constitute. The model of the grammar is, in other words, text- or discourse-driven.

The notion of system

The second of the aspects distinctive to systemic theory to which I have alluded is the notion of 'system'. Many people today would quite conventionally refer to the idea of a 'language system', while not necessarily according it the significance intended here. In SF theory, language is said to be a meaning system, where a system is 'a set of options with an entry condition' (Halliday, 1976: 3). In fact, language is said to be polysystemic, in that it operates through the exercises of clusters of choices or options. To construct an English clause for example, one makes simultaneous choices from the grammar with respect to theme (the point of departure for the message of the clause), mood (and hence the speech function taken up) and transitivity (the type of process, associated participants and any circumstances). The available sets of choices with respect to each of the systems of theme, mood and transitivity are various and often quite complex, and for the most part they are not conscious. The interest for the SF theorist is in looking at how language users exploit and deploy the language choices to make meanings, for the focus is on language as resource, never as set of rules.

I shall say a little here of the various choices with respect to transitivity, theme, mood and modality, for an understanding of these will prove essential for the analyses to be offered in later chapters. However, readers for whom the theory is new will also need to consult one of the several sources on functional grammar listed at the end of this chapter, as this discussion is not definitive.

Transitivity choices involve selections from the various process types which are realized in verbal groups, while the associated participant roles are realized in nominal groups and any circumstances are realized in either prepositional phrases or adverbial groups. Examples of process types are displayed, most of them taken from the classroom texts used in this book. Process types may be material:

we	made up	our own monster sandwiches
Actor	Process: material	Goal

or mental:

you	should consider	this
Senser	Process: cognition	Phenomenon

or behavioural:

we	are writing	a story	about a lost lunch
Behaver	Process: behavioural	Range	Circumstance: Matter

or verbal:

the clock	tells	the time	very accurately
Sayer	Process: verbal	Verbiage	Circumstance: Manner: Quality

or relational:

it	's	an island
Carrier	Process: intensive	Attribute

but also:

the way [[to work]]	might be	[[to sit around this group]]
Value	Process: intensive	Token

or existential:

once upon a time	there were	three bears
Circumstance: Location: time	Process: existential	Existent

The above in no sense exhausts the possibilities, and it is intended only to suggest something of the range of process types, as well as something of the principles for analysis and labelling of items. The functional labels with respect to process types allow us to distinguish the types of processes that occur across a text, to notice the manner in which the types are deployed at different points across the text, and to make judgements about the kinds of experiential meanings in construction. As for the participants involved in the processes, these are also given labels particular to the process types, and the interest again is to distinguish the range of participant roles available. Circumstances are so called because they provide circumstantial information about what is involved in the process.

Process types and their participant roles are important measures of the experiential content found in classroom texts. As already noted, I shall argue in this book that there are two registers (or sets of language choices) at work in classroom texts: those of the 'first order' or 'regulative' register, to do with types of behaviours in the classroom, and those of the 'second order' or 'instructional' register, to do with the 'content' being taught and learned. Examples of clauses in which the process types are primarily of the first order register, and about the participants' behaviour, include the following clause, part of teacher talk to the class:

right okay now we	are going to start	our theme	next week
Actor	Process: material	Goal	Circ: Loc: Time

or a remark by one student to another:

you	've got to follow	the instructions
Actor	Process: material	Range

The second order register frequently finds expression in parts of transitivity other than the process itself as in the following, addressed to a class:

you	'll be making	an exact replica of a catapult
Actor	Process: material	Goal

In the latter case, the material process and its participant role of Actor realize aspects of the students' behaviour, and these are of the first order or regulative register. But the participant role of Goal realizes an aspect of the second order or instructional register (in this case, to do with *catapults* and other types of machines humans have invented), and is to do with the field of information being taught and learned. It is of the nature of all pedagogic activity that some language choices are to do with the behaviours of the participants in the activity, while others are to do with the 'content' or instructional field of information which is at issue. As we shall see in later chapters, the interplay of the two registers, and the manner in which they are realized over long stretches of classroom text, tell a great deal of the kinds of meanings being made as well as the extent to which, and the ways in which, students are learning.

To turn to the interpersonal metafunction, mood choices necessarily involve the speaker in taking up particular speech roles vis-à-vis the listener (Halliday, 1994: 69). For example, teachers or students can offer information:

well today we've got another simple story which is called 'My Lunch',

or demand information:

what's a barrel?

or they can offer a service:

do you want this Stanley knife?

or they can demand a service:

give me the Stanley knife please.

The basic speech functions here are augmented by the various types of responses available (e.g., rejection or acceptance of an offer, acknowledgement of a statement, refusal to comply with a command, for example). For some discussion of the speech functions see Eggins (1994: 149–54). Teachers and students take up various roles vis-à-vis each other across a classroom text, and identification of their respective speech roles becomes one important measure of their relative roles and responsibilities. In practice, since the teacher–student relationship is asymmetric, it is the teacher who exercises particular power in offering information, in eliciting information and in directing the nature of activity, and this, as we shall see, is very marked in the operation of the regulative register.

Other interpersonal resources of significance are found in the uses of modality and of person. Thus, teachers often use high modality to indicate the importance of a course of action to be pursued:

So we've got to do a lot of concentrating.

though sometimes they use low or median modality to make the directions to behaviour more oblique:

Now a lot of work [[that you may have to do]] may be with a partner. Some you'll do by yourself. So you're probably best to sit next to somebody [[that you will work with]].

(The square brackets [[ ]] indicate an embedded or down-ranked clause.)

The interpersonal resources available in English with which teachers and students negotiate and maintain relationships are rich and varied, including various forms of interpersonal metaphor, to be alluded to below.

The person system too has significance in classrooms. Teachers classically use the first person plural when building solidarity with their students in some enterprise to be undertaken:

Well today we've got another simple little story...

while elsewhere they use the first person singular as part of indicating their expectations of students:

I want you to listen to this little tiny story like the one we had yesterday.

Finally, teachers use the second person when overtly directing students' behaviour:

> *You really do need something to write with so if you don't have your own pens and pencils would you collect those please?*

Turning to the textual metafunction, our principal interest in the discussions in this book will be in the manner in which theme patterns assist in the unfolding of the directions taken in the discourse. Theme refers to 'the point of departure for the message' of the clause (Halliday, 1994: 37). It is what the message is about. Theme comes in first position in the English clause, though this does not actually define it. The clause is said to be organized in terms of its theme (its point of departure) and its rheme (whatever is not in theme). The grammatical system of theme is complemented by the operation of the information unit. The latter is a feature of speech, for it refers to the pitch contour or tone produced in speaking. While information units do not correspond completely to any unit in the clause grammar, it happens that the nearest grammatical unit is the clause. As a general principle, what is expressed as given information falls towards the start of a clause, while what is termed new information comes towards the end (see Halliday, 1994: 292–307 for a detailed discussion.) What is new information falling in the rheme in one clause will often then be picked up and reinstated as given information in the topical theme position in a new clause. In unmarked (or typical) situations, what is topical theme conflates with the subject of the clause.

The following text extract demonstrates that topical theme progression is such that what appears as new information in the rheme of a clause often finds status as topical theme in a subsequent clause, thus helping to give connectedness and unity to the text.

She had no lunch to start with,

because it was left at home,

and she thought her mum was going to bring it at lunch time,

and when her mum didn't bring it,

Mrs S rang her mum,

and she wasn't at home,

so her dad brought her lunch

and then her mum remembered

she hadn't brought her lunch ... [text is omitted]

Instances of marked topical (or atypical) themes occur for example, when a circumstance is put in theme position:

Today we're going to start a new unit of work,

and sometimes a marked topical theme is created by placing a dependent clause first, thus giving it thematic status:

Before you start your work, we had better go over what's to be done.

Topical themes are often found in association with both textual themes and interpersonal themes and where all three appear, it is the textual theme that comes first, followed by the interpersonal, and then the topical theme as in:

We'll see how that works ah (topical theme)
as we go through (a textual and a topical theme)
so hopefully you're following the pattern ... (a textual, an interpersonal and a topical theme, respectively) [the row of dots here indicates that words are left out of the final clause].

In classroom talk, thematic progression is often expressed primarily in teacher talk, particularly at the start of lessons, as in the following where textual themes are marked with a double underlining, and topical themes with a single one:

Well now these people are back,
I want you to listen to this little tiny short story like the one we had yesterday.
You know we had 'A Monster Sandwich'
and then we made up our own monster sandwiches.
Well today we've got another simple little story
which is called 'My Lunch'.
And I want you to listen to it ... [text is omitted]

The above is an instance of teacher monologue but, if one turns, for example, to a passage of dialogue involving a group of students working together in building a simple machine, one finds the theme choices are of a different order:

Yvonne: *Want some help?*
Naomi: *It fell apart. [refers to a pulley they are building]*
Aranthi: *I know. Chanoa, Chanoa, you can hold it.*
Katrina: *You hold this. [refers to a bottle]*
Aranthi: *Aren't we using the other one? [refers to another bottle]*
Yvonne: *Okay you know where to cut? [hands the bottle to Naomi]. Cut that there.*
Chanoa: *Ohh, be careful.*

Textually as well as interpersonally such a passage of text is quite different from the passage of teacher monologue. The students indicate that they are directing the course the discourse takes, which is in this case very intimately linked to the making of the machine: hence the extensive uses of exophoric references to matters out of the text and in the context.

Patterns of theme distribution in classroom talk are very revealing, for it is through the theme choices that the discourse is developed and carried forward. Who controls theme, to what ends, and at what points in the lesson, tells a lot about the overall organization of the classroom text and about the relative responsibilities assumed by participants. As we shall see, thematic patterns tend to be distributed rather differently across the different stages of a curriculum genre, reflecting, but also enabling, the various shifts that occur with respect to the operation of the first and second order registers to which I have alluded.

Metaphor in systemic theory and its relevance for a study of pedagogy

The above brief discussion of SF theory has served to sketch in the notion of the metafunctions and their role in constructing and organizing text. Before outlining the SF theory with respect to text, context and genre, it will be appropriate to say something briefly of the role of metaphor, both because it has a significance in the theory and because it is of relevance to the theory of pedagogy that concerns this book. Metaphor in its conventional, lexical sense is accepted in SF theory, but it is the notion of grammatical metaphor, developed in particular by Halliday (1994: 342–67) which represents the more original and innovative contribution to linguistic theory. Broadly, two kinds of grammatical metaphor are recognized: ideational and interpersonal. They occur when the usual or 'congruent' realization of a meaning is given a non-congruent or metaphorical expression.

To take the notion of an ideational meaning first, it will be clear from the examples cited above that a typical congruent way to represent experience is to create clauses that use the verb to realize some process of participating in the world, to use associated nominal groups to realize participants involved in the process, to use adverbial groups and/or prepositional phrases to represent some associated circumstance(s) and to use conjunctions to build logical relationships between the messages of the clauses. The following made-up example represents a congruent realization: *On Tuesday* (circumstance) *the class* (participant) *visited* (process) *the zoo* (participant) *and then* (conjunction) *they* (participant) *went* (process) *to the museum* (circumstance). A non-congruent or grammatically metaphorical way to represent this would be *The class visit to the zoo last Tuesday led to* (or *was followed by*) *a visit to the museum.* In the latter, the two clauses of the congruent realization are compressed into the one, and the conjunctive relation between the two clauses is buried in the verbal group *led to*, while the two processes realized in the verbal groups (*visited*, *went*) have been turned into nominal groups, *the class visit* and *a visit to the museum.* One tendency of such grammatical expression is to create longer nominal groups than would otherwise be present as in: *the class visit to the zoo last Tuesday.* This helps to account for the enhanced lexical density which both Perera (1984) and Halliday (1985) have noted is a feature of written rather than spoken language.

As a general principle, congruent expressions are a feature of speech at any age, while the tendency of adults' language, in particular their written language, is to use the more non-congruent or metaphorical expressions. Capacity to use grammatical metaphor would appear to emerge at the earliest in children in late childhood (Derewianka, 1995; Aidman, 1999; Christie, 2002), though it seems that many students well into adolescence experience difficulty in handling grammatical metaphor in their writing.

As for interpersonal metaphor, this occurs when the speaker uses a metaphorical expression to express interpersonal meanings, as those are congruently expressed in mood or modality choices. Interpersonal metaphor is commonly found in teacher talk, often to give an oblique expression to the teacher's expression of authority. An expression such as 'Would you like to get out your books now?', in teacher talk actually means: 'Get out your books now'. Sometimes, as we shall see in later chapters, teacher authority is expressed even more metaphorically, as when a teacher says to his class:

> The main requirement is for various things [[to be done]].

This is actually a metaphor for 'you must do various things'. The metaphorical expression, whose effect is to hide the teacher's identity, creates an abstraction *the main requirement*, which gives particular strength to the expression of teacher authority.

The classroom texts to be examined in later chapters will show that in the talk of the early childhood classroom the talk is congruent in the ideational sense. Occasional uses of interpersonal metaphor will occur among teachers in early childhood classrooms, though for the most part the meanings are congruently expressed. By the upper primary years the language becomes more metaphorical, both in the ideational and interpersonal senses. Thus, teachers tend to use more interpersonally metaphorical expressions in responding to, and talking with, their students. Equally, ideational metaphor becomes an issue in teaching the various instructional fields of late primary and secondary education.

Text, context and genre

The third of the matters I noted above were distinctive features of SF theory is what is said of the relationship of language – or text – and context. The two terms 'text and 'context' have a particular significance in systemic theory. Historically, this aspect of the theory was built upon the distinction originally made by Malinowski (1923; 1935) between 'context of situation' and 'context of culture', which was in turn developed by Firth. Building from this distinction, the theory of register developed, so that, it was said, any text is a condition of the context of situation which it both realizes, and of which it is a part. The language choices particular to any context of situation are said to be choices in *register*. Three variables of any context of situation are involved in the register choices that are made to realize the text: they are the *field of activity*, the *tenor* of the relationships of participants, and the *mode* of delivery and organization of the message. Language choices of the experiential metafunction are primarily involved in realizing the field; those of the interpersonal metafunction are primarily involved in realizing the tenor; while those of the textual metafunction are involved in building the mode.

Table 1.1, taken from Halliday in Halliday and Hasan, 1985: 26, sets out the relationships.

Table 1.1   Relation of the text to the context of situation

Situation: Feature of the context	(realized by)	Text: Functional component of semantic system
Field of discourse (what is going on)		Experiential meanings (Transitivity, naming, etc.)
Tenor of discourse who are taking part		Interpersonal meanings (mood, modality, person)
Mode of discourse (role assigned to cohension)		Textual meanings (theme, information, language)

Texts and their particular configurations of registerial choices are a condition of context of situation, while for some SF theorists the generic choice is said to be a condition of the context of culture (see Martin, 1992, and also Christie and Martin, 1997, for some discussion). A genre is said to be a staged purposive activity undertaken to accomplish some goal or goals. Genres have their particular character because of the context of culture in which they are found. Thus, for example, almost all societies in the world have trading genres, and probably all are in some sense identifiable as such. However, the trading genres found in particular societies will differ and the differences will be a condition of the context of culture.

The relationship of register and genre may be explained as follows. A genre unfolds, constructing, let us say, an instance of a narrative familiarly found in an English-speaking culture, having the classic structure *Orientation* ∧ *Complication* ∧ *Evaluation* ∧ Resolution (∧ indicates sequence) associated with Labov (Labov and Waletzky, 1967), but also identified as one instance of a story genre by both Plum (1988; 1998), and Rothery (1990). As the structure unfolds, choices particular to the registerial values help construct the various stages. That is to say, these will be choices with respect to the field of experience (be that to do with a lost lunch, a visit to the zoo or indeed any of the myriad of fields available), the tenor assumed towards the listener/reader (is it, for example, hierarchic or non-hierarchic?) and the mode of telling the story (e.g., spoken or written, and if written, is it accompanied by illustrations or not?) The choices with respect to genre and register are not the same, and with a model of linguistic analysis as delicate as that available with the functional grammar, one can tease out the different choices. Nonetheless, such choices are mutually interdependent, for they collectively build the text, giving it its characteristic generic structure, as well as its particular values to do with the field or 'content', the relations assumed with others by the storyteller, and the manner of telling the story.

Genre theory in the SF tradition has been vigorously debated since Martin and his colleagues first started to develop it in the 1980s (see Reid, 1987; Hasan, 1995; Freedman and Medway, 1994; Lee, 1996 for some representative discussions), though it is not my intention to consider the debates here in any detail, on the grounds that they have been widely canvassed elsewhere. In fact, the arguments in this book are built upon the model of register and genre theory as outlined. Classroom activity, it is proposed here, is to be understood as constituting curriculum genres. Furthermore, it is often the case that curriculum genres in turn constitute larger unities referred to as curriculum macrogenres. Curriculum genres and macrogenres are staged, goal-driven activities, devoted to the accomplishment of significant educational ends. They are quite fundamentally involved in the organization of the discourses of schooling.

Genre and pedagogy

The notion of a genre is adopted here for several reasons. First of all, it is used partly because a discussion of the genres found in schooling contributes to the wider, now quite considerable, body of work on genres and their description in the SF tradition (see Christie and Martin, 1997 for a representative discussion). In the general scholarly interest to explain and interpret human behaviours which has achieved accelerated significance in the human sciences over the last century or so, genre theory – including its application in studies of schooling – can claim to offer one possible model for such explanation and interpretation.

Apart from this, the notion of a curriculum genre (and of a curriculum macrogenre) is useful because it provides a principled basis for making selections of classroom texts for analysis and interpretation. How one selects classroom activity and on what basis decisions are made about identifying sequences of activity – and perhaps not others – is of course always a sensitive issue, and one that reflects a great deal of the predilections and assumptions of the researcher. Discourse itself is never neutral, and discourse analysis is also not neutral, for it necessarily involves the imposition of some interpretation upon events. Indeed, the very transcript of the classroom talk (and the video record from which that is drawn), is already removed from the reality, and itself an interpretation of it.

Methods and models of analysis of talk are actually built on theories of human behaviour and society, whether acknowledged or not, and these have consequences for the text selections that are made, as well as the interpretations offered of them. While we can agree, then, that a passage of classroom text is always a selection, we can also argue that a concern for the overall generic structure of some classroom activity involves a commitment to trying to interpret a reasonably complete cycle of teaching–learning activity, tracing and following those shifts and changes in the discourse through which the teaching–learning activity is effected. The goal, as I shall seek to demonstrate in later chapters, is to follow how the classroom genre unfolds, through its various elements of structure and phases within these. The model of genre used here requires that one avoid, as far as possible, making arbitrary selections of passages of text. Even where (as will be true in this book) one cannot reproduce a complete classroom text, one must collect and analyse the whole text (or as much of that as is feasible), so that what one says of those passages selected for presentation and discussion is informed by an analysis and interpretation of the whole text. I should note here that I am aware that even the term 'whole text' is in a sense indeterminate, and subject to some challenge. To be clear about this, I use it to refer to a complete unit of curriculum activity, which will typically extend over several lessons, sometimes lasting a week or a fortnight, and sometimes taking as long as a whole school term.[1] Its presence in the discourse will be marked by some clearly initiating stage which signals the commencement of some new learning about a topic, and it will also be marked by a clearly defined closure, expressed for example, in completion of a piece of work which normally has significance as a tool for evaluation of the students' learning. Only when one has such a complete text for analytic purposes, I shall argue, can we make reasonable judgements about the meanings made in the overall teaching–learning cycle and about the significance and placement of any language usages.

In this context, I note that Edwards and Westgate (1994: 144–6), discussing proposals for developing patterns of talk other than those that rely on constant use of questions directed to students, refer to the work of Dillon. An extract from classroom talk provided by Dillon is cited, demonstrating what can happen when students engage in what Dillon calls 'Discussion'. The talk, involving what one gathers are secondary students talking about Louis XIV's treatment of the Huguenots, is indeed on the evidence very impressive, as the students each offer substantial contributions to the discussion and the teacher takes what might be termed a facilitating role. But this is only an extract, and the very references made in the text indicate a considerable degree of prior learning, in which one assumes the teacher and students adopted rather different roles and constructed the experiential information rather differently. It is not that one wants to dismiss the achievements of the teacher and students in the text extract, but it needs to be understood for its status in the much longer stretch of classroom activity – talking, reading and researching – which must have heralded it, and which presumably contributed to some logogenesis.

I should note that both Wells (1999) and Green and Dixon and their colleagues (1993) have made similar claims to those made here about the importance of following teaching–learning activity over long sequences of time. The orientation adopted here is in that sense compatible with theirs. However, I would argue that a grammatical analysis as delicate as that provided by the SF grammar allows a very fine interpretation of the meanings made and the nature of the relationships of participants in the discourse. That method of grammatical analysis, together with the genre theory which it illuminates, can also assist in development of a more general theory of pedagogic practices.

Another reason for using the notion of genre theory adopted here concerns the nature of the two registers I have suggested operate within the curriculum genre. The notion of the two registers owes most to the work of Bernstein (e.g., 1990, 1996, 2000) and his observations about the nature of pedagogic discourse. The concept of a pedagogic discourse is part of a complex set of proposals Bernstein developed over some years, devoted to explaining 'the production, reproduction and transformation of culture' (Bernstein, 1990: 180). Pedagogic discourse and pedagogic relationships in his theory include a range of fields of activity and their agents much greater than those of schooling, though the discussion here concerns only schools. A pedagogic discourse is instrumental in building and shaping consciousness, and schools are agencies of 'symbolic control', though they are by no means the only examples of such agencies. It is of the utmost importance to analyse and explain how the pedagogic discourses of schooling work, how access to forms of knowledge is made available, how such forms are variously distributed to persons in a culture and how they function to shape consciousness. A pedagogic discourse operates by taking forms of knowledge from elsewhere and 'relocating' these for the purposes of the initiation of others. All societies, Bernstein claims, have forms of knowledge that are 'esoteric' and 'mundane' (Bernstein, 1990: 181), and in contemporary western societies the control and development of the esoteric knowledge is mainly found in universities. For the purposes of pedagogic activity, at least some of the forms of esoteric knowledge found in universities are taken and relocated for the purposes of teaching and learning in schools. The processes of relocation are realized in a pedagogic discourse, which is defined thus:

> We shall define pedagogic discourse as the rule which embeds a discourse of competence (skills of various kinds) into a discourse of social order in such a way that the latter always dominates the former. We shall call the discourse transmitting specialised competences and their relation to each other *instructional* discourse, and the discourse creating specialised order, relation and identity *regulative* discourse. (Bernstein, 1990: 183; his italics)

The instructional discourse is said to be 'embedded' in the regulative discourse, where the relationship of the two is suggested thus: ID/RD (Bernstein, 2000: 183). Pedagogic discourse is said to be 'a discourse without a specific discourse', for it has no discourse of its own. Rather, the pedagogic discourse is said to be 'a principle for appropriating other discourses and bringing them into a special relation with each other for the purposes of their selective transmission and acquisition' (Bernstein, 2000: 183–4).

Adapting Bernstein's terms, I shall argue that the pedagogic discourse found in the curriculum genres of schooling functions in such way that it is realized primarily in a first order or regulative register, to do with the overall pedagogic directions taken, their goals, pacing and sequencing, and a second order or instructional register to do with the 'content' and its specialized skills at issue. The first order or regulative register, it will be argued, 'projects' a second order or instructional register. The choice of the term 'register' rather than 'discourse' reflects the particular SF theory involved. The choice of the term 'project' rather than 'embed' also reflects the linguistic theory. Bernstein's choice of the term 'embed' fits uneasily in a linguistic theory which uses the notion of 'embedding' in a different sense; it is to do with the ways some linguistic items – very commonly clauses – are said to be embedded or down-ranked, because they function not as independent clauses, but as components of the larger elements of the constituent structure of the clause. The notion of 'projection' seems to fit more appropriately than that of 'embedding', drawn as it is from the SF proposals about clauses that 'project' (Halliday, 1994: 215–91) Where projection occurs (as in mental and verbal process clauses), 'the secondary clause is projected through the primary clause, which instates it as (a) a locution, or (b) and idea' (ibid: 219). A made-up example would be:

He said//	*that he did not know the answer to the question*
Projecting clause	projected clause

A clause that projects in some sense takes something said or thought before and reinstates it. Hence the notion of projection is used metaphorically to refer to the relationship of the two registers in the pedagogic discourse.[2] A field of knowledge and its associated activity is taken, relocated and in some sense therefore 'projected' for another purpose and another site.

Like Bernstein, I shall argue that the pedagogic discourse of a curriculum genre is indeed one, though I shall also seek to demonstrate how the two registers are realized linguistically differently at different points in the overall construction of the pedagogic discourse. This, I shall suggest, tells us a lot not only about the manner in which pedagogic knowledge and relationships are constructed, but it allows us to make judgements about the relative success of the different models of pedagogy and of the pedagogic subject that appear to apply.

Chapters 2 and 3 will look at curriculum genres in the early childhood classroom, and here I shall use the model of classroom discourse analysis to examine and critique aspects of the ideologies of much that applies in early childhood education. Here, among other matters, I shall invoke Bernstein's (2000: 41–63) useful discussion of 'competence' models of the person which have had considerable impact in a great deal of the practices of early childhood education of the last 30 to 40 years. In that such models have tended to propose and perpetuate a view of persons possessed of discrete capacities or 'competences' capable of development in reasonably decontextualized ways, they have often tended to trivialize the practices of teaching and learning, deflecting attention away from the sustained effort over time that is required for effective learning. Chapter 4 turns to some examination of two curriculum macrogenres of the upper primary school, devoted to the teaching of natural science and social science respectively. The two macrogenres unfold in linear fashion, each moving towards a culminating task, so that there is a strong sense of incremental learning realized in the discourse and its associated activities. In these two cases, the nature of the pedagogy and the model of the pedagogic subject can be shown to be quite different from what applies in Chapters 2 and 3. While the differences are in part a consequence of the fact that the students are older, they are also a consequence of the operation of a rather different kind of pedagogic discourse – one that is much more overtly committed to apprenticeship into specialist areas of knowledge than is true of the early childhood examples, involving among other things, mastery of a technical language, and some requirement for sustained effortful learning over time. In both cases, forms of logogenesis apply, and the pedagogic discourse works such that the regulative register appropriates and speaks through an instructional register. Chapter 5 turns to a macrogenre of the mid-secondary years, examining students in a Year 9 geography class, and following their teaching–learning activities over a period of six weeks. The macrogeneric structure in this case is of interest not least because it unfolds in a manner that is not linear, but 'orbital' (a term taken from Iedema, 1997 and White, 1997, 1998 in particular). The structuring of the discourse in this case allows for an apprenticeship into aspects of the instructional fields of geography, though the processes by which this occurs are termed 'accretive' rather than incremental.

Several themes emerge through the chapters, and these are in turn revisited in the final chapter. Such themes involve a concern for the values of knowledge, an argument for the importance of curriculum practices that are strongly classified and strongly framed, a model of the pedagogic subject as one who is apprenticed, and finally, a model of the teacher as authority.

For readers unfamiliar with SF theory, there are, fortunately, now available several sources of information on the systemic functional grammar:

Halliday, M. A. K. (1994) (2nd edn.), *An Introduction to Functional Grammar*. London: Arnold.

Eggins, S. (1994), *An Introduction to Systemic Functional Linguistics*. London: Pinter.

Gerot, L. and Wignell, P. (1994), *Making Sense of Functional Grammar*. Sydney: Gerd Stabler.

Bloor, T. and Bloor, M. (1995) *The Functional Analysis of English: A Hallidayan Approach*. London and New York: Arnold.

Thompson, G. (1996) *Introducing Functional Grammar*. London and New York: Arnold.

Butt, D., Fahey, R. Feez, S., Spinks, S. and Yallop, C. (2nd edn.) (2000), *Using Functional Grammar: An Explorer's Guide*. Sydney: National Centre for English Language Teaching and Research.

Notes

1. Of course, a case could be made for regarding the whole year's work as a complete text, or even, more ambitiously, the whole course of a class's learning over all the years of schooling. Certainly, as methods of creating transcripts of talk speed up and as the several computer programs now available for parsing and analysis are improved, it will be possible to develop larger units for analytic purposes.
2. I should note that Halliday (1978: 143–4) has also used the terms 'first and second order fields', though not in the sense intended here. His account referred to a football game where the game itself is the field of activity, and any verbal interaction among the players is the first-order field. But in a discussion where the talk is about the game after the event, this he calls a 'second order of field'.

2 Early childhood: first steps in becoming a pedagogic subject

The entry to school learning

Life transitions are always challenging, sometimes even painful, and the various transitional stages associated with schooling are among the most important in the lives of children in English-speaking societies. The initial movement into formal schooling when children are aged 5 or 6 must be deemed the most significant in many ways, because it represents the start of an initiation into the school as an institution, the influence of whose subsequent phases will last for as many as 10 to 13 years, concluding when children are aged at least 16 years, more commonly today 18 years. The transitions from early childhood education to the middle years of schooling and again from the middle to the upper primary years are in their ways also significant, though neither matches in its significance the later transition from the primary to the secondary school, bringing with it the requirements to move to another, often bigger school, and to adjust to the demands of a different curriculum and school day.

For many children, the movement into formal schooling is often presaged by a period of time spent in a pre-school setting of some kind, and this prepares young children for at least some of the practices and expectations of schooling. Nonetheless, there is a sense in which the entry to school is still a significant point, marking a break with aspects of the past, and leading to development of new habits, practices and understandings of many kinds. The first year of formal schooling tends to have a name that marks it out as different from the later stages of schooling. In Australia for example, the terms 'preparatory grade', 'reception' and 'kindergarten' are all in use in the various states, and similar terms are used in other parts of the English-speaking world. While the various names probably signal little to children as young as five, they serve to suggest a lot in the community, and the schools themselves, about the goals and expectations of the first year of school. The reception or preparatory year is intended to effect the transition from participation in family and community, where parents, extended family and community network have been the principal educating agencies, into the school, where teachers assume the principal, officially sanctioned educating roles. Associated with this transition will be a movement into learning officially sanctioned and defined notions of acceptable pedagogic practice, with corresponding notions of a pedagogic subject position, and of a pedagogic knowledge.

There are many senses in which the pedagogic subject position established in the early years is particular to those years, yet it is also the case that many features of the early pedagogic experience endure, so that the pedagogic subject position is in some senses also distinctive. Teacher authority is established very early, and though it will be expressed very differently by the time students reach the upper years of the secondary school, the essential role and character of the teacher as 'in charge' of what is taught and learned, when it is taught and learned, how it is taught and learned, and, in particular, of how students' learning is evaluated, does not change. The pedagogic subject position available to the learner is necessarily constrained by the nature of the relationships assumed with respect to various teachers and school institutions over the years of schooling; a particular kind of consciousness is constructed, involving the building of a willingness and capacity, ideally at least, to accept methods of defining what counts as knowledge, what counts as acceptable ways of working with the knowledge, and what counts as acceptable performance in demonstrating a capacity to use such knowledge. Quite critical to the building of these matters is the nature of the relationship of teacher and students: the teacher is the authoritative figure, and she (it normally is a woman in early childhood education) orchestrates what happens in the classroom, managing both what will be learned, and what constitutes acceptable behaviour in its learning.

A great deal of effort in early childhood classrooms goes into initiating young children into acceptable practices for schooling. Young children learn about organization of time and space, as these are established for the purposes of schooling; they also learn acceptable ways to dispose their bodies within the terms of these socially defined notions of space and time. In fact, physical dispositions change, often quite markedly, as students and teachers move through the school day. Thus, the children learn about: ways the school day is broken into activities, lasting for regular periods of time, and generally marked by a closure of some kind which frequently involves movement, sometimes a move to a different part of the room, sometimes a move out of the room and into the playground, sometimes a slight change in physical disposition, designed perhaps to allow the children some physical shift before progressing to some new phase of activity. (Mehan, 1979, documented similar matters in his study of a primary classroom.) Patterns of acceptable movement about the classroom and school building are also established, as are acceptable behaviours for interacting with others. Teacher directions to do with acceptable behaviours are very audibly foregrounded in a great deal of teacher talk, constituting one aspect of the realization of the regulative register. With the passage of the months after children enter school, many of these directions become less foregrounded, the requirements for acceptable behaviour having been established. In that those requirements now tend to function at a tacit level, this is evidence that the regulative register has been effective: it still operates of course, and can always be explicitly invoked by a teacher should a desired pattern of behaviour need clarification. Green and Kantor-Smith (1988) made similar observations of children in early childhood situations.

The early childhood curriculum typically shows evidence of fairly weak classification of knowledge, in that what counts as valid educational knowledge often consists of contents or areas of knowledge which are not marked by clear boundaries (Bernstein, 1974: 204), the one from the other. For example, units of work devoted to what the teacher in her school programme might call 'language arts', 'social science' or even 'natural science' will frequently be developed by drawing on the same broad areas of experience or 'themes' like foods, where students might learn about what constitutes healthy foods, what foods we like to eat, how they are prepared and perhaps when and why we eat them.

Just as the boundaries within the curriculum in terms of what constitutes pedagogic knowledge are often not strong, so too the boundary between what constitutes the knowledge of home and family and that of the school is often blurred in early childhood education. This is part of an often deliberate attempt to build strong connections between family and school, so that that which is family and community experience is often in some sense recontextualized or 'relocated' for the purposes of school learning. The development of such a model of the early childhood curriculum is a post-Second World War phenomenon, and more specifically it seems to have emerged in the 1960s and 1970s, given official support in England for example, among other agencies, by the Plowden Report (1967) devoted to *Children and their Primary Schools*. The authors of the Plowden Report insisted, among other matters, that 'knowledge does not fall into neatly separate compartments' (Plowden Report, 1967: 187), and the general thrust of their advice was towards a curriculum marked by weak classification of knowledge. That report, influential in Australia as well as England, gave considerable support and credibility to the notion of an early childhood education whose curriculum was weakly classified.

Linked to the emergent ideologies of the 1960s and 1970s about language, language development and language education, the model of the early childhood curriculum that came to predominate in many parts of the English-speaking world attached a particular importance to self-expression in the young learner, and to the fostering of opportunities to use language for learning as one important aspect of such self-expression. Dixon (1967), in his evocatively titled book *Growth through English*, captured something of the spirit of the time, while calls for adoption of 'language across the curriculum' policies in schools, and/or policies that stressed the 'role of language in learning' had considerable impact on models of the curriculum for the primary school generally, and in time for the junior secondary school as well. Nowhere was the loosening of the principles of classification of knowledge more marked than in the curriculum of the early childhood years, conventionally regarded as covering chronological years 5 to 8. Furthermore, within the general terms of the loosely classified curriculum, for reasons already alluded to, language development came to assume a new significance in the thinking of many curriculum planners and teachers. It was against this newly acquired interest in language development that, among other matters, activities such as 'morning news' or 'sharing time' came to assume importance in early childhood curriculum planning, because of their assumed role in promoting language growth or language competence. Such a general commitment to promotion or 'facilitation' (often the preferred term) of language growth, while in some senses attractive, is also in many ways naive and misplaced. It denies issues of social class, ethnicity and familial background and their profound influence upon the meaning orientations available to different children in their language uses. In consequence, it wrongly assumes a parity of potential capacity and performance available to all children in meeting the requirements of schooling. (See Bernstein, 2000: 41–63, for a recent discussion of the problems in educational notions of 'competence'.) In practice, schooling privileges certain meaning orientations rather more than others, as Bernstein (2000) and Heath (1983) have both proposed, and as both Williams (1995) and Brown (1999) have recently demonstrated, the former with respect to early literacy practices, the latter with respect to early numeracy practices.

In that the early childhood educational programme often blurs the distinction between home and school knowledge, inviting young children to draw on their family and community experiences for the purposes of pedagogic activity, the pedagogic relationship is to this extent rather weakly framed (Bernstein, 1974: 205–6). That is because the students enjoy some capacity to select those areas of personal knowledge that are relocated in the school as pedagogic knowledge, and the teacher accepts, even encourages this. (See Baker and Perrott 1988, for a discussion of the role of morning news as an activity primarily concerned with initiating the young into the knowledge and culture of schooling, though, they argue, it is ostensibly an opportunity for the children to introduce and develop their own topics of interest.) The capacity of the children to select personal experience for morning news-giving is in fact a little illusory. That is because, while the capacity of the children to select experience for (re)telling in this activity may appear reasonably open, there are in fact powerful tacit requirements constraining the choices of acceptable fields of personal experience for (re)construction in the early childhood classroom. The nature of the framing is thus stronger than might at first appear to be the case. In practice, the fields that teachers most reward in such activities as morning news are to do with happy events, such as a family party, a wedding, a visit to the zoo or a circus, staying with friends, an amusing incident with friends or family, the acquisition of and/or display of some new objects or perhaps a new pet. Talk of sad or unhappy events is generally discouraged (though Michaels, 1986, cites a child with a sad event), and a very strong expectation applies that young children will present themselves as happy, able and willing to share essentially celebratory news. Cazden (1988: 7–28) offers a discussion of 'sharing time', based on her own work and that she undertook with Michaels. She argues that sharing time is to be valued as providing 'a context for the production of narratives of personal experience' (ibid: 8), and she suggests that few other occasions in the school day allow children to engage in such activity.

I shall argue that a particular ideology of the young child is at work in the pedagogic subject position of morning news: the young child is ideally happy and pleased with life, engages in what are seen as acceptably 'wholesome' activities, and is able to offer some sustained account of these for the relatively public forum of the classroom. As I shall seek to demonstrate below, at least some children are indeed able to perform in these terms, though it remains the case that others are either unable or unwilling so to perform: the particular meanings to be made in morning news are in fact not equally available to all. Moreover, and rather ironically, given the justification offered for such activities in terms of affording opportunities to children to (re)construct 'their own experience', they frequently turn out to be among those activities in which teachers can provide least assistance to children with difficulties. That is because the fields to be selected for (re)construction, drawn as they are from outside the school, and often from intimate familial contexts, are frequently not even known to the teachers, so that assistance in some (re)building of these is not easy to give.

This chapter and the next will examine some of the features of the pedagogic subject position intended to be established in early childhood education. This will be done by reference to two different curriculum genres, selected because they are found extensively in early childhood classrooms, and because they exemplify many of the characteristics of an early childhood programme with its principles of weak classification and framing. One such genre, to be discussed in this chapter, is what is variously called 'morning news', 'news time', 'sharing time' or 'show and tell' (though the activities captured in these names are realized linguistically rather differently); the other, to be considered in Chapter 3, is an early literacy genre, devoted to the teaching and learning of writing.

Among other matters, I shall argue of both types of curriculum genres that they have been instituted in early childhood education in recent years as aspects of an educational theory to do with promoting 'language growth' or 'language competence', where this is seen as an end in itself, developed in a manner regardless of meaning orientations available to the learner, and regardless of the particular contexts of situation involved. This is a tendency particularly marked in the weakly classified and weakly framed curriculum of much early years education. That is because, regardless of what 'content' is to be dealt with, and what claims on learning and thinking such 'content' might be held to have, development of language competence will be held to be both a desirable and an achievable goal. A difficulty in such an educational theory is that it leaves poorly defined and articulated both what might be valid goals for teaching and learning, and what particular capacities in using language might best serve those goals. Competence is not an end in itself, promoted in some fashion apart from social relationships, the meaning predispositions of the learners, contexts for learning or goals for teaching and learning.

The morning news genre

The custom of holding a morning news or sharing time session in the early part of the school day is historically relatively recent. It appears to have emerged in the English-speaking world by the 1960s. The Plowden Report (1967: 210) alluded in passing to several means of promoting speech in children, including the holding of 'the "news" period', while Mehan (1979: 26) reported a 'show and tell' activity in the American primary classroom in which he did his major ethnographic study in 1974–5. It appears to have been adopted in Australia in the late 1960s. The emergence of morning news was a feature of the changing curriculum of the 1960s and 1970s, and it was justified in terms of: the opportunities it was said to give young children to talk about experiences familiar to themselves; the freedom it was alleged to allow students to select personally significant experiences from family and community settings and to bring these into the school; and the benefits it was therefore thought to confer in allowing students opportunity both for creative self-expression and for development of competence in oral language. To this day, this sort of justification is still offered for morning news or sharing time.

I shall argue that to some extent such a justification holds, at least for some children who appear to enjoy the experience of sharing news in the relatively public forum of the classroom. However, as I have already indicated, I shall also argue that in this, as in other activities, schooling privileges some students rather more than others. The ability to narrate about experience is itself an important one for living and for learning. I should note, by the way, that as I use the term 'narrate about experience' here, I intend no particular commitment to a discourse structure, and certainly not to narrative, as Labov and Waletzky (1967) for example, might have intended when analysing oral narratives; I use the term in a reasonably general sense to capture uses of language to 'tell about experience' in some sustained and coherent way. The task of learning to reconstruct experience in a manner that is comprehensible to others who were not involved in the experience is a considerable intellectual challenge, and some children clearly take longer than others to learn it.

Michaels (1986), already referred to above, examined the tasks for young children in learning to participate in the 'adult conversational world', and noted that, while the learning commenced in the family, the school had certain formal requirements in development of competence in this area. She identified the daily 'sharing time' session as an occasion when children could practise making selections of appropriate topics as well as appropriate discourse structures that helped apprentice them to the world of schooling, including its literate modes. Michaels also provided evidence that teachers, who tended to hold essentially white, literate models of what constitutes acceptable narrating or telling about experience, were inclined to privilege those children (normally white) who held similar models, while often failing to recognize and support the models for topic choice and discourse structure of the children of the more oral, Black social groups. The latter general conclusion accords with many of the findings of Bernstein (1971, 1973) and also of Heath (1983), Delpit (1995) all of whom, arguing from dissimilar theoretical frameworks, have demonstrated that young children operate with very different modes of meaning-making and communication, depending upon social class background, familial status and/or ethnicity, and they are in fact differentially rewarded by schooling. Williams (1995, 2001) has also provided evidence of very different meaning orientations in children of different social class backgrounds, having consequences for their early literacy learning.

I should note that the school in which the activities in this chapter and those in Chapter 3 were recorded was in a reasonably poor area of the city in which it occurred. Numbers of the children were drawn from non-English-speaking backgrounds, and the major bread-winners in most families had skilled or semi- skilled occupations. Skilled workers included one father who was a locomotive driver, for example, while others who were not so skilled worked as farm labourers or in local factories. The families, while not well off, were by no means destitute, and the school enjoyed the warm support of the community that it served.

The classroom in which the instance of morning news to be examined occurred was one in which open shelves ran around three walls. The students left their bags and lunches, as well as stacks of writing materials, and boxes of pencils on these shelves. Books and wall displays relevant to themes being pursued in lessons were on display and frequently changed. Small settings of chairs for children to sit in quiet areas in two corners of the room were provided Arranged in three groupings were sets of tables and chairs for the children to sit at, mainly for writing and doing maths. In the central area of the room the space was kept clear of any furniture, and as the floor was carpeted, the children were able to sit there for such activities as morning news, and also for those time of the day (normally in the afternoons) when the teacher read to them. The teacher's desk was at the front of the classroom, slightly to one side of the board, and it was accompanied by her chair. The teacher used the chair quite frequently, for such activities as marking the roll, and for reading to the class. She vacated it for the morning news sessions, allowing the news giver to take it and hence to adopt what was understood to be a reasonably privileged position.

The schematic structure of the morning news genre

Morning news was held in the morning after the class roll had been marked and lunch orders collected. The total session, devoted to roll call, lunch orders and morning news-giving, lasted about 40 minutes. A morning news genre is a curious one in some ways, in that it typically has other genres embedded in it. Its schematic structure may be displayed thus, where the names of the various elements of structure suggest the experiential meanings, and the sequence, indicated by ∧, suggests the textual organization of the genre:

Morning News Initiation ∧ *[Morning News Nomination* ∧ *(Morning News Greeting)* ∧ *Morning News Giving* ∧ *Morning News Finish]* π ∧ *Morning News Closure*

Interpersonally, the genre operates in such a manner that it is the teacher who directs activity to start and who also directs its closure, while it is in the 'middle' stages that the student selected as news giver operates with some independence:

Teacher direction – – – – – –> Student activity – – – – – –> Teacher direction

It is argued that the experiential meanings in this, as in any curriculum genre, may be described as 'constituent' or 'particulate' in that they constitute the 'content' of the genre, while the textual meanings, to do with the overall sequencing and patterning of the elements, may be described as 'periodic' or 'wave-like'. Finally, the interpersonal meanings may be said to function 'prosodically', operating fluidly throughout the text. Such a characterization owes most to the work of Halliday, and some explanation will be in order.

Discussing the nature of a text, Halliday (1979: 2000) suggested that it may, metaphorically at least, be understood as functioning like a clause. A text has a configuration of meanings that are similar to the meanings of the clause, though there is an important difference: a clause is a 'lexicogrammatical object, a structure of wording', while a text 'is a semantic object, a structure of meaning' (Halliday, 1982: 225). In systemic theory, as already discussed in Chapter 1, language is said to be metafunctional, in that some meanings are experiential, some are interpersonal and others textual. Experiential meanings, according to Halliday, may be thought of as 'constituent' or even 'particulate', following the ideas of Pike (1959, cited by Halliday, 1979: 73): they constitute the 'content' of the clause. Interpersonal meanings operate in a manner that is 'prosodic', in that they function fluidly or in a 'field-like' manner, throughout the clause. Textual meanings, to do with the organization of the clause as a message are 'periodic', or 'wave-like', giving shape and order to the way the meanings in the clause are made relevant. Matthiessen (1988, 1992) has offered a related discussion, in which he suggests the textual metafunction operates rather like a 'pulse', and that it 'ripples through the experiential structure' of the clause (1988: 165).

Turning to the elements of structure of the morning news genre, it will be seen that the Morning News Initiation is the opening element. In this, it is the teacher who commences the activity, normally with a statement such as the following, both of which were produced by two different teachers:

Okay, now it's news time.

or

News time? Who's got some news?

In that it is the teacher who initiates in this way (and never the students) we can see even in such a simple instance that it is the teacher who controls the regulative register, directing the course of events and the students' behaviour.

Beyond the initiating element, the genre moves into a recursive phase (indicated with the brackets [ ] and the symbol π), because in the course of the activity several news givers will have an opportunity to perform. The Morning News Nomination refers to the element in which the news giver is identified. Typically the children (a number of whom, but not all, are keen to contribute) will put up their hands, signalling both in their gestures and facial expressions their desire to be chosen. The teacher nominates the first child for the role of morning news giver, but, at least in the classrooms studied here, beyond that it will be the task of the morning news giver who has just concluded to nominate a successor. The Morning News Greeting is an optional element (this is denoted with the use of the rounded brackets – ( )), in that the morning news giver is often required to greet the class, as was the case in the classrooms studied here:

> Student: *Good morning, boys and girls!*
> Chorus: *Good morning, Susy!*

The salutations are very vigorously stated, and it seems there is an expectation that the children practise 'good manners' in such a vigorous exchange of greetings. This is in fact one manifestation of the operation of the regulative register. The Morning News Giving element proceeds, such that one of several possible genres is selected by the news giver, and it is thus found to be embedded within this element. Some news givers recreate some aspect of experience, such as an incident that occurred over the weekend or a pleasurable event, such as the arrival of a new baby, or, as we shall see, staying with friends and their families). In both instances, the genre requires capacity to recreate (hence 'narrate about') some sustained sequence of activities. In these cases, the language is constitutive of the activity of news giving, although gesture, facial expression and general physical disposition of the news giver are significant in establishing the overall success with which the language is used. Other news givers tend to bring in objects, such as toys or some new possession(s), display these and talk about them. In such cases, the language is ancillary to the display and viewing of the object(s), and this is really an instance of 'show and tell', which is in fact one of the several names sometimes used of the morning news session. Where the morning news giver is less successful, he or she tends to rely on the teacher's help in drawing out statements from the child; this often therefore constitutes a kind of interview genre, where it is the teacher who does the interviewing, and the news giver offers very short responses to teacher questions. The Morning News Finish comes when the news giver has completed what he/she has to say and, at least in the classrooms sampled, this is signalled by the child:

News Giver: *Finished!* (said on a high rising note, suggesting that the student is still in performance mode)

Then, the next cycle of news giving commences, with the appointment of another news giver. At least in the classrooms studied here, as already noted, the last news giver nominates the new one:

News Giver: *Stephen.* (said on a falling tone, suggesting that the performance is over, and it is time to relinquish the news giver's post)

It is the teacher who determines when the activity has lasted long enough, and she thus signals the Morning News Closure:

Teacher: *Right, that's all we have time for today. It's time to do some maths.*

or

Teacher: *Very good. Time to stop and do our writing today.*

The example I shall show here of a successful news-giving activity involved a student I shall call Susy, who had been nominated by the previous news giver. Susy was a very successful news giver, who plainly enjoyed the role, appeared to prepare for it by often bringing in items to show and tell, and was listened to by the other children with considerable attention. So successful was Susy on this occasion that the teacher allowed her to produce two genres within her news giving – a privilege not normally granted to any child who struggled with the role or who appeared not to hold the interest of the other children. The first of the two genres Susy produced is an instance of show and tell, while the latter is an instance of an anecdote, first identified in adult storytelling by Plum (1989, 1998). The text is displayed in Text 2.1, where I have labelled the two genres, and provided some linguistic commentary beside each. I shall examine each of the two embedded genres in turn. I shall firstly identify the overall schematic structure in each case, and then offer some analysis of the ways the schematic structure and the various register choices involved build the text. Before I proceed, some observations need to be made both about the operation of the two registers in morning news, and about the method I shall adopt in outlining the linguistic analyses to be offered.

Text 2.1

(Susy, having been nominated, walks from her place on the floor to take up the chair at the front of the group, carrying a plastic bag full of toys and other objects)

Susy: Good morning, boys and girls.
Chorus: Good morning, Susy.

Show and Tell

Susy: My sister's got a little pet. She reckons it's her pet. (*displays a toy racoon*)
Jodie: What is it?
Susy: A racoon.
T: Oh, how do you know it's a racoon, a racoon?
Susy: 'Cause it's got a striped tail.
T: Yes, and they've also got that striped part.
Jodie: And they've
                   ] overlap
T: around their eyes that looks like a bandit, doesn't it?
Susy: I've got a frog. (*displays it*)
Veronica: A koala. (*Susy displays this*)
Another child: A koala.
Susy: And I've got a monkey, and he sucks its thumb with both fingers. And my sister tried to make him twist its head but it can't. (*She displays the monkey as she says this*)
Anthony: What does it say? (*refers to some writing on the monkey*)
Tony: You know what monkeys do? They get fleas out of other monkeys and eat it.
Joseph: Yuk!
Stephen: His fingers doesn't stay in. (*The fingers of the monkey are in its mouth, though they tend to fall out*)
Anthony: Susy, I've got a question.
Susy: What?
Anthony: It's got a sign on it. What does it say?
Several children: What does it say?
Susy: It says 'Beware Gongo loves you', and on the back it says 'Gongo'. And my uncle gave it to us.
T: Why does it say 'Beware Gongo loves you'?
Veronica: Have you got another bangle? (*Susy has displayed a bangle*) Can they go anywhere? (*refers to whether you can put them somewhere apart from on an arm*)
Susy: And last night
                   ] overlap
T: Susy, why does it say that? Do you know?
Susy: No.
Anthony: I've got a new question.
Susy: What?

Regulative register realized in the opening salutation:
Good morning, boys and girls.
Good morning, Susy.

Instructional register in the show and tell genre realized:
Interpersonally in a series of declarative and interrogative mood choices in which Susy offers information re: her toys:
My sister's got a little pet,
or others elicit information by asking questions and Susy replies:
What is it?
A racoon,
and
What does it say?
It says 'Beware Gongo loves you', and on the back it says 'Gongo'. And my uncle gave it to us.

Experientially in transitivity choices which build information re: the field of Susy's sister's toys:
And I've got a monkey, and he sucks its thumb with both fingers. And my sister tries to make him twist its head but it can't,
or which sometimes build related fields, stimulated by talk of the main field:
You know what monkeys do? They get fleas out of other monkeys and eat it.
No, men can wear bangles.
My dad doesn't wear bangles.

Logically in a series of simple additive conjunctive relations:
<u>and</u> on the back it says 'Gongo'
<u>and</u> I've got a little plant an empty pot plant
<u>and</u> I've got a pad to write.

Textually in a series of mainly unmarked topical theme choices:
<u>my sister's</u> got a little pet
<u>she</u> reckons it's her pet,
<u>his fingers</u> doesn't stay in.

text continues

Text 2.1 – *continued*

Anthony: Is that a girl or a boy? (*Points to the monkey*)
Susy: I don't know.
Several: Boy!
Joseph: It's a boy!
Jodie: Boys can't wear bangles!
Anthony: I hope it's a girl.
Stephen: No, men can wear bangles.
Olivera: My dad does.
Frankie: Yeah Mr P does.
Tony: My dad doesn't wear bangles. (*A series of indecipherable exchanges follow for a few seconds, re whether men can wear bangles.*)
Susy: (*reaches into her bag again*) And I've got a little plant, an empty pot plant, and I've got a pad. (*displays a writing pad*)
Anthony: To write what?
Susy: I don't write. My sister does.
Anthony: What does that say? (*points to writing on pad*)
Susy: 'Chrissy', and she done some scribble round it.
Anthony: Oh, can't she draw better than that?
T: Shh! Right, that's enough, don't forget your manners.

Anecdote
Susy:

Orientation
And at Tracey's house, not yesterday but the day before, I sleeped at her place because Mum was looking after Paul.

Events
and Paul slept in my bed and Chrissy slept in her bed, and Mum and Dad slept in their bed, and I slept in Tracey's bed. And in the morning we jumped on Uncle Dougie, and we called him lazy bones, and we called him lazy bones all day.
Tracey: Who, Dougie?
Susy: Uncle Dougie, and we called my dad lazy bones, because we was the first one up, because Bradley came and jumped on us,

Crisis
and then < <when he jumped on us> >, we all got up and Bradley was screaming, 'All aboard, all aboard, the shark'll eat you!' and we was dancing all around the bed and we was jumping up and down

---

several that are both topical and interpersonal:

what is it?
why does it say 'Beware Gongo loves you'?
and a number of interpersonal themes:
<u>*Susy*</u> *I've got a question*
<u>*have*</u> *you got another bangle?*
<u>*do*</u> *you know?*

Instructional register in the anecdote genre realized in

Textually, in the adoption of a marked topical theme, indicating a move to a new genre;
and <u>at Tracey's house, not yesterday but the day before,</u> I sleeped at her place,
while with two exceptions the other topical themes are unmarked. The two exceptions are:
and <u>in the morning</u> we jumped on Uncle Dougie
and
and then ≪ *when he jumped on us* ≫ *we all got up,*
where in the latter case, a new element of structure is heralded.

Interpersonally, in a mood shift so that Susy takes up the declarative mood as of one who is informing or telling others. (There is one instance only where another child uses the interrogative mood to seek information about a person in the story: *Who? Dougie?*)

text continues

Text 2.1 – *continued*

Reaction/Completion

and then me and Tracey said 'Bradley go back to bed and Uncle Dougie and Auntie Eda'll get a headache', and he didn't! (*pronounced very emphatically on a high rising note, and with a loud laugh.*) He kept on screaming! (*Considerable laughter from the whole class greets this, lasting for several seconds*)

Morning News Finish

Susy: Finished. (*said on a high rising note*)

Experientially, in transitivity choices which build events in material processes:

I slept in Tracey's bed

Bradley came and jumped on us

when he jumped on us, we all got up

we was dancing all around the bed,

or an occasional verbal process:

Bradley was screaming, 'All aboard, all aboard, the shark'll eat you',

or several instances of the same identifying process:

we called him lazy bones,

and in associated participant roles that identify self or family members.

Logically, in a series of clauses linked mainly by additive or temporal conjunctive relations:

and Paul slept in my bed

and Chrissy slept in my bed

and mum and dad slept in their bed

and I slept in Tracey's bed

and then we called him lazy bones all day

For reasons outlined in Chapter 1, the pedagogic discourse is said to have two registers – the regulative and the instructional – the former to do with the overall ordering, sequencing and management of the discourse, and the latter to do with the particular field of experience taken up in the pedagogic activity. In the morning news genre the regulative register operates overtly to initiate the activity, to organize the sequence in which news givers take their turns and to close the activity. It is within the Morning News Giving element itself that the instructional field comes to the fore, and it is this which the news giver selects and develops. The regulative register continues to operate tacitly during the news giving, as I have already noted, and in the text discussed here there is one point at which it operates overtly, when the teacher corrects unacceptable behaviour. Nonetheless, it is the instructional register that is primarily to the fore in the Morning News Giving element: hence the linguistic analysis will mainly discuss its realization. Apart from this, it should be noted that in offering the linguistic analyses, I shall move through the various metafunctions (already explained in Chapter 1), seeking to demonstrate how each is involved in the construction of the overall text. I should note, however, that I shall not necessarily proceed by examining the operation of the metafunctions in the same order in either the text to be examined here, or indeed those looked at in later chapters. While all the metafunctions are important, it proves helpful to consider them in different ways in various genres, depending upon the particular configurations of linguistic choices concerned.

Show and tell

Strictly, show and tell has no distinctive generic structure, since it is the activity of displaying the objects which determines the overall ordering and staging of the pattern of talk, rather than any particular schema that unfolds to achieve goals. For convenience, we will nonetheless refer to a 'show and tell genre', noting that its structure is extremely simple:

Show ∧ Talk π

Show involves physical display of an item or items, while Talk involves the telling about the object, as well as any exchanges with the news giver's audience about the object(s). The pattern is recursive.

The opening salutation is outside the show and tell genre. Where it occurs, it realizes the regulative register, for it has a significance in shaping behaviour. Apart from the general goal of developing language competence, early childhood teachers regard the morning news session as an important activity in which to impress upon young children their responsibilities in such matters as attending to each other, addressing each other politely, and generally being quiet and still while others are speaking. The opening salutation is a small if important realization of the regulative register, intended to impress upon children their obligations in addressing each other politely. It is because of its significance in this sense that some early childhood teachers, at least, insist upon the exchange of greetings each time a child gets up to speak, even though such a requirement is rather excessive, given that the children interact so freely with each other on a daily basis. The one instance at which the regulative register is realized as the text unfolds, occurs when the teacher indicates that the remark made by a child is unacceptable:

Shh! Right, that's enough, don't forget your manners!

I have said that the structure rests on the physical display of objects and the accompanying talk. Hence, without preamble, Susy displays a toy and says:

My sister's got a little pet. She reckons it's her pet.

To which a child responds:

What is it?

This sets a recursive pattern for the rest of the text, while it also establishes the interpersonal functioning of the text. Thus, it proceeds through an interplay of declarative and interrogative mood choices, as Susy informs her listeners of what she has to display and responds to questions:

T: *Oh, how do you know it's a racoon, a racoon?*
Susy: *Cause it's got a stripey tail.*

Sometimes, so animated is the talk as it proceeds, other children offer remarks:

You know what monkeys do? They get fleas out of other monkeys and eat it,

and on the talk proceeds in a highly interactive manner.

It will be noted that all the clauses in Susy's show and tell are constructed in grammatically congruent ways.

Experientially, the text constructs simple personal experience, where this involves initially several possessive processes, relevant to establishing ownership of the objects:

My sister	's got	a little pet
Carrier: Possessor	Pro: possessive	Attribute: possessed
it	's got	a stripey tail
Carrier: Possessor	Pro: possessive	Attribute: possessed
I	've got	a monkey
Carrier: Possessor	Pro: possessive	Attribute: possessed
I	've got	a little plant
Carrier: Possessor	Pro: possessive	Attribute: possessed

There are a few other relational processes. One such process is identifying, while some attributive processes help establish characteristics:

she	reckons	it	's	her little pet
Senser	process: cognition	Carrier	Pro: intensive	Attribute

what	is	it	
Value	Process: intensive	Token	

is	that	a girl or a boy
Pro: intensive	Carrier	Attribute

A few material processes establish what toys and/or their owner 'do':

he	sucks	his thumb		
Actor	Pro: material	Goal		

my sister	tries to make	him	twist	its head
Initiator	Pro: causative	Actor	Pro: material	Goal

while some verbal processes have a role in establishing what some writing 'says':

| on the back | it | says | 'Gongo' |
| Circumstance: location: place | Sayer | Pro: verbal | Verbiage |

| what | does | that | say? |
| Verbiage | Pro: | Sayer | verbal |

Participant roles are constructed in very simple nominal groups, and they identify *Susy*, her *sister*, the toys (e.g., *a racoon*) and occasionally family members of children in the class, such as *my dad*. Almost no circumstances are constructed, the one exception occurring when Susy says of her sister and her writing : *she done some scribble round it*. This is of some interest, because as we shall see, Susy does provide some circumstantial information in her anecdote. The demands of this genre, depending as it does very considerably upon visible display of the objects, are apparently such that Susy feels no need to provide circumstantial information.

For related reasons to do with the activities of displaying objects, the text makes limited use of conjunctive relations, apart from occasional uses of the additive conjunctive, where the intention is to provide some connectedness to the other objects already displayed, as in:

and I've got a little plant, an empty yellow pot plant.

Textually, Susy's most significant topical theme choices signal the introduction of items on display and, with one exception, her topical themes are unmarked:

My sister's got a little pet
I've got a frog
and I've got a monkey
and I've got a little plant
and I've got a little pad.

The one marked topical theme occurs when she says:

and on the back it says 'Gongo'.

She has in fact little need of marked topical themes, given that the object is simply to display and comment. Other theme choices, part topical and part interpersonal, help to sustain and forward the talk:

what is it?
what does it say?
oh how do you know it's a racoon?
what does it say?

Textual theme choices are relatively few and where they occur they are realized in structurals (the same language items in fact, as those in which the conjunctive relations are realized):

and I've got a monkey
and I've got a little plant
and I've got a pad.

The mode is dialogic, where the language uses are ancillary to the display of the objects.

Overall, the show and tell genre is a linguistically simple text type, whose success depends very considerably upon satisfactory selection and display of some object(s), of a kind likely to appeal to one's audience, although capacity to comment upon the objects and to answer questions about these is clearly very important. It is in some ways surprising that Susy selected her little sister's toys: other examples of show and tell I observed normally involved the news giver in displaying some object(s) owned by the child, rather than another, younger child. Why might Susy select the toys of a younger child, and what are we to make of the activity overall? Susy must have chosen the field because she was aware firstly, that it would be approved by her teacher and fellow students. But it is also clear that she had another reason for her choice: the field selection allowed Susy to acknowledge, but also gently laugh at, the activities of a younger sibling, one who was not yet old enough to join the ranks of the 'bigger children' who had started school, and who were members of this class. One child, it will be noted, was rather scornful of Susy's sister's drawing: *Oh, can't she draw better than that?* and, as we have already seen, the teacher, not happy at this, responded, *Shh! Right, that's enough, don't forget your manners.* The importance of the relative 'bigness' and sense of 'being older' of Susy and her class mates was at issue here, comfortingly affirmed by reflection upon what a smaller and younger child was capable of doing (or alternatively, of not being able to do so well) when compared with older children.

The second of Susy's genres – an anecdote – was remarkably different linguistically from her first genre though, as we shall see, issues of childhood, this time in terms of relationships with adults, were again very much to the fore in Susy's field selection. Where children are given some capacity to select from fields of personal experience to talk about, the skilled ones at least will find ways obliquely to acknowledge the authority of adults and point to ways they sometimes challenge that authority. Before I commence the discussion of Susy's anecdote I should offer some explanation of the genre.

Anecdotes were first identified and described in detail by Plum (1989, 1998) who studied oral storytelling in adult Australian native speakers of English, and he adopted the term 'anecdote' to distinguish a particular type of story he found from a number of other stories he collected. At the time the best known oral narrative genre, identified by Labov and Waletzky (1967) and later developed by Rothery and Martin (e.g., Martin and Rothery, 1980;

Rothery, 1990) in examining children's writing, was said to have the structure of:

(Abstract) ∧ Orientation ∧ Complication ∧ Evaluation ∧ Resolution ∧ (Coda).

According to Plum, anecdotes, like narratives, are intended primarily to entertain, yet the manner in which the two structures unfold, and the fundamental purposes of the two differ very considerably, particularly in terms of the interpersonal meanings involved in each type of genre. Both crucially introduce some complication or crisis, yet the two differ in the way they handle the crisis and achieve some sense of completion. Plum (1989: 225) argued that while 'both narrative and anecdote are focussed on a crisis, narrative alone creates a balanced movement of rising tension, sustained suspense and falling tension', as in the Complication, Evaluation and Resolution pattern. He held that the anecdote has a crisis element, but it has no resolution. On the contrary, lacking such an element, the success of the anecdote depends upon a shared but essentially non-verbal response to the crisis, acknowledged by the interlocutors in a burst of laughter, a gasp of shock or horror, or even a sudden silence. Anecdotes, as Plum described them, are in particular associated with the oral mode, because they rely so much upon the face to face participation of storyteller and audience, and upon their shared awareness of the significance and/or challenge of some critical event. I have, incidentally, found evidence of such genres in the oral storytelling of adolescents (see Christie and Soosai, 2001, chapter 2) and I conclude that such genres have considerable value and significance at all stages of life, including among the adults in whom Plum originally described them. The elements of structure of the anecdote may be displayed thus:

Orientation ∧ (Events) ∧ Crisis ∧ Reaction ∧ Completion.

The Orientation establishes persons in some sense of temporal and/or spatial setting. The Events element is an optional one, for, according to Plum, sometimes there is only an Orientation, followed immediately by a Crisis. The Crisis introduces a problem whose significance is that it offers some challenge to the usual order of events (a characteristic also of the Complication element in a narrative, though in the latter case, there is some return to usuality, achieved in the Resolution); the Reaction indicates a response to the Crisis, and the significance of that Reaction relies upon a shared appreciation of the horror or the humour of that Crisis, expressed as I have noted, in laughter, a gasp or even in silence. No Resolution is offered. Beyond that, the anecdote has a final element termed the Completion, whose function is to 'round off' the genre. In the case of Susy's genre, her tale concerns the events that occurred when she stayed with certain family members on a Saturday night (though she doesn't mention this night was involved), so that, on the Sunday morning, when all the adults might well be looking to sleep rather later than during the working week, they were disturbed because her cousin Bradley, her friend Tracey and she herself were all behaving rather boisterously. Incidentally, the family relationships for anyone not knowing the family involved (as some in the classroom obviously did) are a little confused, reflecting the very intimate family knowledge that was really being shared. The point or 'punchline' of Susy's anecdote rests on the implicit under-standing that young children should not yell and make a loud disturbance in the mornings when the adults in the household want to sleep on for a while. Where children persist in such behaviour, they risk very sharp reproof for being naughty. It is the shared sense of naughtiness – in this case apparently unchecked – which makes Susy's little tale very enjoyable to her peers, and even her teacher smiles.

Susy's anecdote

The schematic structure of Susy's anecdote, following Plum's description outlined above, is as follows:

Orientation ∧ Events ∧ Crisis ∧ Reaction/Completion

The shift in Susy's text from show and tell to an anecdote genre is in many ways made most markedly in the textual choices and the mode of communication. Where the show and tell was dialogic, this text is monologic, as of one who talks uninterruptedly to an audience (save for one point at which a child seeks clarification regarding the identity of a person in the story). The Orientation is signalled textually, partly through the use of the structural *and*, but mainly through a marked topical theme which advises Susy's listeners that she is shifting into a different stage of her news giving, which she is foregrounding:

And <u>at Tracey's house, not yesterday but the day before</u>, I sleeped at her place...

The subsequent Events element involves a series of textual and topical themes, one of which is again marked (indicated with double underlining), and the effect of all of which is to help create a continuous flow of event:

<u>and</u> Paul slept in my bed
<u>and</u> <u>Chrissy</u> slept in her bed,
<u>and</u> Mum and Dad slept in their bed,
<u>And</u> I slept in Tracey's bed.
<u>And</u> <u>in the morning</u> we jumped on Uncle Dougie,
<u>and</u> <u>we called him</u> lazy bones,
<u>and</u> we called him lazy bones all day.
<u>and</u> <u>we</u> called my dad lazy bones,
<u>because</u> we was the first ones up,
<u>because</u> <u>Bradley</u> came and jumped on us

The move to the Crisis is again indicated with a marked topical theme, this time realized in an enclosed dependent clause:

and then ≪ *when he jumped on us* ≫ * *we all got up*
and Bradley was screaming, 'All aboard, all aboard, the shark'll eat you!'
and we was dancing around the bed
and we was jumping up and down.

* The symbols ≪ ≫ indicate an enclosed hypotactic or dependent clause. Such a clause is said to be enclosed because it is removed from what would be the more usual or 'unmarked' position for the clause, and displaced, in this case, in order to make it thematic. The unmarked way to represent the two clauses involved here would be 'and then we all got up when he jumped on us'.

The final stage, building both Reaction to the Crisis and Completion of the genre, uses simple textual and unmarked topical themes:

and then me and Tracey said, 'Bradley go back to bed and Uncle Dougie and Auntie Eda'll get a headache',
and he didn't,
he kept on screaming.

Experientially, the text, like the show and tell genre, relies heavily upon building the experiences of family and friends, so that it is they who are generally identified in the various participant roles in transitivity throughout the genre: *Tracey, Mum and Dad, Chrissy, Uncle Dougie*. The majority of the process types are material and they feature strongly in building both the Orientation and the Events element, for example:

I	slept	at her place
Actor	Pro: material	Circumstance: location: place
Bradley	came	
Actor	Pro: material	
and	jumped	on us
	Pro: material	Circumstance: location: place

though three instances of the same identifying process are also used in these two elements:

we	called	him	lazybones
Assigner	Pro: intensive	Token	Value

we	called	him	lazy bones	all day
Assigner	Pro: intensive	Token	Value	Circumstance: Extent: time

we	called	my dad	lazybones
Assigner	Pro: intensive	Token	Value

A verbal process appears in the Crisis, adding to the building of activity which is also built in more material processes:

and	Bradley was screaming: All aboard . . .
	Sayer Pro: verbal

we	was dancing	all around the bed
Actor	Pro: material	Circumstance: location: place

As already noted, the 'punchline' comes when, in the Reaction/Completion stage, Susy reports that she and Tracey told Bradley to go back to bed:

and then	me and Tracey	said
	Sayer	Pro: verbal

Bradley	go	back to bed
	Pro: material	Circumstance: Location: place

and	Uncle Dougie and Auntie Eda	'll get	a headache
	Behaver	Pro: behavioural	Range

She goes on to employ another material process, this time with an instance of a negative polarity, and this is followed after a pause, and with considerable amusement in her voice, by another behavioural process realizing Bradley's naughty behaviour:

and	he	didn't	(go back to bed)
	Actor	Pro: material	

he	kept on screaming
Behaver	Pro: behaviour

Interpersonally, the whole text relies at all stages upon Susy's use of the declarative mood, as she tells her tale; in speech functions terms, her role is to inform her listeners. However, it is in the final stage that the text works most powerfully interpersonally. It is here, Susy having identified Bradley's failure to do as asked, so that he apparently continued to make a noise and disturb the adults, that the whole class bursts into laughter, sustained for several seconds. Thus, by implication, did one child disturb and challenge the usual course of events which would require that he not be rowdy and disturb adults, especially on a Sunday morning: and the particular pleasure for these young children is that he apparently got away with it. Susy, while careful to identify Bradley as responsible for the naughty behaviour, leaves a general understanding that she was herself complicit in it, and certainly inclined to rejoice in it. The other children in the class understand the nature of adult authority and they are aware of the general expectation that they obey it, so that they enjoy the telling of a tale in which adult authority has been mildly challenged.

To return for the moment to an aspect of transitivity, it will be recalled that in the discussion of the show and tell, I noted that Susy made little use of circumstantial information, and that she used considerably more in the anecdote. We can see that in the latter case, she makes extensive use of circumstances of place, albeit in a repetitive way

I sleeped at her place
Paul slept in my bed
Chrissy slept in her bed
Mum and dad slept in their bed
I slept in Tracey's bed
we jumped on Uncle Dougie
Bradley came and jumped on us
we was dancing all around the bed
we was jumping up and down
Bradley go back to bed

The other circumstances she uses are of two of time:

not yesterday but the day before, I sleeped...
in the morning we jumped on Uncle Dougie...

Stories of personal experience will no doubt make considerable use of circumstances of time and place, for it is in these that a great deal of the circumstantial information of interest to interlocutors is constructed. This accounts for Susy's greater use of them in her second genre. It also provides some of the linguistic evidence with which we can establish the presence of a different types of genre from the first example.

Finally, to return to a matter I raised with respect to the show and tell genre, it will be observed that the language is again grammatically congruent, and this is what one would expect of children as young as Susy and her class mates.

We may now summarize the details of Susy's Morning News Giving element. Firstly, it consists of two genres – a show and tell and an anecdote – each of them drawing rather differently upon the linguistic system in order to build their meanings. Secondly, the two genres reveal that such a child, generally successful as she was in morning news giving, recognized and selected fields of personal experience that were within the general range of appropriate instructional fields for such an occasion. They were about family members and, in the first case, in particular about the possessions of one family member. Thirdly, the two genres had some interest because they revealed how a skilled news giver could take familiar, commonplace experience and give it a significance in terms of the values of early childhood. On the one hand, the first genre reinforced the sense of relative capacity enjoyed by Susy and her peers by drawing attention to the lesser capacity of a child still too young to come to school. On the other hand, the second genre acknowledged adult authority yet also celebrated one occasion on which such authority was apparently successfully challenged, though not in a manner that earned a reproof from the teacher. Both genres were constructed with some verve, bringing pleasure to the audience of students and teacher who all laughed at Susy's morning news giving.

At this point it will be worth asking what principles of evaluation appear to apply in morning news, for these are relevant to determining what constitutes successful adoption of the pedagogic subject position for this genre.

Success in the role of morning news giver: principles of evaluation

It will be recalled that in Chapter 1 I argued, following Bernstein, that a pedagogic discourse operates in such a way that discourses from some setting beyond the school are taken and 'relocated', to use Bernstein's word, for the purposes of the pedagogic activity. Furthermore, it was suggested, the pedagogic discourse is realized through the operation of the two 'registers' in such a way that the regulative register 'projects' the instructional register. It is the regulative register, in other words, that creates the pedagogic goals for an educational activity, shaping the pacing and sequencing of the activity and, in particular, setting the principles of evaluation for that activity. Earlier in this chapter, I observed of early childhood education in which morning news is a common practice, that the curriculum is weakly classified, in that its areas of knowledge are not strongly 'insulated' from each other. I also observed that it is weakly framed, in that it is open to children to make selections of experience for morning news giving, though I have also said that such selections are more constrained than might at first appear. Finally I have observed of morning news that it is intended to promote oral language competence, in a manner believed to enhance personal development and learning. Critical to the pedagogic discourse as Bernstein writes of it, are the principles of evaluation that will apply as a necessary feature of its operation. I have examined one instance of morning news giving involving two genres, and I propose on the basis of that to consider those principles of evaluation that appear to apply. 'The key to pedagogic practice', Bernstein (1990: 186) suggests 'is *continuous evaluation*' (his italics).

Given that the curriculum for morning news is weakly classified and framed, the principles of evaluation, while capable of being established, are not in fact ever well enunciated, so that the measures of success that apply tend to remain tacit and part of the 'hidden curriculum' of early schooling. I would argue that the relative absence of explicit criteria of evaluation is at least one ground for concern about the practice of morning news. Those children who, in terms of prior life experience, are relatively well prepared for the language of schooling, often enjoy participation in such activities because, although the criteria to guide performance are not made clear, they are enabled to deduce the practices required for successful participation. However, many children do not benefit from the morning news activity, while the claimed advantages of enhanced oral capacity very frequently elude them. About this, I shall have more to say below. First let me turn to what constitutes success, and hence the evaluation criteria that apply.

As we have seen, success depends upon, and is evaluated in terms of, capacity to move to the front of a class group and engage in the relatively public task of initiating, developing and sustaining a coherent text, such that some field of personal experience is (re)created for several minutes. The language of the text may be ancillary to some activity, such as a display of objects, or it may be largely constitutive of the task, as when the news giver recreates personal experience. The speaker is required to be audible, interesting, ideally amusing and capable of selecting a field of experience that involves happy or entertaining event. Formal requirements the successful news giver must accept in order to be enabled to assume the role include a willingness (i) to put up a hand and politely await a turn to be nominated, (ii) to move to the front of the group, (iii) (at least in the classrooms reported here) to exchange a salutation with other class members, (iv) to give the news, (v) (again at least in the classrooms reported here) to nominate a subsequent news giver and (vi) to accept the need to return to the floor along with other class members.

Other class members, also evaluated for their success as listeners, must listen politely, ask questions where appropriate, and generally be attentive. It will be recalled that, at only one point in the text we have examined, the teacher called one student to order, and it will also be recalled that she invoked the importance of not forgetting *your manners*, since he had made a remark deemed unacceptable. His problem was not that he had been inattentive, or that he had not offered comments or questions: his problem was that his comment was not of the sort the activity required or rewarded.

The ideal pedagogic subject position in morning news, then, is that of one who can successfully select an aspect of personal experience, chosen for its generally happy, celebratory or amusing significance and (re)create it in a sustained sequence of talk, while also observing the proprieties that should be observed in facing the audience of one's peers. The corresponding subject position for the other class members is that of attentive listeners, though some genres admit questioning or making comments, where these, as we have seen, must also remain within the proprieties for 'good manners' that apply.

Non-success in morning news giving

What of those students who do not achieve the necessary competence as morning news givers? How are we to explain them? Elsewhere (Christie, 1997: 144) I have referred to the case of the early childhood teacher (not the one whose classroom activity is used in this chapter) who turned to a boy whom I shall call Ken, who never volunteered for morning news giving, and commented that he 'never had anything nice or interesting happen to him'. The remark was rather hurtful, but apart from that, it begged many other questions. The topics that were selected for morning news in the classroom in question (much like those in the room reported here) all concerned commonplace activities of a kind that may well have been (and probably were) a feature of the life of the boy in question: such activities as visits to a family member such as a grandparent, going to a party, the acquisition of a new toy or pet, and so on. If they were an aspect of Ken's life, we must assume that he either didn't want to participate in telling news himself, or that he was unable to do so, constrained perhaps by a predisposition to organize and construct meanings in other ways from Susy, reflecting his rather different orientations to experience and meaning construction. I should note, by the way, that Ken was always willing to listen politely to others in morning news, and indeed talked quite animatedly among his friends at other times of the school day. Whether he was unable or unwilling to participate in morning news in one sense does not matter to this discussion: the fact is that as an activity intended to promote oral language competence morning news simply failed in his case.

As I noted much earlier, morning news is not an activity in which the interested teacher might give much help to the student, and this is a consequence of the condition that applies by which the responsibility for the field selections, as well selection of the relevant genre, is left to the children. Gray (1999) has argued very powerfully the value of shared experience in classrooms where teachers are to work with students in promoting their language and learning. Shared activities permit what he terms 'inter-subjective sharing' (ibid: 38), following D'Andrade (1987), for it is in the sharing that joint construction of meaning is made possible, such that students are assisted to learn, practise and, indeed, rehearse the language necessary for some task(s). Gray's particular preoccupations, at least in the reference cited here, are with the teaching and learning of literacy, rather than oral language, to Australian Aboriginal children, though the general principles he proposes he would argue apply as much to oral language learning, and as much to other children.

A situation in which the curriculum is so weakly framed as morning news can place an unreasonable burden upon the child who is expected to talk about experience in some sustained way, particularly where the object is to recreate some event. The teacher, not party to the events to be talked about, is often unable to assist the child in selecting or reconstructing happenings.

Another child, whom I shall call Christopher, often brought to school some object(s) to display at morning news, and he evinced considerable interest in being chosen for the role of morning news giver. Yet he never managed to develop much facility for the role and could not really be deemed a competent morning news giver. Here I shall display one of many morning news sequences involving Christopher and another teacher. Christopher always managed his Morning News Greeting in a loud voice:

Christopher: *Good morning.*
Chorus: *Good morning, Christopher.*

But beyond this he rapidly became largely incoherent, reluctant to do much with the toys he had brought with him, inclined to cover his face with a hand, presumably out of shyness, and the teacher thus adopted what I much earlier referred to as a kind of interview genre, in which she did most of the talking.

Christopher having produced a toy car, the talk proceeded thus:

Christopher: *I've got a car.*
T: *What's that make it go, does it?* (points to mechanism on the side of the car for winding up the toy)
Another child: *I know.*
T: *Well, let Christopher tell please. Oh that's really good, isn't it?* (Christopher has wound the key, creating a mechanical noise) *What's the number on the front, Christopher?*
Christopher: *Five.* (It is in fact 50)
T: *Yes, but what's the whole number?*
Christopher: *Um.* (covers his face)
T: *It's a big number.*
Another child: *I know.*
Several children: *Fifty.*
T: *Right, well you tell us Kelly.* (asked because she didn't call out like the others)
Kelly: *Fifty.*
T: *Right, number 50 in the race. What else have you got there?* (points to a brown

paper bag containing other cars, which Christopher displays without comment)
T: *Where did you get them?*
Christopher: *My dad.*
T: *Your dad* (slight pause while she waits for him to say more; receiving no comment, she goes on) *Well, how did you get them? I mean, did you buy them?*
Christopher: *No, I don't know where he gets them.*
T: *Lots of lovely, lovely cars. Are there many local ones?* (a reference to the fact that racing cars sometimes bear the names of the towns where their owners reside)
Christopher: *Mmm* (appears quite uncertain)
T: *Which is your favourite team?*
Christopher: *Umm* (again hides his face)

Various children, hearing this as a request for information about football rather than motor racing teams, call out the names of their favourite football teams' names, though Christopher remains silent.

T: *Right well, you pop them all in and put them over on the shelf.* (Christopher does as he is told, then returns to his place on the floor)

The teacher here concluded the news giving, principally because it seemed Christopher would not do so.

Space will not permit any linguistic analysis of this little text. Instead, I shall comment on some matters that are revealing. As a general principle the successful morning news giver, whether retelling event or displaying some object, needs to elaborate upon experience in the desired manner. Christopher seems incapable of elaborating upon his experience as, for example, in responding to the teacher's questions about where the toy cars came from. One is tempted to think that Susy, asked a similar question about her toys, would be capable, not necessarily of saying where they came from (if she genuinely didn't know) but of nonetheless responding to the question by drawing on related experiences in some way that would not leave her unable to expand on the point. She might, for example, acknowledge that she didn't know where her dad got the toys, but she might then go on to talk of related experiences marking those occasions when other toys were purchased perhaps, or perhaps she might refer to the shops where such things are often bought. This ability to introduce and draw upon wider experiences is one dimension of what is involved in 'narrating about' experience in some way. It is not that Christopher is necessarily incapable of drawing upon such experience, but it would seem that he is not equipped in terms of prior life experience to recognize that this might be a legitimate, even a useful thing to do. Williams (1995, 2001), referred to earlier, and following Bernstein's work, has suggested that young children function with different meaning orientations, depending upon familial background; those of professional backgrounds tend to be enabled, in building any one text, to draw into and inform its construction by reference to other texts and experiences, whereas those of non-professional backgrounds are less likely to do so. This is a tendency, of course, and it does not always apply to all children: that is to say, not all children of professional families are enabled to produce sustained talk which elaborates upon experience, just as not all children of non-professional families are unable to do so.[1] Susy, who was always a vocal child, was capable of producing texts which involved drawing upon and narrating about experience in a sustained way, and we may conclude that she had certain orientations towards the construction of meanings in texts which were not available to Christopher.

Again the experience of Gray (1999) referred to earlier, is relevant here: if the object is to encourage children to develop facility in talking about the features of some object or perhaps about how it works, then, working with extremely deprived Aboriginal children, he has demonstrated that this requires considerable modelling and rehearsal with the teacher or some other significant adult. Teacher and student(s) need to work together with the object(s), and/or with any shared experience they might need to recreate; they need to rehearse the talk required to deal with the object or experience, often over periods of several days, revisiting the activity, but in such a way that it remains enjoyable and that the student(s) slowly assume a growing responsibility for using the necessary language. Along the way, Gray builds in constant reference to other texts, often quite demanding ones, and he reads these with the children, drawing on them for joint construction of written texts about the object(s), and revisiting them frequently for their values in informing different types of activities; he thereby allows the students to experience opportunities in informing the engagement with the object(s) or experience by constructing other meanings about it. By implication at least, the possibilities are made available to children for working on any one text and experience by reference to other related ones. To engage in such a way, so Gray would argue, is one manifestation of scaffolding – a term he takes from Bruner (1983) though many other writers use it today.

One of the several problems of a morning news activity using an object for show and tell is that it tends not to admit sufficient scaffolding.[2] Such an occasion by its nature is essentially a 'one-off ' activity, having no prior educational 'lead-up', and equally, having no planned 'follow-up'. In such a case, the activity of displaying a toy offers limited educative value either to the news giver or his audience, and at least in the case of a child like Christopher, it served to leave him much as he had been before the activity started. Indeed, Christopher made negligible gains in morning news (a view generally held by his teachers) though, rather sadly, he continued to volunteer for the role.

Competence as an educational goal

As I noted earlier, central to the pedagogic goals of such an activity as morning news lies the commitment to its claimed values in promoting oral language competence. Conceptions of 'competence', so Bernstein (2000: 41–63) suggests, were incorporated extensively into educational theorizing over the latter half of the twentieth century dating from the 1960s on, and they were borrowed from many scholars, as various, for example, as Piaget, Hymes, Garfinkle, Chomsky and Lévi-Strauss. Though their scholarly preoccupations were very different, they all contributed to the articulation of a particular model of 'competence' in education which involved several ideas: the notion that competence was available to all, suggesting that 'all are inherently competent and all possess common procedures'; a related notion that the subject operates creatively in constructing 'a valid world of meanings and practice', and that difference, not deficit, explains variations in performance; 'an emphasis on the subject as self-regulating, a benign development', and an associated idea that such development is not promoted through formal instruction; a sceptical view of hierarchical relations, such that for many contexts the function of the 'socializer' (in education of course, the teacher) is understood as 'facilitation, accommodation, and context management'; and finally, a shift to a perspective that is essentially of the present, having consequences for changed conceptions of both the past and the future (Bernstein, 2000: 43). The influence of the latter shift of perspective for educational theory and practice, as I understand the matter, is that it tends to stress the immediate in terms of skills, understandings and performance, while diminishing the significance of capacities developed in some more sustained way over time, where they will carry some sense of their developmental history; it also carries no sense of possible future ways of either using the capacities involved or of amending or developing them further in the light of experience.

All these characteristics of competence as Bernstein identifies them seem to me to be identifiable in the morning news activity, with its weak classification and framing. Competence is indeed seen as a 'good', capable of being achieved by every child, and while the notion is superficially attractive, it denies the fact that not all children will be able, or prepared by life experience and opportunity, to 'possess common procedures' to go about the morning news task. It is not helpful to pretend otherwise. As for the second of Bernstein's features of the notion of competence, it is also true that all students are held, theoretically at least, to operate creatively in constructing 'a valid world of meanings and practice', though in fact they perform very variably, and at times the differences are explained in terms of 'difference', not deficit. While I am not, by the way, arguing the virtues of a deficit model over a difference one, in the cases of children such as Ken and Christopher, I do point out that to explain their cases in terms of 'difference' is not in itself a sufficient strategy, since it implies that the teacher has no responsibility to do anything to intervene in the situation: difference is all. The third and fourth of Bernstein's features of the notion of competence are very much at work in morning news: it is true that through the regulative register there is a strong pedagogic goal to do with observing 'good manners' and with following the proprieties, as well, as we have seen, with offering sustained telling about experience. The expectations for following desirable procedures are very much to do with 'context management' and with general 'accommodation' of the children. However, save that the instructional field should be about acceptable areas of experience, there is no teacher intervention at all, and this is seen as a virtue: the teacher's role is that of 'facilitation' only of language performance. As for the last of Bernstein's features of competence as an aspect of educational theory, as I have said, I take this to refer to the ways in which a great deal of educational theory and practice appear to uphold the virtues of what I might term 'the immediate performance' in the classroom, be that a 'one-off' morning news giving or perhaps a 'one-off' writing activity, undertaken with no prior learning experiences being drawn upon, and no subsequent related learning experiences to be pursued. In such cases, no sense of developmental progression in understanding or in mastery of skills is planned for, or even thought to be necessary. Teaching–learning activity in such a circumstance is endlessly about the 'here and now', and never about sustained growth and development in understanding, which will necessarily take place over time.

Conclusion

This chapter has sought to open discussion of how a pedagogic subject position is constructed in educational settings by examining the early childhood educational activity of morning news, chosen because it has become a familiar aspect of much educational practice in the English-speaking world. As such, it is of interest, both in terms of the ideology of early childhood education it upholds, and in terms of the opportunity it offers to explore how meanings are constructed in at least one early childhood activity devoted to facilitation of oral language capacity. For reasons I alluded to much earlier in this chapter, I would argue that it is important that children develop capacities in using language to narrate about experience, for such capacities, among others, are desirable for living and for learning. I have examined one instance of morning news giving in which one child demonstrated her competence to take up the role of news giver, and I have suggested that for the child involved it may well have been a useful activity: it was at any rate an enjoyable one for Susy and her classmates.

The question I would hope this chapter has raised is this: are the educational principles and theory on which activities such as morning news are based the most efficacious for teaching and learning oral language? Morning news is but one activity in an early childhood curriculum which is often marked by weak classification and framing of knowledge. Such a curriculum is remarkable among other matters, for the lack of a distinctive character or definition accorded different areas of knowledge, or the kinds of associated skills students might need for handling such areas of knowledge. On the contrary, such a curriculum attaches a virtue to facilitation of some generally conceived 'competences', including language competences, and it sacrifices or denies what might otherwise be opportunities to teach clearly focused areas of knowledge, as well as to teach useful skills relevant to those areas of knowledge. There is no reason why schools should ruthlessly deny children opportunities to talk, or even to write, about areas of personal experience. Indeed, much time-honoured teaching practice has started with what children know and are familiar with, and, using this as a basis, has moved on to extend their understandings beyond the known and the familiar. However, personal experience is an insufficient basis on which to develop a school curriculum or to provide an entry to the 'uncommonsense' knowledge of schooling. Let us by all means seek to develop the abilities of children to use language successfully for the purposes of learning, but let us do so by providing them with significant bodies of knowledge to work with, and by challenging them to learn the necessary skills to handle and use the knowledge. This is a process that can commence when children first come to school.

Notes

1. Hasan (1989) and Williams (1995) both provide very convincing statistical evidence to support the claim that there is a strong correlation between social class background and capacity to function with meaning orientations that predispose the subject to build elaboration upon experience.
2. Adendorff (1999) who studied morning news activities in early childhood classrooms in South Africa, found evidence that some teachers, at least, deliberately intervened in situations where children displayed toys, moving them into rather more independent or 'decontextualized' uses of language, of a kind useful for some rehearsal of the language of literacy. Where this occurred, it might be said that some form of scaffolding did apply.

3 Early literacy teaching and learning

Introduction

In my earlier chapters, I outlined the general theoretical framework being pursued here, as a basis for exploring and analysing classroom discourse. Briefly, the theoretical framework proposes a model of pedagogic discourse such that it unfolds through the operation of two registers. In Chapter 2, I used the method of analysis to demonstrate the ways in which the pedagogic discourse was realized in an instance of early childhood education, with a particular focus on what I termed the morning news genre. I sought to reveal how the regulative and instructional registers operated, suggesting that the former 'projects' the latter, in that it is responsible for initiating teaching–learning activities, for ordering and sustaining them and for providing the principles by which participation in morning news is evaluated. The instructional register, on the other hand, identifies the instructional field(s) or 'content' selected for taking up in the act of morning news giving. I argued that the morning news activity is an unusual one in some ways because it gives rise to a genre embedded within the overall genre: it is realized linguistically quite differently from the regulative register, so that there is a very limited overt association of the two. This is a consequence of an activity in which a value attaches to leaving responsibility for the selection of the instructional field to the news giver. Thereby also, I suggested, are some of the causes of problems in such activities as morning news, for they deprive the teacher of opportunity to intervene in the teaching–learning activity, leaving an often unreasonable responsibility for field selection and its organization upon the young learner. As discussions in other chapters in this book will seek to argue, successful teaching–learning activity occurs when there is a very intimate association of the two registers at significant developmental stages across the genre, or across the macrogenre, where the latter larger unity applies. I suggested that the emergence of activities such as morning news had been a result of the adoption of weak principles of classification and framing in early childhood education, and I claimed that the principles of analysis adopted were useful in exposing the limitations of such weak classification and framing.

In this chapter, pursuing the last point a little longer, I aim to examine one other instance of a genre drawn from early childhood education. I have elected to examine this for several reasons. Firstly, the analysis will serve to reveal how the two registers operate in a very different early childhood activity from morning news. Secondly, since the activity selected is also enacted as an aspect of a curriculum that is weakly classified and framed, it will again serve to reveal the limitations of such classification and framing, even though, as I shall demonstrate, the two registers have more convergent expression than was true in the text devoted to morning news. Finally, it will allow further reflections on the issues of curriculum design and models of teaching–learning activity which I began to address in Chapter 2.

An early writing genre

One frequent feature of the weakly classified early childhood curriculum is that it is often built around a weekly or fortnightly 'theme' with a range of loosely connected activities which make up the language arts, social and natural science elements of the educational programme. Writing activities undertaken within a writing genre constitute an aspect of the language arts programme. In such a genre, a function of the regulative register is that the young learn to write as one aspect of their growing literacy development; a function of the instructional register is that it provides an appropriate topic for writing about. The object overall is that children learn to write, normally in some imaginative way, about the instructional field, though the advice provided to do with the nature of the writing task, as distinct from the topic about which to write, is often very general.

The general instructional field selected for the week in the case of the genre I have chosen was 'healthy foods'. One other activity during the week (alluded to by the teacher in the text to be examined) involved making 'healthy sandwiches' in the classroom as part of the science/health programme. The activity in the genre to be considered involved the teacher reading the children a short story about a boy who lost his lunch, and their using this as a stimulus to the writing of their own imaginative 'stories' about lost lunches.

Like many instances of early childhood writing genres that I have collected, this one was accomplished in one teaching–learning episode or lesson. The lesson would constitute one of a loosely connected series, in that, as just noted, other lessons in the week or fortnight were devoted to the same broad theme. But even where it did constitute an activity in a series of activities loosely connected in terms of the instructional field choice, it was not normally easy to see much evidence of a progression from one activity to another. There was in other words, no obvious logogenesis at work across lessons and in consequence the genres the lessons realized were essentially discrete. Written texts produced were not awarded any special attention once the writing was completed, though while the children were actually engaged in doing the writing, they received assistance from their teacher with such things as spelling. The act of writing was itself deemed sufficient, for this was taken as evidence of learning and hence also, of development. Bearing in mind the suggestions made by Bernstein and cited in Chapter 2, regarding the model of 'competence' that emerged as a development of the radical and progressivist educational theories from the 1960s on, one can understand how such a model might emerge; it is expressed in a commitment to the teaching of writing to the young, where the writing is all, and where any criteria constraining the nature of the writing tasks, or offering principles for evaluation of performance of those tasks are very weak, and at best tacit to the educational activity.

The lesson that realized the early writing genre to be examined occurred some 45 minutes into the school day, and the children had been sitting at the teacher's feet while she had marked the roll, collected money for school lunches and organized the morning news session. It occurred in the same school as the morning news genre considered in Chapter 2, though the teacher was not the same person. The classroom was very similar to that in the morning news activity, involving various wall displays which were frequently changed, students sitting in groups of four or five at tables facing each other, sets of shelves in which books, posters and writing implements were displayed, and an open space in the middle of the room, where the children could sit grouped in front of the teacher for activities such as morning news but also for the reading of stories. In the genre involved here, the children were in fact grouped in front of the teacher.

I should note, before commencing discussion of the classroom genre here, that the teacher was in many ways a good one, capable of generating animated classroom discussion about the story book she used. In my view, the skills she undoubtedly possessed could have been considerably enhanced had she had a sense of more strongly classified curriculum with which to work and to guide her pedagogy. That she did not, I would stress, reflected the particular ideologies of early childhood and curriculum that had constituted a part of her own training as a teacher, and such ideologies were widely held among the other teachers at her school.

The overall schematic structure of the early writing genre as identified in the classrooms of a number of different teachers is as follows:

Task Orientation $\wedge$ (Task Reorientation) $\wedge$ Task Respecification π $\wedge$ Task

Teacher initiation ⟶ *Teacher–student activity* ⟶ *Student independent activity*

In the Task Orientation the teacher points overall pedagogic directions. She takes a dominant role, introducing what is to be done, and generally marshalling the energies of the students towards the achievement of a common purpose. The regulative register is clearly foregrounded in teacher talk, though the instructional register is also realized, since what is to be written about must find some expression, and indeed the story read does provoke responses from the children. The Task Reorientation is a reasonably uncommon element in such a genre; hence it is shown as optional. It occurs in the text to be examined here, where this element involves re-reading the story read to the class in the Task Orientation. In terms of the instructional field constructed, it does not establish much that is different from the Task Orientation. The Task Specification element is recursive; there are two Task Specification elements in this text, and both registers are realized in these, though it is primarily the instructional field that is addressed. Finally, the Task is the element in which the children make a marked move in their physical disposition in that they move away from the floor in front of the teacher and return to their desks and chairs, where they write their texts. In this element the instructional register has no expression in the talk, though it is foregrounded in the written texts the students are to write. In this element, the teacher moves about the room providing help, normally in spelling, but occasionally in making suggested changes to sentence expression.

The text, with some omissions as noted, and with some accompanying commentary and analysis is set out in Text 3.1, where elements of structure are also clearly labelled. In this discussion, I shall draw from the text, developing aspects of the analyses more fully where necessary, and below adding more extensive commentary on what the analyses reveal. As was the case in the discussions in Chapter 2, I shall address aspects of the realization of the full range of metafunctions, though the order in which I consider these is dependent upon those features that seem most salient. I should also note, before commencing the discussion, that though an occasional interpersonal metaphor is used by the teacher, the text is throughout grammatically congruent in the ideational sense. That is to say, the clauses in both teacher talk and student talk realize their meanings in congruent ways, while the clauses are in turn regularly linked through overt conjunctive relations.

The Task Orientation

In the opening of the Task Orientation, the teacher displays the little book called 'My Lunch' (see notes on accompanying text). Two students have just returned to the classroom after taking class lunch orders to the canteen, and the teacher's opening both alludes to their return and signals the start of a new curriculum genre: *Well now these people are back, I want you to listen to this little tiny short story like the one we had yesterday.* I shall comment on the way in which the two registers operate to realize the pedagogic discourse in this opening element.

With respect to mode and the textual metafunction, it is notable first of all that the teacher takes up a monologic mode to begin and, secondly, that she uses a cluster of textual theme choices, some realized in continuatives, others in structurals, as well as two marked topical themes of time (shown with a double underlining), all of which serve to establish both some connectedness with the activities of yesterday and some sense of progression into the new activities:

Well now *these people are back...*
You know we had 'A Monster Sandwich' and then we made up our own monster sandwiches
Well *today we've got another simple little story...*
And *I want you to listen to it.*
So *listen what happened...*
and *we'll think of something...*

Time and sequence of events in time are something of a preoccupation of teachers: hence the two marked topical themes here: *now* and *today*. It is the teacher's prerogative to determine the timing and sequencing of activities, so the frequent and overt references to these things in teacher discourse help to reinforce her authority in the pedagogic relationship, as well as to give definition to the particular activity to be initiated, marking it as clearly apart from the earlier activities. In addition, because of these things, time references also serve to help define the pedagogic subject position available to the students. Below, when we examine the details of the Task Specification 1, I shall draw attention to another instance in which the teacher invokes considerations of time to reinforce her authority in correcting a student's unacceptable behaviour.

Apart from the matters mentioned, teacher authority is apparent too, in the realizations of theme in both the experiential and interpersonal senses. Experientially, teacher authority is apparent in the frequent uses of *I,* as in:

I want you to listen,

though in the manner of all teachers, this one frequently uses *we* instead, as in:

well today we've got another simple story...

As already noted in Chapter 1, wherever teachers use *I,* they intend to indicate their authority to direct, while their uses of *we* are intended to build solidarity with the students in the common enterprise of working on whatever task is in hand.

Looking more generally at the interpersonal metafunction and its realization, we can see that the text is for the most part in the declarative mood, where the teacher's role is primarily to impart information. Contributions from the students would not be welcome in such an opening stage in a curriculum genre, and since the children in this text are in Year 2,[1] and have by now spent over two years at school, they need little reminding that it is not the time for them to talk. Teacher authority is most marked in the uses of an interpersonal metaphor of command:

I want you to listen,

though it is also apparent in the occasional imperative:

So listen what happened...

68

Text 3.1

Task Orientation

Teacher sits on a chair facing the children grouped on the floor at her feet and displays a book.

T: Well, now these people are back [a reference to Rebecca and Simon who have been sent to the school canteen with the class lunch orders, and who have now returned], I want you to listen to this little tiny short story like the one we had yesterday. [displays a book] You know we had 'A Monster Sandwich', and then we made up our own monster sandwiches. Well, today we've got another simple little story which is called 'My Lunch'. And I want you to listen to it, what happened to the little boy's lunch. Who came and took the lunch, and what happened to it, and then what happened to the little boy after he found he had no lunch at all. Because when we finish reading this story, something's going to happen to your lunch today, or we're going to pretend that it does. So listen what happened to this boy's lunch and we'll think of something that could happen to our lunches, our beautiful healthy sandwiches. [She then reads the story 'My Lunch', showing the pictures as she goes, as they constitute significant elements of the book, supplying additional information to that of the actual text.]

' "Where's my lunch?" "It's not here. Miss Gill, look!" ' [As the text unfolds, the lunch is told by a dog, and the boy whose lunch it is, is told by his teacher, Miss Gill, that he can have some lunch from a shop; the pictures display him selecting things to eat.] What sort of lunch has he ended up eating?

Kelly: Spaghetti bolognaise.

T: He's chosen lots of things. [looking at the pictures] He's got a plate of [indecipherable] and a plate of strawberries and an apple and spaghetti.

Stephen: Strawberries.

Frankie: Hot dogs.

Veronica: He's got some milk.

T: He went along into a take-away into a take-away food shop and he could choose what he might like.

Kelly: It looks like a canteen.

Jeffrey: That is a canteen, it is...

T: It's like a canteen. It says 'eat here or take away', and he can choose spaghetti or salad or olives or onion...

Frankie: He took a lot.

T: He's chosen lots of things – had a special 1. What was in his lunch that the dog ate?

Kelly: Healthy sandwiches.

Stephen: Spaghetti.

T: It looked like he had spaghetti in his sandwich. [Several children laugh at this] There's the dog with his head in the bag and there's all the spaghetti falling down around his ears. Perhaps he has a spaghetti sandwich. [A number of comments from the children greet this, too animated and too many to record]

Regulative register realized in:

Interpersonally in interpersonal metaphors of command: *I want you to listen...*
grammatically congruent commands:
So listen...
Experientially in processes to do with desired behaviour:
you to <u>listen</u>...
when we <u>finish</u> ...
we'll <u>think</u> of something...
Textually in teacher continuatives:
<u>well now</u> these people...
<u>well</u> today...
<u>and</u> I want you to listen...
Instructional register realized in:
series of clauses, overtly linked through temporal, additive and causal conjunctive relations, as well as some projected clauses:
<u>and</u> what happened
<u>and then</u> what happened
<u>after</u> he found...

Instructional register again realized:
interpersonally in exchanges of information:
what sort of lunch has he ended up eating?
he's got some milk
Gosh, that looks like nice food.
experientially in processes that construct details of the story:
he went along into a take-away
it looks like a canteen
textually in a series of topical theme choices that identify aspects of the field and help carry the discourse forward:
he's got some milk
that is a canteen
it's like a canteen
he's chosen lots of things

text continues

Text 3.1 – *continued*

Joseph: Gosh, that looks like nice food.

Jodie: He's eating all different things.

Christian: She's [the teacher] eating too.

Task Reorientation

T: All right, I'll read it through one more time. Now listen carefully to what happens. [T rereads the story, making and accepting comments on it as she goes.]

[**Text is left out here**.]

Task Specification 1

T: Now what I want you people to think about is something coming along and taking your lunch, or something happening to your lunch so that you couldn't eat it. Not a dog, that's in the story. Well, you can have a dog if you want, but it'd be better if you think of something else. Frankie, put the comb away. The time to do your hair is at play time. [Frankie has been playing with a comb, and surreptitiously doing his hair for a few seconds. He puts it in his pocket] All right put your hand up if you've thought of something that could come and take your lunch, or something that could happen to your lunch. [no one raises a hand] Have you ever had a day when you've had no lunch to eat? Jodie? [she nods] What happened, Jodie, when you had no lunch to eat?

Jodie: Mum didn't bring it up. She left it at home.

T: Left your lunch at home on the bench, and her mum didn't bring it to school, and she had no lunch. And what happened?

Jodie: Found no lunch.

T: And then what happened?

Jodie: My mum brought my lunch.

T: And who else brought your lunch?

Jodie: Dad.

T: She had no lunch to start with, because it was left at home, and she thought her mum was going to bring it at lunch time, and when her mum didn't bring it, Mrs S rang her mum, and she wasn't at home, so her dad brought her lunch and then her mum remembered she hadn't brought her lunch, and she brought lunch too, so she ended up with two lunches. She ate the lot.

Joseph: What did she have?

T: [looks at Jodie] You had – I can't remember – you had a sausage roll and doughnut.

Jodie: I had a very nice lunch. I had a sausage roll and a jam doughnut and a [indecipherable]

T: Mm, so that was an extra-special thing. Who else has ever had no lunch, and then something's happened that they've had a different lunch? [no one raises a hand] Emily? What happened yesterday?

Emily: My sister left hers on the dressing table.

T: And what happened when she found that she had no lunch? Was she happy? What was happening to her?

Regulative register realized:
textually, in teacher textual themes to point directions:
now what I want
well, you can have a dog...
interpersonally in an interpersonal metaphor of command to direct behaviour:
Now what I want you people to think about is...
Grammatically congruent commands:
Frankie, put the comb away.
associated with an impersonal metaphorical command:
The time [[to do your hair]] is at play time.
and **interpersonally** and **experientially** in a grammatically congruent command and process of cognition, also directing behaviour:
all right put your hand up
if you've thought of something that could happen

Instructional register realized:
interpersonally, teacher interrogatives to provoke talk re: the field
Have you ever had a day...
what happened, Jodie...
And what happened...
And who else brought it?

logically in a series of clauses overtly linked through a number of conjunctive relations building the field:
she had no lunch
because it was left...
and she thought...
and when her mum...
so her dad brought her.
and then her mum...
and she brought lunch...
so she ended...

text continues

72

Text 3.1 – *continued*

Emily: She was crying.

T: She was crying and she came to me, and what did I say?

Emily: She could have one from the canteen.

T: What else happened to you?

Emily: The day I put the lunch in the school bag and brought the other school bag instead.

T: Mm, and what happened that day? Emily had two school bags at home, and she put the lunch in one school bag, and took the other school bag to school. And when she looked in her bag, no lunch. And what happened that day?

Emily: I got a lunch from the canteen.

T: You had a special lunch order.

Task Specification 2

T: All right, hands down. Thinking caps on. Get these brains working, They're nearly Grade 3 brains. I don't have to tell them everything to think. You have to get them working, you have to be responsible for what you're thinking. Now what you're going to do – you're – it can be something that really happened to you. Joseph, you're really spoiling the grade. [addressed because he is not paying attention but instead looking out of the window. He is sitting at the back of the group and somewhat apart from the other children. He does as he is told and 'wriggles up' closer to the group] No wriggle up please and start listening. You'll get back to your place and you won't know what to do. What I want you to think about is something that – it might be something that really happened to you, one day you found you didn't have any lunch, or it might be something like this little boy in the story, a dog came into the school and took your lunch out of the school bag, so he ended up with a wonderful lunch that the teacher had to buy him, or it might be something different altogether. You might have a monster coming in and taking it [A murmur of laughter from several children] You might have someone with the same bag eating your lunch, and then you didn't like the lunch that they had in their bag, so that you had to get something special. You might have – perhaps put your lunch down outside to play a game, and some animal, a cat or a dog or some person steps over it, and squashes it or...

Simon: A bird?

T: Or a bird. Yes, you could have a bird take your lunch. Or somebody might throw your lunch away by mistake.

experientially in a series of processes that reconstruct events of the field:
she ate the lot
what happened yesterday?
she was crying
my sister left hers on the dressing table

textually in a series of topical and interpersonal themes identifying aspects of the field or seeking information about it
I had a very nice lunch
she was crying
what happened that day,
and associated construction of a dialogic mode.

Regulative register realized:
interpersonally in elliptical imperative mood choices creating commands:
all right, hands down
thinking caps on
imperative mood choices creating congruent commands:
get these brains working
metaphorical commands:
I don't have to tell them everything to think.
you have to get them working
you have to be responsible for what you're thinking. . .

Instructional register realized:
interpersonally in a series of clauses using modal operators to build possibilities in field construction:
one day you found. . .
or it <u>might</u>. . .
or it <u>might</u> be something different. . .
you <u>might</u> have a monster coming in. . .
you <u>might</u> have someone with the same bag. . .
you <u>might</u> have – perhaps put your lunch. . .
or you <u>could</u> have a bird. . .
or somebody <u>might</u> throw your lunch. . .

experientially in process types that build possible events in a story:
one day you found you didn't have any lunch,
a dog came into the school
and took your lunch out of the school bag

textually in topical themes that identify potential participants in the story:
you might have a monster coming,

text continues

Text 3.1 – *continued*

Task

T: Right, who's got something in their head that they're going to write about? Oh, I can see some eyes popping. Looks like they've got beautiful stories in there, ready to be written down. Well, you can do it straight in your blue books. Now if you need some help with the spelling, have your jotter beside your spelling books, so that if you've got words in there that you've already asked how to spell, you can look them up.

Susy: What about if they're in your folder?

T: You can have your other spelling sheets besides you and your folder. All right, let me see who's going to be first. [Moves to the board] Now here's your heading: 'What happened to my lunch?'

[At this point the children get up from their positions on the floor and move back to the shelves where they collect their writing books before they go to their desks and sit down to write. The writing activity, accompanied by a degree of quiet talk, proceeds for another thirty minutes, during which time, if the children have finished, they are encouraged by their teachers to draw pictures illustrating their stories. When the bell goes for the morning recess, they place their books back on the shelves and leave the room.)

---

and textual themes that carry the discourse on:
one day you found you didn't have any lunch,
or it might be something like this little boy in the story,
a dog came into the school
<u>*and*</u> *took your lunch out of the school bag,*
<u>*so*</u> *he ended up with a wonderful lunch*

Regulative register realized:
interpersonally in opening teacher interrogative
who's got something in their head [[that they're going to write about?]]
and in associated metaphor:
Oh, I can see some eyes popping

experientially in a series of processes all to do with behaviours to be undertaken:
stories... ready to be written down
can do it straight in your blue books
have your jotter beside you

textually in textual themes that help direct the course of the behaviours:
<u>*right*</u> *Who's got something...*
<u>*well*</u> *you can do it...*
<u>*now*</u> *if you need some help*

Instructional register is not realized at all in this last element.

There is at least one other sense in which teacher authority is marked in this opening element: it is in the consistent use of positive polarity. The effect is that the discourse builds a strongly assertive sense of what is to be done, one which appears to admit of no deviation from the path of activity that is being established. Such is the process by which energies are marshalled and directed towards the task in hand.

Incidentally, positive polarity is a common feature of opening teacher talk in all curriculum genres, throughout the years of schooling, and even within university settings. It is a function of the pedagogic relationship, at least in educational settings, that the teacher defines in a reasonably categorical way what is to be done, and, by implication, necessarily excludes other possibilities.

Thus far, much of the discussion has focused on the regulative, rather than the instructional register, and one would expect that, since this will be most marked at points of teacher initiation as here, or teacher summary or closure. Yet the instructional register begins to be realized, as is apparent if we look in particular to the ideational metafunctions, both experiential and logical. Initially the experiential information is to do with the general field of language pedagogy, rather than with the instructional field of sandwiches and lunches, and its character is thus of the regulative register. Thus, the teacher tells the students:

I	*want*	*you*	*to listen to*	*this little tiny story*	*like the one [[we had yesterday]]*
Senser	*pro: cog.*	*Behaver*	*Pro:* *behavioural*	*Range*	*Circumstance: Comparison**

(* Here, as elsewhere, where the clause involved is an embedded one, no transitivity analysis of the embedded clause will be offered, in the interests of conserving space.)

Incidentally, I have here displayed the transitivity process using italics, to suggest the operation of the regulative register; at points where the instructional register is displayed in transitivity, I have used plain text. On occasion, as will be seen later on, the two will be found to be expressed in the same clause. I shall adopt the same method for signalling the two registers in later chapters in the book.

It will be noted that this clause complex foregrounds the regulative register, for it is all to do either with teacher requirements for behaviour realized in process types (*I want you to listen to*) or with the referent involved in the participant role of Range (*this little tiny story*): the reference to the book, though it uses the specific item *this*, does not in itself capture anything of the instructional field. As the teacher discourse proceeds, the regulative register remains foregrounded, though the instructional field for writing starts to be foreshadowed. Look for example at the participant roles in the following clause complex, in which the shift is made from the rather general referent *another simple little story*, in the participant role of Goal, to an identification of the name of the story in the participant role of Token, *My Lunch*, whose effect, though the latter referent is still of the regulative register, is to introduce a greater degree of specificity, while also foreshadowing the nature of the instructional field:

Well	*today*		*we'*	*ve got*	*another simple little story*
	Circ: loc: time		*Actor*	*Pro: material*	*Goal*
which	*is called*			*'My Lunch'*	
Value	*Pro: identification*			*Token*	

The regulative register reappears in teacher direction to behaviour:

and	*I*	*want*	*you*	*to listen to*	*it*
			Behaver	*Pro: behavioural*	*Range*

though she then moves on into the details of the story, when the instructional field is foregrounded. Metaphorically at least, we can argue that thus is the instructional field 'projected' through the regulative register:

what	happened to		the little boy's lunch
Actor	Pro: material		Goal
who	came		
Actor	Pro: material		
and	took		the lunch
	Pro: material		Goal
and	what	happened to	it
	Actor	Pro: material	Goal
and then what		happened to	the little boy
	Actor	Pro: material	Goal
after	he	found	
	Senser	Pro: cognition	
he	had		no lunch
Actor	Pro: material		Goal

Experientially, these seven clauses make use of six material processes (and one of cognition) to help build a series of events, where, in terms of the logical metafunction, those events are linked in four uses of additive and/or temporal conjunctions. Overall, both experiential and logical choices thus help to construct a 'narrative-like' sequence, of a kind that the teacher unconsciously favours for story writing, though despite this, the model provided in the book is of quite another order. The story presents its meanings very considerably in a series of pictures depicting the boy, the dog that took his lunch, the teacher, Miss Gill, to whom he complained and who helped him purchase a new lunch. Furthermore, the verbal story unfolds throughout in dialogue such as the opening: *Where's my lunch?* Occasionally, the speech in the dialogue is reported through a projecting clause, such as '*What can I eat?*' '*I will see*', *said Miss Gill.* (not reproduced in the text as displayed) For the most part, the text is simply direct reporting of speech. The dialogue is ancillary to the pictures, and together the two build the sequence of events. Such a sequence, however, does not make use of additive and temporal conjunctive relations of the kind that the teacher models, indicating that the teacher constructs a sense of narrative sequence rather differently from the book.

The two registers converge in the remaining clauses in the opening teacher monologue before the commencement of the reading:

Because ≪ *when*		*we*	*finish reading*	*this story* ≫
		Behaver	*Pro: behavioural*	*Range*
something	's going to happen to	your lunch	today	
Actor	Pro: material	Goal	Circumstance: time	
or	*we*	*'re going to pretend*		
	Senser	*Pro: cognition*		
that it	does.			
Actor	Pro: material			

In this clause complex, two clauses involving a behavioural process (*we finish reading*) and a process of cognition (*we're going to pretend*) direct the behaviours the students are to engage in, while in the other two clauses, the process types are both material and they help realize aspects of the projected imaginary instructional field to do with what *happens to your lunch*. Three instances of conjunctive relations, causal (*because*), temporal (*when*) and contrastive (*or*) help to construct the connectedness both of the clauses and of the two registers. Thus do the two registers converge to build the pedagogic discourse, and this convergence is sustained for a few more seconds before the teacher starts to read:

| *So listen* | | [[what | happened to | this little boy's lunch]] |
| *Pro: perception* | | Phenomenon | | |

| *and we* | *'ll think of* | *something* [[that could happen to our lunches, our beautiful healthy lunches |
| *Senser* | *Pro: cognition* | *Phenomenon* |

Note the way in which in these clause complexes, it is the regulative register, to do with operationalizing student behaviour, which is foregrounded in the two mental processes, and it is the instructional field which is realized as the Phenomenon in each case. The relationship of the two clauses in each case captures something of the relationship of the two registers they help to realize.

At this point, the teacher then reads the story 'My Lunch', showing the pictures as she goes, as they constitute significant elements of the book, supplying additional information to that of the actual text: 'Where's my lunch? It's not here. Miss Gill, look!'

It will be apparent that the reading of the story and the display of its pictures stimulates dialogue about its details, and hence about the instructional field. Experientially, the process types realize aspects of the behaviour of the participants in the story:

| He | 's chosen | | lots of things |
| Senser | Pro: cognition | | Phenomenon |

| he | 's got | some milk | |
| Possessor | Pro: poss. | Attribute: poss. | |

| he | took | a lot | |
| Actor | Pro: mat | Goal | |

Interpersonally, the text sees shifts in mood as teacher and students ask questions and offer information.

Textually, the sequence is marked by one opening theme that is both interpersonal and topical:

What sort of lunch has he ended up eating?,

while other topical Themes realize aspects of the tale:

It looks like a canteen
he took a lot,

The Task Reorientation will not be considered here, on the grounds that it involves reading the text again with some commentary offered of a kind similar to that revealed in the Task Orientation. Its analysis would add little to the overall argument.

Task Specification 1

Turning to the first Task Specification, we can see that the regulative register is once again to the fore, though again as before, the instructional register finds some expression, and as this element proceeds, there is a steady shift towards a foregrounding of the latter register. As is generally true at the opening of an element of schematic structure, the teacher's mode is monologic, though as the element proceeds, the text becomes dialogic when the teacher draws the students into talk of the instructional field. As in the opening of the Task Orientation, the teacher selects a cluster of textual theme choices, realized in the main in continuatives, but in one case in a structural, to move the discourse and hence the activity forward:

> _Now_ what I want you people to think about is something ...
> _Well_, you can have a dog if you want ...
> _but_ it'd be better if you think of something else.
> _All right_ put your hand up ...

It is of interest to note that in many curriculum genres textual themes are a feature of teacher talk, not student talk, and this is not peculiar to early childhood classrooms. The explanation of course is not that students are incapable of using such themes, for they certainly produce them in other contexts of situation. Rather, the unequal distribution of such things as textual themes in classroom talk reflects the particular authority of the teacher, and the fact that it is her prerogative to direct the course that activities will take, while it is the students' responsibility to accept directions. It does not follow, nor am I suggesting, that classrooms in which teachers make frequent use of textual themes are necessarily undesirable because they appear to deny the students to direct the course of activity. On the contrary, I would argue that teachers must exercise authority in directing their students' learning. The test of whether such linguistic patterns as frequent uses of textual themes in teacher talk are desirable or not will depend entirely upon the complete classroom genre of which they form a part, the points at which they appear in the text, and their role in the overall organization of meaning. In Chapter 4, we shall examine one classroom text in which the students made extensive use of textual theme choices as they jointly negotiated and developed a shared task.

The opening clause in the Task Specification is of interest, textually, interpersonally and experientially, for it employs linguistic resources which, while of course found elsewhere, are nonetheless very distinctive to pedagogic discourse:

[[what I want you people to think about]]	*is*	[[something coming along [[and taking your lunch, [[or something happening to your lunch [[so that you couldn't eat it.]]]]]]]]
Value	*Pro: identifying*	*Token*

I say that the clause is very characteristic of pedagogic discourse, at least as that is realized in teacher talk, because it involves an identifying process, both of whose participant roles are realized in embedded clauses, where their function is to 'pack in' a great deal of relevant information in a tight and economic way. (The first of these participant roles also of courses constitutes the opening topical theme for this element.) Teachers use such resources at times of summarizing what has gone on and/or signalling the start of a new phase whose success depends on some grasp of what has been covered in the talk or activity immediately prior. Such is the case here. Identifying processes will be used elsewhere in a classroom discourse apart from the teacher opening, though their distribution is undoubtedly less common, and they are not for the most part commonly found in students' talk. On those occasions where they do appear in student talk, they do not normally realize aspects of the regulative register: rather they realize some aspect of the instructional register, often for example to do with offering some definition of a technical term found in the instructional field. Teachers use identifying processes not only for their experiential role in compressing a lot of information, but also because, interpersonally, they offer a categorical statement of what is to be the case. In this sense, combined with the use of the positive polarity referred to in examining teacher talk at the start of the Task Orientation, the teacher strongly asserts what she intends, and this assertion is strengthened by the interpersonal metaphor involved in the expression *what I want you people to think about is something coming along and taking your lunch...* which actually means 'you must think about something coming along.'

Before pursuing further the features of what it is that is to be thought about, I want to comment briefly on another aspect of the interpersonal in the opening remarks of the teacher in the Task Specification 1. I refer to the point at which the teacher turns to Frankie, who has been surreptitiously playing with a pocket comb, and corrects him:

Frankie,	*put*	*the comb*	*away.*
	Pro-	*Goal*	*-cess: material*

The time [[to do your hair]]	*is*	*at play time.*
Value	*Pro: int.*	*Token*

Teacher authority is overtly marked here in: the use of the vocative (most commonly employed by teachers as a management device); the use of the imperative in the first clause; and the use of the identifying process in the second clause, allowing the teacher to create a general principle *[[the time to do your hair]]*, expressed in the participant role of Value. I have remarked already the significance of the ways in which teachers define the temporal: it is their right to determine those times at which actions will be carried out, just as it is their right to determine the spatial arrangements by which the students will act. The teacher's intervention here is an explicit expression of the power she enjoys in handling matters of time, and of the ways she uses that power to reinforce her authority in directing the students' behaviour. Such power is involved in defining the pedagogic subject position, and what can and can't be done at particular points in the school day. As Bernstein remarked more than once, spatial and temporal relationships and their definition are very much at issue in the building of pedagogic subjectivity.

The matter to be 'thought about' in this element, as indeed in other elements of this genre, concerns an imagined loss of one's lunch, and the next few clauses, before the entry to dialogue, are intended to develop ideas about this. Nowhere, it will be noted, does the teacher actually say that the object is that the children are to do some writing, though the children are quite aware that this is the case. In fact, the absence of any overt teacher reference to the requirement for writing here or in the Task Orientation element, is a measure of the tacit operation of the regulative register. The children are so familiar with the pattern of talk about a possible task for writing, normally undertaken on a Wednesday morning, as is this example, before they return to their desks, that they understand the requirement without its being made explicit. Nonetheless, the omission of any references to the nature of the writing task, apart from one teacher reference to *beautiful stories* which are *to be written down* in the Task element itself, is a matter for concern for other reasons. It is a characteristic of such a curriculum genre: in the weakly classified curriculum that applies, some discussion of imaginative experience for writing about will occur, though the features of the written text to be produced – its structure and organization – remain implicit to the talk. In consequence, the principles for evaluation of performance remain largely invisible, though they can often be deduced from the teacher's manner of guiding the students' talk. Here, as I have noted earlier, when the teacher guides much of the talk, she seems to favour overt temporal sequence of events, though the model of the story in the story is actually different: its sequence depends upon a series of clauses all of which constitute dialogue, and they support the details of the story as established in a sequence of pictures.

The teacher spends a few seconds defining the potential field for writing about, starting with an elliptical clause using negative polarity (*not a dog*), then going on:

| that | 's | | in the story | |
| Carrier | Pro: attributive | | Attribute: Circumstance | |

| *Well,* | *you* | *can have* | | a dog |
| | Possessor | Pro: possessive | | Attribute: possessed |

| *if* | *you* | *want* | |
| | Senser | Pro: affect | |

| *but* | *it* | *'d be* | | *better* |
| | Carrier | Pro: attributive | | Attribute |

| *if* | *you* | *think of* | | *something else* |
| | Senser | Pro: cognition | | Phenomenon |

After the brief correction of Frankie, the teacher launches the students into dialogue, though it will be evident that it is she who both directs the talk and who does most of the work in rehearsal of narrating of event. An imperative signals the entry to dialogue:

| *All right put* | | *your hand* | *up* |
| | Pro: mat- | Range | -erial |

if you 've thought of something [[that could come
                              [[and take your lunch,
                    or something [[that could happen to your lunch.]]]]]]
Senser Pro: cognition   Phenomenon

Here, as is the pattern in many other places, it is the regulative register that is paramount in an opening textual theme (*all right*), in a choice of the imperative mood and in the process of cognition to direct student behaviour, while it is the instructional register that is expressed in an embedding within the participant role of Phenomenon.

The absence of an immediate response to the teacher's question causes her to call upon one child's personal experience as a means of developing the possible field for writing. She asks Jodie:

| have | you | ever had | a day [[when you've had no lunch [[to eat?]]]] |
| Pro- | Behaver | -cess: behavioural | Range |

and when Jodie nods, she goes on:

what	happened	Jodie,	
Actor	Pro: material		
when	you	had	no lunch [[to eat]]
	Possessor	Pro: possessive	Attribute: possessed

The following sequences of clauses, relying heavily on contributions first from Jodie and later from Emily, use mainly material processes: experientially, it is events that are in reconstruction here. I shall not set out all the details of the process types, confining myself instead to drawing attention to the way in which the teacher actively, though not entirely consciously, constructs logical relationships between the events by drawing mainly on additive and temporal conjunctive relations, but also on some that are causal and consequential. Interestingly (with one exception in the case of the second child, Emily), the two children involved, while contributing experiential information as requested, do not contribute to the building of the logical relationships between events. They are capable of this, but they do not so. In that the teacher produces these, it is clear that it is she who is determining the logic by which the discourse unfolds:

> T: *Left your lunch at home on the bench,*
> *and her mum didn't bring it to school,*
> *and she had no lunch.*
> *And what happened?*
>
> Jodie: *Found no lunch.*
>
> T: *And then what happened?*
> *Who had to ring up your mum and dad?*
>
> Jodie: *Mr H.*
>
> T: *And then what happened?*
>
> Jodie: *My mum brought my lunch.*
>
> T: *And who else brought your lunch?*
>
> Jodie: *Dad.*
>
> T: *She had no lunch to start with,*
> *because it was left at home,*
> *and she thought her mother was going to bring it at lunch time*
> *and ≪ when her mum didn't bring it ≫ Mrs S rang her mum,*
> *and she wasn't at home,*
> *so her dad brought her lunch,*
> *and she brought lunch too,*
> *so she ended up with two lunches.*

The same pattern applies when, a few seconds later, the teacher draws Emily into the talk:

T:	*What happened yesterday?*
Emily:	*My sister left hers on the dressing table.*
T:	*<u>And</u> what happened*
	<u>when</u> she found that she had no lunch? Was she happy? What was happening?
Emily:	*She was crying.*
T:	*She was crying to me*
	<u>and</u> she came to me
	<u>and</u> what did I say?
Emily:	*She could have one from the canteen.*
T:	*What else happened to you?*
Emily:	*The day I put the lunch in the school bag*
	<u>and</u> brought the other school bag instead.
T:	*Mm... <u>And</u> what happened that day? Emily had two school bags*
	<u>and</u> took the other school bag to school.
	<u>And</u> ≪ <u>when</u> she looked in her bag ≫ no lunch.
	What happened that day?

Thus is a field for writing about modelled by recourse to reconstructing some recent events in the lives of two class members, while at least some of the elements of the probable schematic structure of a story are also modelled in teacher talk. Directions for writing are less well developed, however, and principles for evaluation are not made clear. In addition, as we shall see below, the model for constructing a story is not in practice taken up by the children in their writing.

The Task Specification 2

The second Task Specification starts with a series of teacher utterances which realize the regulative register. Note the two opening elliptical clauses (the second using a metaphor):

T: *All right, hands down. Thinking caps on,*

and the strong obligation placed upon the students, partly in an imperative mood choice in a clause which uses another metaphor:

Get these brains working,

and partly in the series of clauses using modality (underlined), and one instance of negative polarity:

They're nearly Grade 3 brains.
I don't have to tell them everything [[to think]].
You have to get them working,
you have to be responsible for [[what you're thinking]].

This is the first point in this text where such teacher uses of modality have appeared. Their presence is evidence of two matters. Firstly, it is evidence, along with other linguistic features, that a new stage in the curriculum genre has been reached. Secondly, it is evidence that the teacher is using considerable moral suasion to build and appeal to a particular pedagogic subject position. In the building of such a position her process types are very revealing:

You	*have to get*	*them (the brains)*	*working*
Initiator	*Pro-*	*Actor*	*-cess: material*
(You	*must think)*		
Senser	*Pro: cognition)*		
you	*have to be*	*responsible for [[what you're thinking]].*	
Carrier	*Pro: attributive*	*Attribute*	

The material process (really a metaphor for 'you must think') imposes the obligation *to work*, while the second, attributive process, carries a strong moral imperative in the choice of Attribute – the students must be *responsible for what they think.*

The available linguistic resources for building authority in English are considerable. Authority, at least within the pedagogic relationship of schooling, is expressed rather differently, depending on the age group of the students, as well, no doubt in part, on the identity of the teacher and the manner in which he/she chooses to construct the role and relationship. One general observation about authority, however, may be made, in the pedagogic relationship, regardless of the age of the students: it is that authority is most successful in its expression when it enjoins good practice in positive terms which suggest a 'moral good' of some kind. The expression of authority is least successful when, for example, it relies upon excessive uses of negative polarity (*you are not to do that*) and/or frequent uses of attributive processes that build essentially negative attributes (*you are disobedient/badly behaved/irresponsible*). In such cases, a moral position is certainly expressed, but it is expressed in negative terms. The pedagogic subject is most powerfully persuaded by uses of essentially positive linguistic resources. It does not follow that successful teachers make no use of negative linguistic resources. On the contrary, good teachers sometimes use them well, mainly because they use them sparingly, where their effect is to help give reasonably effective definition to what constitutes acceptable behaviour, normally by making very clear what is not acceptable.

As for the pedagogic positions in construction in the clauses cited above, it will be clear that a powerful value prevails such that the ideal pedagogic subjects are 'industrious' in that they get their brains to 'work' hard, and in the sense that they assume 'responsibility' for their own thinking. A very strong work ethic, much valued in English-speaking societies, would seem to be operating here.

An instance of the way in which the teacher uses some negative evaluation of behaviour to correct one child is provided a few seconds after the clauses just examined when the teacher invokes a strong judgement about behaviour. I earlier noted that teachers use vocatives sparingly, and their use is essentially as a management device. Note the way in which the process type used in addressing Joseph invokes the 'good' of the grade or class of which Joseph is a member, and which, by implication, he is placing at risk:

Joseph,	*you*	*'re spoiling*	*the grade*
	Behaver	*Pro: behavioural*	*Range*

Two imperative mood choices follow in clauses which also construct desired behaviours:

Now	*wriggle up*	*please*
	Pro: material	
and	*start listening*	
	Pro: behavioural	

Joseph, an essentially obedient child, does as he is told, and hears without comment the further advice of the teacher:

You	*'ll get*	*back to your place*
Actor	*Pro: material*	*Circumstance: location: place*
and	*you*	*won't know*	*what to do.*
	Senser	*Pro: cognition*	*Phenomenon*

In any pedagogic discourse, the regulative register has two aspects. One is to do with what constitutes acceptable behaviour, so that, for example, in the text being examined here, the students are to *put up their hands*, or to *start listening*. The other aspect concerns 'doing the task', whatever that may be, where the latter aspect has to do with developing patterns of constructing experience, methods of reasoning, ways of addressing questions, ways of offering explanations, and so on, which as we shall see in later chapters, manifest in different ways, depending upon the 'content' or area of the curriculum being studied. In an early childhood classroom such as the one discussed here, which is devoted to teaching literacy, matters relevant to 'doing the task' involve mastering aspects of literate behaviour, more specifically the writing of stories. The two aspects of a pedagogic discourse, in this case the one to do with what constitutes acceptably attentive behaviour, the other to do with the adoption of acceptably literate behaviour, are equally important, and both are part of the 'moral regulation' that Bernstein argues is fundamental to the operation of a pedagogic discourse (1990: 184).

[[what I want you to think about]]   is   *something that –*
          Value   Pro: intensive   *Token*

it   *might be*   something [[that really happened to you]]
Carrier   *Pro: attributive*   Attribute

one day   you   found
Circumstance: Location: Time   Senser   Pro: cognition

you   didn't have   any lunch
Actor   Pro: material   Goal

or   *it*   *might be*   something like this little boy in the story
       Carrier *pro: attributive* Attribute

a dog   came   into the school
Actor   Pro: material   Circumstance: Location: Place

and   took   your lunch   out of the school bag
         Pro: material Goal   Circumstance: Location: Place

so he   ended up   with a wonderful lunch [[that the teacher had to
                         buy him]]
Actor   Pro: material Circumstance: Manner

or   *it*   *might be*   something different altogether
         Carrier *Pro: attributive* Attribute

Hence it is that while in one sense there is a break in the flow of the discourse as the teacher corrects Joseph, in another sense the overall intention to dispose the students towards writing their stories proceeds: they must be attentive, but equally they must think about the details of their stories. This is signalled in the teacher's talk when she commences another identifying clause involving embedded clauses in the participant roles. The clause is actually aborted when she hesitates and starts again, though setting out what she says as I have serves to illustrate the intention. The three uses of modality, which are underlined, help to establish the building of possibilities for writing here.

Other possibilities for writing follow, provoking some expressions of amusement from the children, though notably they are all constructed by the teacher:

---

you   *might have*   a monster [[coming in [[and taking it]]]]
Behaver   *Pro: behavioural*   Range

you   *might have*   someone with the same bag [[eating your lunch]]
Behaver *Pro: behavioural*   Range

and then you   didn't like   the lunch [[that they had in their bag]]
   Senser   Pro: affect   Phenomenon

so that   you   had to get   something special
            Actor   Pro: material   Goal

you might have – perhaps put   your lunch   down   outside
Actor   Pro: material   Goal   Circumstance: location: place

to play   a game
Pro: material   Range

and some animal, a cat or a dog   steps   over it
or some person
            Actor   Pro: material   Circumstance
                                                      location
                                                      place

and   squashes   it
           Pro: material   Goal

One child, Simon offers a possibility in the elliptical clause, *A bird?*
Overall, the second Task Specification has served to move the students

further towards the goal of writing stories. Unlike the first Task Specification, this element is constructed mainly in teacher talk, so it is largely monologic. It begins with strong moral imperatives upon the students to work, and proceeds to construct possible sequences of events that the students might use for writing their stories. Hence it is the instructional register which is mainly foregrounded here, though it will be noted that several clauses involve a convergence of the two registers, as for example in a clause such as:

> *it might be something [[that really happened to you]],*

where the opening participant role of Carrier and process realize the regulative register, while the instructional register is realized in the role of Attribute. The regulative register is significant here, both in opening the element and in determining the manner in which information is sequenced. But it realizes little information to do with the nature of the task for writing itself, where that might for example concern the overall organization of the target text, its linguistic structure or its goals.

The Task

The Task element opens in teacher monologue, in which the regulative register is foregrounded and the instructional register is not realized at all. The students do not need to be directed to get up from their positions on the floor, incidentally, for this expectation is clearly understood as an aspect of the regulative register which is functioning at a tacit level. Two instances of textual themes expressed in continuatives signal direction of behaviour:

> *Right, who's got something in their head [[that they're going to write about]] ?*
> *Now ≪ if you need some help with the spelling . . . ≫ ,*

while in other ways the teacher seeks to build a degree of excitement, even energy, for the task of writing. She employs an interpersonal metaphor when she says: *who's got something in their head that they're going to write about?*, for this actually means 'I hope you have something you have thought of to write about'. Her subsequent three clauses reflect observation of the students' bodies, and the apparent evidence she suggests they reveal of their preparedness to write *beautiful stories*:

oh	*I*	*can see*	*some eyes popping.*
	Senser	*Pro: perception*	*Phenomenon*

looks	*like [[they've got beautiful stories in there [[ready to be written down]]*
Pro: attributive	*Attribute: Circumstance: Manner*

The remaining teacher directions concern advice about how to handle matters of spelling:

Now	*≪ if you need some help with the spelling ≫*			
	Senser Pro: cog. Phenomenon Circ: Matter			
have	*your jotter*	*beside your spelling books,*		
Pro: material	*Goal*	*Circumstance: Location: Place*		
if ≪ you 've got	*words*	*in there*	*[[that you've already asked how*	
			to spell]] ≫	
Actor Pro: material	*Goal*	*Circumstance: Location: Place.*		
you	*can look*	*them*	*up*	
Behaver	*Pro: behav-*	*Range*	*-ioural*	

The teacher writes the heading for writing on the board, and this represents the only point at which the instructional register is realized in this element.

The written texts are of course an essential part of the Task element, and it will thus be important to examine several of those that emerged. What evaluation principles appeared to apply? It will be necessary to spend some time considering these before examining some of the stories written by the children.

Principles of evaluation of the written stories

As I suggested in Chapter 2, the principles of evaluation that apply in any educational activity will be of major importance in understanding what is going on in the activity, for this tells us what is rewarded and valued. Since the curriculum here is both weakly classified and weakly framed, the criteria for judging what constitutes success are not well articulated. By examining closely what the teacher says at several points in the classroom talk, we can identify at least two matters relevant to the task. Firstly, the students are to write *beautiful stories* about something happening to their lunches, where the events might have really happened, or they might be imaginary. A value would seem at times to attach to demonstrating imaginative capacity, though elsewhere in the text the students are told that *it (the story) might be something that really happened to you.* Secondly, they can elect one of two possible models for the structure of the tale, though these are not explicitly stated at any time. One model is implicit in the teacher's talk, where she appears to favour overt sequencing of events through frequent uses of additive and temporal conjunctive relations to reconstruct events in the lives of the children. The other model, offered in the pages of the little book read and displayed, builds the story, verbally at least, through sets of dialogic exchanges. These are ancillary to accompanying pictures and, together, the pictures and dialogue create the sense of narrative sequence. No directions are given to advise students to take up either model. Furthermore, no metalanguage is used to talk about the organization of the stories to be written. In the event, most students in the class adopted the model from the little book read to them, with its absence of strong narrative sequence, at least in a verbal sense. Others adopted a conventional narrative structure, more characteristic of the imaginative stories they had been read from time to time in the past. Few actually adopted the model implicit in the teacher's talk.

The written texts

Students who opted for the model in the little book they had been read in the lesson, wrote like Olive:

My Lunch
My lunch is gone, Mrs Drummond. I had a look in my bag but it isn't in there. I will ring up Mum and if she isn't home I will take you to the canteen and you can buy yourself enything (anything) you like.

Another child, Tony, wrote the following:

My Lunch
'Miss Cooper my lunch is gone. I had it in my bag and its gone. Peter saw a koala sniffing at my bag I think he might tas (have taken) my lunch. Miss Cooper kan (can) I go to the ganteen (canteen) so I col by safing (could buy something).'

One can see in these two examples, how much the model of the dialogue in the little book has been pursued. Without the accompanying illustrations, such texts lack a proper sense of completion. Another text, written by Stephen, was in at least two senses more complete. He opened with an orientating sentence, and he also closed his text by bidding his readers farewell:

My Lunch!
My mum made a beautiful lunch it was lunch time I went to get it. When I came back in I said Miss Cooper my lunch has dissapeared (sic). Well we will have to look for it. What's that noise. Oh no an elephant has eaten my lunch. You bad elephant go back to your zoo. What will I do now. You can go to the shop. By by (sic)

This text was accompanied by a good picture of an elephant eating some food.

Of the children who opted for the model of imaginative tales, one reasonably complete example was provided by Joseph. I have set it out to reveal the elements of schematic structure, adopting the names for labelling such elements that Rothery (1991) provided:

What happened to my lunch?

Orientation/Complication
Ones (once) I forgot my lunch in my room
Resolution
Miss Phillips phoned my mum my mum brought my lunch to school then
Santer (Santa) cam(e) to school Santer put his sack on the ground so did I.
Santer gave out toys.
Complication
Santer picked up the (w)rong sack then I didn't have ane (any) lunch.
Resolution
Then I had a lunch order I had a pie and a drink

This text adopts reasonably completely the conventional narrative
structures found in many children's tales. It might be thought to be closer
in character to the model unconsciously provided by the teacher, though it
does not make extensive use of additive and temporal connectedness, of the
kind the teacher modelled. It is likely that Joseph had in mind other models
in creating this text.

As it happens, Joseph had written the following narrative while in Year 1,
a year before he wrote this text, that time based on the model of 'The Little
Red Hen' which his then teacher had read to him:

The little brown bear

Orientation
Once upon a time the little brown bear found some ap(ple) seed and
plant(e)d it
Complication
W(h)en the apples grow (grew) who will help pic(k) the apples.
Resolution
Not I said the dog Not I said the pig Not I said the rat. Then I will.
Complication
Who will help me eat it I will and I will
Resolution
No said the bear I will eat it myself

It is hard to escape the conclusion here that Joseph already had a
reasonably developed model of a narrative structure, of a kind employed in
tales of imaginary experience. He may well have benefited from writing the
text in the classroom genre examined in this chapter, as text types repay
many revisits in the course of a school career. Indeed, I would argue they will
very usefully be revisited at different points over the years of one's schooling,
but that will surely be when opportunity is provided to reflect upon both the
language that is used and the structure that is created. However, such matters
require use of a metalanguage; moreover, they require some sense, possessed
by the teacher and hence developed in the students, of what might constitute
progress and change in controlling and using the structure. These can then

become measures of what constitutes evidence of success as students work over time. Such matters were not available in the classroom talk we have examined. Had they been present, they would have been overtly realized through the regulative register, and the relationship of this register to the instructional register would have been such that the two converged in a sustained way as teacher and students together shaped both a target text for writing and a possible field or fields for writing about.

To return for the moment to the issues of evaluation that applied in the classroom genre we have been examining, all the written texts produced by the children, whether complete or not, were accepted as 'good' by the teacher. There are good reasons to be supportive of the efforts of young children learning to write, and hence good reasons for being accepting of their efforts. It would not have been helpful to condemn or fail to accept the children's efforts. However, I suggest that with a better developed sense of what might constitute a suitable target text, the teacher could have used the children's written efforts as a basis for further talk, further learning and further writing. As I noted much earlier, she showed herself in many ways a good teacher, and with a clearer sense of pedagogic goals it is apparent that she could have directed the students' learning rather more effectively.

Conclusion

The lack of explicitly stated criteria for writing the target text and the lack of well articulated principles of evaluation in classroom genres of the kind examined, I have already suggested, reflect an ideology of the early childhood curriculum which has done both teachers and students a disservice. Among the many problems the weakly classified and framed curriculum tends to beget is its failure to provide clear criteria by which educational growth and progress might be measured and maintained over time. This is both a cause and a symptom of the fact that teaching–learning activities of the kind analysed in this chapter are essentially discrete or 'one-off' affairs. Without principles to guide sustained teaching and learning over time, teachers will necessarily fall back on arranging individual lessons as events having no status and significance other than what they achieve at the time. For the most part, future activities based upon such events will not be contemplated: students might for example, be encouraged to read each other's texts; the teacher might select one example and involve the whole class in developing it, reviewing and extending its structure. Alternatively, she might choose to model the target structure overtly in the first place, involving the students in developing a simple metalanguage for developing their own texts and for examining others' texts. In the classroom we have studied here, it is true that the teacher referred in the final element to class spelling books, and to the need to use them as a resource to help in writing: she also offered assistance with spelling as the children were writing. These are not trivial things to do, though in themselves they are not sufficient as steps to develop literacy learning. Enhanced and sustained literacy development over time will ideally involve much extended work, developing a metalanguage for classroom use. The developmental work involved will be marked by full use of both a regulative and an instructional register, where the two will operate in intimate association over significant periods of time. Where such a development occurs, classroom texts will also demonstrate logogenesis. Later chapters will explore these matters more fully.

Notes

1. It will be recalled the children commenced school in the preparatory year.

4 Pedagogic discourse and curriculum macrogenres

Introduction

In the previous two chapters I have examined the operation of a pedagogic discourse in instances of two types of curriculum genres. Both the morning news genre and the example of an early writing planning genre examined were, I argued, instances of discrete or 'one-off' activities, having little sense of a planned pedagogic connection to previous work, and limited implications for future pedagogic activity. The two examples were drawn from early childhood education and, while I suggested that several of their features reflected particular ideologies that have characterized a great deal of early childhood education, I should make clear I do not propose that such discrete genres are uniquely an aspect of early childhood education.[1] On the contrary, curriculum activity that is expressed mainly in discrete curriculum genres carrying little sense of progression and development in learning is found in teaching and learning at all levels of schooling. This can be the case even where teachers and their students engage with the same broad instructional field over several weeks of work. Unless there is evidence of significant change and development in understanding and in learning of a kind that marks an entry to new forms of 'uncommonsense knowledge' (Bernstein, 2000: 28–9) then it is difficult to justify seeing the series of teaching episodes that emerges as more than a collection of discrete genres, often of an ineffective kind. 'Uncommonsense knowledge' is best understood if we contrast it with 'commonsense knowledge': the latter is knowledge that is familiar and readily available, while uncommonsense is unfamiliar, even esoteric, and it involves use of a specialist or technical language. Development of control over uncommonsense knowledge requires effort over time, and it normally requires the intervention and guidance of a mentor. Pedagogic processes that lead to development of such knowledge are quite other than those that focus on acquisition of 'competence' of the kind referred to by Bernstein, and discussed in Chapter 2. That is because, as I sought to argue in the latter chapter, competence-driven models of pedagogy, among other things, tend to give little significance to the developmental stages in which new areas of knowledge need to be learned. In addition, they downplay or diminish the authority of the teacher in the important work of guiding development by identifying and pointing pedagogic directions, providing information and advice and evaluating progress.

There will be evidence of educational development if one is able to trace changes in the language used across a sequence of curriculum genres, creating growth in the *logos*: a process in fact, of *logogenesis* (Halliday in Halliday and Martin, 1993: 18), a term to which I alluded in Chapter 1. This is a useful term, perhaps best understood if contrasted with the other kinds of genesis Halliday identifies: *phylogenesis*, having to do with the language system and its evolution over time; *ontogenesis*, having to do with the growth, maturity and eventual death of language in the individual. In contrast to these two, logogenesis refers to the unfolding of the text itself, moving from its beginning to its middle and its end. Where a series of genres is intimately connected, such that logogenesis occurs, the genres will be significantly interdependent, creating a larger unity termed here a curriculum macrogenre. This chapter seeks to explore the nature of curriculum macrogenres, examining some of the linguistic evidence we can provide for their presence, and also arguing the importance of developing models of curriculum activity which are built around macrogenres. I shall commence this discussion by considering the notion of a macrogenre, before proceeding in later sections to consider two examples of curriculum macrogenres.

Macrogenres

The notion of a macrogenre was first proposed by Martin (1994, 1995), and his proposal emerged in the main from work he had undertaken with Rothery (e.g. 1980, 1981) and others in exploring the written genres of schooling, especially those of primary and junior secondary science. He had observed the tendency of what he termed 'elemental' genres such as recounts, reports, explanations or procedures to create larger unities in written texts – as for example in school science textbooks. A taxonomic report that classifies and describes some creature, for example, will often be followed by some explanation of its life cycle. There may in addition, depending upon the field, be provided a historical recount to do with the manner in which the creature was found and identified, or even perhaps a procedure to do with how to keep and maintain the creature in some state of captivity. The larger unity created by a text that incorporates several 'elemental' genres Martin termed a 'macrogenre'. The argument with respect to the presence of macrogenres, like that for genres as exemplified in Chapters 2 and 3, depends upon a metaphorical use of the SF grammar, introduced already in Chapter 2. As I have already noted, Halliday (1979, 1982) argued that a text could be thought of metaphorically at least, as like a clause, in that it has meanings that are experiential, interpersonal and textual. As we have seen, I have argued that curriculum genres can similarly be thought of as involving meanings that are experiential, interpersonal and textual, all reflecting the values of the three metafunctions involved.

One metafunction, thus far not invoked at least for the purposes of generic description, remains to be considered, for its particular significance, both in arguing from the grammar, and in developing an argument about the notion of a macrogenre. This is the logical metafunction. For a number of reasons, the logical metafunction is rather different in character from the others, though its relationship to the others – in particular the experiential metafunction – cannot be overlooked. Where the experiential metafunction is involved in representation of the world and its experiences, using the resources of transitivity and of lexis, the logical metafunction is of a different order, for it is involved, not directly in the building of the meanings within the clause, but rather in the more abstract business of building connectedness between the meanings of clauses. As noted in Chapter 1, such a logical connectedness is realized in those resources in the grammar which are involved in two different sets of relationships: those to do with the interdependency or taxis between clauses; and those to do with the logico-semantic relations between clauses brought about by either projection or expansion. Clauses are to be understood as standing in relation to each other in particular ways through the clause complex relationship. And, so the argument proposed by Martin goes, genres can in like manner be said, metaphorically, to stand in relation to other genres, thus creating the larger unity that is the macrogenre.

Martin's proposals regarding macrogenres were made, as I have noted, mainly from work on written genres, and though he referred in passing to a curriculum macrogenre he had identified in work with Rothery, he did not explore classroom texts in any detail. Furthermore, the written texts he examined which he said constituted macrogenres, were relatively short, and, compared with spoken texts, reasonably easy of parsing and analysis. For the purposes of undertaking analysis of classroom talk I find the notion of a curriculum macrogenre a useful one. It provides a means to trace the developments and changes within large tracts of classroom talk and activity over very long periods of time. Yet the challenges in terms of methodology are quite considerable, and I did allude to these in chapter 1, where I discussed methodological questions to do with how texts are selected for close scrutiny and analysis.

Any spoken language poses challenges not normally faced in examining written language, and the challenges are greater in the classroom, not least because, even with the best recording equipment, it is hard to capture all that is said. Moreover, recording and transcribing classroom talk in a sequence of lessons that might run for a full school term of 10 weeks is itself an arduous thing to do. But what is even harder is finding ways to present, analyse and interpret such long texts as emerge. It is of course impossible to present the full texts to be examined in this chapter, for example, and one is always in that case open to the charge that one has made selective choices from the text the better to enhance any argument one might want to make. Yet I am also of the view that, if we are really to understand the nature of teaching and learning, and in particular to interpret and explain how teachers manage to effect important changes in their students' understanding, we must be bold enough to view the relatively 'big sweep' of classroom talk that typically characterizes a unit of curriculum activity. No doubt in the future, as computer facilities improve, and as computer-based programs for parsing large quantities of text at speed develop, some of the time-consuming aspects of classroom data analysis will recede. The problems to do with the best ways to compress and represent significant passages of the texts will remain. Despite these problems, I can claim that the notion of a macrogenre – as indeed of a genre – is a powerful one for text analysis purposes. It provides a principled basis upon which to collect very long sequences of classroom text and, correspondingly, a basis upon which to select those passages one does choose for close text analysis. Without such a model, it is difficult to make judgements about such matters as: the role that language plays in the construction of knowledge through the different stages of activity; the negotiation of relationship of teacher and students or students with each, over time; the ways in which students learn over time; the principles of evaluation of performance in learning that apply, how they are applied, and the extent to which they prove useful. All these matters require large sweeps of language in order to make valid judgements.

A successful instance of classroom activity across a sequence of lessons – sometimes lasting for several weeks – can be shown to be a curriculum macrogenre, made up of numbers of 'elemental' curriculum genres, all of them linked in some kinds of relationships. Martin suggested that in practice, it is the logico-semantic relationships associated with projection and expansion that are more sensitive for the purposes of genre relations than are the relations of interdependency. My own observation is that, within a curriculum macrogenre, the elemental genres are interdependent, though there is no real issue of their status one to another in terms of taxis; that is because matters of the relative equality or inequality of genres do not seem to apply. In addition, with respect to the relations within curriculum macrogenres, it seems that those of expansion are the most relevant. This is because, as we shall see below, in a curriculum macrogenre an initiating genre will typically be followed by some genre(s) that provide elaboration, or extension or enhancement upon either the original initiating genre or upon one or other of those in the 'middle' of the total structure, or sometimes upon both.

Curriculum macrogenres

Not surprisingly, curriculum macrogenres have certain features in common with curriculum genres. Most notably, they have a 'beginning, middle, end' pattern, which unfolds through various shifts in the language: some options in language use are opened up, while others are often abandoned, marking changes in the nature of the pedagogic subject position in construction and in the forms of cognition associated with this position. A curriculum macrogenre will typically have an initiating genre (which may last for one or more lessons) whose function is to establish overall goals for the teaching and learning, predisposing the students to address certain issues, defining possible strategies for work, and generally charting the course the programme of work is to pursue. The opening genre normally has a series of phases or stages within it, all important to the definition of tasks and the establishment of a framework for working, as well as indicating those criteria for evaluation that apply in judging students' performance. An ultimate task to be completed is very often established in prospect in this initiating genre, as a necessary aspect of establishing the evaluation principles that will apply. It is the 'middle' genres that show the greatest variation from one macrogenre to another, depending upon the overall goals of the programme of work, the nature of the instructional field and the age of the students. There may be one or more than one 'middle' genres, and these will typically involve several lessons. The middle genres are often recursive in character: this is because it is in the 'middle' genres that much of the essential work is done, and that is at times recursive. The final genre (sometimes taking more than one lesson) will provide some clear sense of a closure, normally requiring of the students completion of some task(s). On occasion, depending upon the skill of the teacher, and the directions to be taken in future work, the closure of one curriculum macrogenre may be used to announce the opening of another, in that overt reference is made to skills developed and/or issues examined which will be taken up again in another curriculum activity. Even where no such overt connection is required – as for example, when teacher and students move into a new instructional field – there will in practice always be opportunities to work with and draw upon recently developed capacities and understandings in addressing the new. Interpersonally there will be shifts across the macrogenre, as students progress towards successful apprenticeship in their learning: the general direction involves a movement from overt teacher direction towards a developing assumption of independence on the part of the learner.

What of the relations of the genres to each other within the macrogenre? I shall outline one rather prototypical model of a successful curriculum macrogenre which I have found in many primary and secondary classrooms, though it is certainly not the only one. It may be represented as in Figure 4.1.

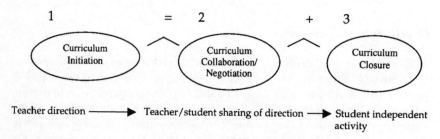

Figure 4.1   Prototypical model of a curriculum macrogenre

The Curriculum Initiation, as already noted, initiates activity, establishes goals, crucially predisposes the students to work and think in particular ways, defines the ultimate task or tasks, though normally in general terms, and it indicates the evaluation principles that will apply. The middle genre – which I sometimes term the 'Curriculum Collaboration' and sometimes the 'Curriculum Negotiation' – involves pursuing the work necessary towards achievement of the tasks. This might involve reading of selected materials, researching in libraries, viewing films, interviewing people, going on field trips, reading a class novel, conducting experiments, constructing models and/or charts, or any of a number of other activities, depending upon what is being taught and learned. The reason for using either the term 'collaboration' or 'negotiation', is that, depending upon the context, one or other of the two terms is better: 'collaboration' is a term I use where, as we shall see, students actively cooperate in the pursuit of a task and the teacher has a secondary role, normally in providing support; the term 'negotiation' seems more appropriate for those situations in which students and teacher actively work together. The Curriculum Collaboration/Negotiation stands in a relation of elaboration to the Curriculum Initiation, while the Curriculum Closure stands in a relationship of extension to the Curriculum Collaboration (signalled by using Halliday's notation '=', and '+', respectively, 1994: 220).[2] I have made no attempt here to represent the various stages or phases within the genres, so that this figure provides a very simplified account of what the prototypical curriculum macrogenre looks like.

The pattern for the structure of the macrogenre in Figure 4.1 is essentially linear, or perhaps serial: that is to say, the sequence reveals a set of genres that unfold one after the other in a manner that reflects their unfolding in real time. Not all genres and not all macrogenres are necessarily linear in character, nor do they necessarily lead to a culminating task or tasks. White (1997), Iedema (1994, 1997) and Martin (1996) have suggested an alternative model of genres, which is termed 'orbital'. Martin, White and Iedema all worked together in a major project in Sydney in the early 1990s, from which the observations about orbital structures derived. White based his observations about orbital structures mainly on analysis of narrative structures found in news stories, though he has also (1998) argued that the orbital pattern applies in other kinds of written texts. Iedema did a study of the language of administration, in particular the administrative memos on which so many contemporary office and business practices depend. Martin's observations covered a range of written texts.

In Chapter 5 I shall examine a curriculum macrogenre which is orbital in structure, while in this chapter I shall continue to develop this discussion of macrogeneric structure by reference to examples which are linear. I shall proceed by examining two examples of macrogenres, drawn from the upper primary school years. I shall look for evidence of the realization of each of the major genres involved, providing illustrations from the classroom texts, though the discussions of the texts will necessarily be constrained in the interests of saving space.

I should preface the following discussion by noting that the two instances of curriculum macrogenres to be examined involved teachers who were using a 'genre-based' pedagogy of a kind that has achieved success in many parts of Australia in recent years, though it has also achieved some success in other parts of the English-speaking world. A genre-based pedagogy has been discussed, exemplified and/or explained in many places, including for example, Derewianka (1990), Christie et al. (1990a, 1990b, 1990c) Christie and Martin (1997), Macken-Horarick (1997), Christie in Christie & Misson (1998), Martin (1999), Unsworth (2000), Butt et al. (2000). Systemic theory and genre pedagogy have also of course attracted several critics, such as Reid (1987), Freedman and Medway (1994) and Lee (1996), while others (see for example some of the collected papers edited by Cope and Kalantzis (1993) have sought to offer critiques with a view to revisions of genre-based approaches. No lengthy discussion of the rationale for genre-based approaches to pedagogy will be offered here, on the grounds that very adequate discussions are offered in many other places. However, I shall provide a brief explanation, partly for any reader for whom it may be new, and partly in the interests of clarifying the teacher's goals in the macrogenres. Because it is so functionally orientated, the pedagogy produces very audibly marked regulative and instructional registers, and these are also important aspects of a curriculum which is both strongly classified and strongly framed. A genre-based pedagogy seeks to be a very transparent one: the pacing and sequencing of activity are very deliberate, while the principles for evaluation, as far as is possible, are made explicit.

So-called genre-based approaches to pedagogy draw upon SF analyses which identify features of different text types or genres and the ways they realize different contexts of situation. The description of a genre that emerges from the linguistic analysis names each of the stages or elements found in the overall schematic structure. Each stage or element of structure is said to have functional significance: that is, it serves some important social and human purpose by helping to organize and shape the meanings of the text type. The goal of a genre-based pedagogy is to teach the features of the genre(s) relevant to the particular subject discipline being taught in the school curriculum. The genre and its characteristics will be taught as part of the regulative register: that is to say, it will be taught as instrumental to the mastery of some method of marshalling and organizing information or ideas. It will also be taught as instrumental to the mastery of the instructional field that constitutes the 'content' of the curriculum.

Before proceeding to discussing the macrogenres here, I should note that the two were recorded in two upper primary classrooms in the same city, though in different schools, and the two teachers were not known to each other. Both schools had similar architecture, and the two classrooms in which the teaching–learning took place were very similar. Students sat in working groups of two or three at tables, looking towards the teacher's area, which was marked by the presence of a blackboard and teacher's table and chair, while cupboards and shelves lined two walls, used for storage of books and equipment. There was no carpeted area for the children to sit on the floor of the teacher, and this reflected the fact that the students were of the upper primary school: as students grow older, their teachers tend not to group them in clusters on the floor in the manner found in the junior primary school.

The students were drawn from communities in which most parents worked, the mothers often in part-time capacities. The major bread-winners held occupations as skilled workers such as carpenters while others held white-collar positions in the local public service. A few students were from non-English-speaking backgrounds, though they were not for the most part recent arrivals.

Curriculum Initiation

The Curriculum Initiation institutes activity for the whole curriculum macrogenre. It is realized in both the regulative and the instructional registers, the one to do with overall pedagogic goals and purposes, the other to do with the particular instructional field that constitutes the 'content' of the programme of work. As a usual principle, the language begins by foregrounding the regulative register and, while the instructional field finds some expression, it is of a reasonably general nature. The opening genre normally has several elements or stages, and their overall purpose is to move the students towards achieving some clarity and specificity about the nature of their tasks. Teachers differ very considerably in the manner in which the Curriculum Initiation and its elements are realized. In the case of an upper primary science curriculum macrogenre (developed in nine substantial lessons over a fortnight) devoted to teaching and learning about the principle of the mechanical advantage conferred by machines and referred to here as Text 4.1, the Curriculum Orientation has three elements: the Task Orientation, the Task Specification and the Task Conference. Each of these in turn has further phases made distinctive through the changes in language use from one element to another. Regrettably, I have abandoned the attempt

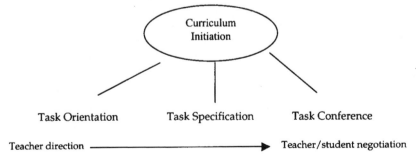

Figure 4.2 Simplified model of the Curriculum Initiation in Text 4.1

to display or discuss the phases within each of the main elements in the Curriculum Initiation in Text 4.1 because of lack of space (a longer discussion can be found in Christie, 1998). I should also note that as the discussion proceeds it will become apparent that I have used only small selections from the text and the subsequent one, and that, while I continue to draw on the systemic grammar for analytic purposes, I shall make only partial use of its resources.

The Task Orientation starts, very characteristically, in teacher monologue:

Text 4.1 (extract only)

T: *Right, OK now we are going to start our theme next week, but we are actually starting a bit earlier because of it. The main requirement is for various things to be done.[3] The main one is on science day....[inaudible] So we've got to do a lot of concentrating. There will be two pieces of writing, one is a procedural text.... [inaudible] The other one is to write an explanation as to why parts of a machine work. So a bit of concentration. Um, you can start by looking up the basis of how the machines work in a series of science books.... [inaudible] For instance a catapult. You'll be making an exact replica of a catapult, not the full size of course. Think about it. This* is *your problem for the next couple of weeks. The other thing you might do is making a lift or wishing well or even a Spanish windlass, it's basically a barrel.*

From the point of view of the textual metafunction, one can see how the cluster of continuatives here serves to drive activity forward:

<u>right, OK now</u> we are going to start our theme next week,
<u>but</u> we are actually starting a bit earlier because of it.
<u>so</u> we've got to do a lot of concentrating
<u>so</u> a bit of concentration.

Experientially, note how much the regulative register (shown in italics, as in earlier chapters) is foregrounded in the process types, some of them material and behavioural:

we	are going to start	our theme	next week
Actor	Pro: material	Goal	Circ: location: time

but	we	are actually starting	a bit earlier	because of it
	Actor	Process: material	Circ: loc: time	Circ: reason

but others are identifying, and in these the Value is very significant:

the main requirement	is	for various things [[to be done]]
Value	Pro: intensive	Token

the main one	is	on science day ... [inaudible]
Value	Pro: intensive	Token

the other one is	[[to write an explanation [[as to why parts of a machine work]]]]
Value Pro: intensive	Token

This	is	your problem	for the next couple of weeks
Token	Pro: intensive	Value	Circ: duration: time

Nominal groups such as *the main requirement* or *the main one* are very forceful expressions in teacher talk, and indeed participants of this kind are very centrally involved in the operation of the interpersonal metafunction here. As a general principle, teachers make sparing, if effective, use of identifying processes. They are involved, on occasion, in establishing technical language, either to do with the instructional register, or with the regulative register. Where they are used, as here, to build an aspect of the regulative register, their effect is to express directions that are categorical: some course of action is to be pursued, where other possibilities are not to be entertained. In fact, the first of these three identifying processes is really an interpersonal metaphor, where the more congruent realization would have been: *you must do various things*. The text extract is interpersonally powerful in other ways, as for example, in the process which involves a use of high modality (underlined):

So	we'	ve got to do a lot of concentrating
	Senser	Process: cognition

and in the later elliptical realization of the same process: *So a bit of concentration,* as well as in the congruent use of the imperative mood in:

Think about	it
Pro: cognition	Phenomenon

Technical language relevant to the regulative register finds some expression in this extract, and one can see how it is alluded to first in a general nominal group (*two pieces of writing*), and then in two nominal groups that build greater specificity (*a procedural text; an explanation [[as to why parts of a machine work]]*). These are in fact both parts of the uncommonsense knowledge of the regulative register. Their function is to signal an important aspect of the eventual task.

The instructional field is realized in the discourse, though in a manner which gives it secondary significance in the overall organization of the talk, and this one would expect at this point where broad pedagogic directions are at issue. It occurs, for example, in an embedded clause in the participant role of Token, where again it is realized in a general nominal group (*parts of a machine*):

the other one	*is*	*[[to write an explanation [[as to why*
		parts of a machine *work]]]]*
Value	*Pro: intensive*	*Token*

Then later the instructional field achieves greater specificity in the manner in which it is constructed, for technical language relevant to the field comes into play:

> *Um, you can start by looking up the basis of how the machines work in a series of science books . . . (inaudible)*
> *For instance a catapult.*
> *You'll be making an exact replica of a catapult, not the full size of course*
> *The other thing [[you might do]] is [[making a lift or wishing well or even a spanish windlass]]*
> *it's basically a barrel.*

In summary we can say that it is the regulative register that is foregrounded in the opening, while the instructional field has some expression, and this reflects the status of the two vis-à-vis each other as a general principle: it is the regulative register that determines the pacing, sequencing and overall management of the pedagogic activity, and it also establishes the criteria for eventual evaluation of the learning. It will be apparent too, that the curriculum discourse here is marked by strong classification and framing. The strong classification is apparent in the way in which *science* and *how machines work* are audibly established in the discourse, by implication setting the concerns here apart from the other concerns of the week's activities. It is strongly framed, since the strong moral imperative to do with such expressions as *the main requirement*, or *we've got to do a lot of concentrating* effectively define what will be the focus of activity, excluding other possibilities. Interpersonally, the teacher makes clear his role in determining how the students will proceed in their learning.

Before I leave the concerns of this opening, I should also note the significance the teacher gives to considerations of time, as in:

> *OK now we are going to start our theme next week, but we are actually starting a bit earlier because of it.*

and,

This is your problem for the next couple of weeks.

In the discussions in Chapter 3, I noted how the teacher invoked considerations of time at one point to discipline a child whose behaviour was unacceptable. Teachers define the pace of activities in schools, establish the spatial dimensions that apply in adopting work practices, and define periods of time in which activities are to be undertaken. Considerations of time and space are both involved in defining the pedagogic subject position in construction, and they are one aspect of the realization of the regulative register. Such considerations serve to build structure and definition to the day, the week, the month, and so on.

The Task Orientation moves through a series of stages in which the students: view a film that explains the operation of machines; jointly construct with their teacher a taxonomy of types of machines displayed on the board; and establish the general principle that lies behind uses of all machines, namely the principle of mechanical advantage. The language changes considerably through these phases within the Task Orientation, moving from teacher monologue in the opening, to dialogue and the classic IRE pattern (discussed in Chapter 1) as in a series of exchanges about types of machines in the film:

> T: *What other, what other machine did he use in the movie that was a wedge or an inclined plane?*
> Yvonne: *Chisel.*
> T: *Chisel, right (writes on the board). Excellent. Now is there anything you can think of?*

towards another phase in which, having discussed the types of machines, the teacher moves back to monologue for a sequence in which he states, *And each machine is used to give you a mechanical advantage (writes 'work-mechanical advantage' on the board).*

In the whole fortnight, incidentally, the IRE pattern occurs only once, and it is in this case essential for the work of jointly constructing groupings of the types of machine: this work helps build a shared instructional field, on the basis of which the students can move forward to a new level of work and of understanding. That new level is expressed in the adoption of the abstraction, *mechanical advantage*, which is an instance of grammatical metaphor; its emergence marks a shift, having consequences for the learning of the students. That is to say, they have moved away from the specificities of different types of machines towards identifying the more abstract principle that lies behind their use.

The Task Specification returns to the nature of the task for the students alluded to in the opening, as we saw above, but this time introducing a much greater use of specificity: sheets are distributed outlining the *variety of problems* that students can take up in making simple machines, such *as a pulley, a robot, a windlass or a lift.*

The Task Conference involves a lengthy passage of animated talk among the students, much of it hard to capture with the recording equipment, though involving exchanges with the teacher such as:

> Kate: *We're doing the robot people.*
> T: *Who is this?*
> Kate: *Our group (points to herself and three other girls)*

The language is at this point very different from that used in either the Task Orientation or the Task Specification, both because it is dialogic and because it requires a great deal of negotiation among the students; it is they who largely determine the direction of activity at this point, rather than the teacher. They emerge with their groups established and the tasks for each group for the rest of the fortnight known.

Overall, I would argue that the Curriculum Initiation in this case has succeeded in that it has established clear goals for the students with respect to both the regulative and the instructional register. Technical language relevant to both fields has been used, and even in the relatively early steps involved, the processes of logogenesis have commenced: considerable shifts in the language uses have occurred, and a major concept (*mechanical advantage*), critical to an understanding of the instructional field has been introduced. Thus does the discourse start to do its work in shaping: the nature of the tasks for the students, the kinds of understandings they are to develop, the principles of evaluation that will apply, and hence the nature of the pedagogic subject position at issue.

I have said that teachers differ in their manner of realization of the genres in a curriculum macrogenre. In order to illustrate the point, I shall now turn to some consideration, again of extracts only, from another curriculum macrogenre, this time drawn from the upper primary social sciences. For the purposes of this discussion I shall refer to the classroom text involved as Text 4.2, and I should note that again I can offer only a very partial discussion of this (a longer discussion is available in Christie, 1997).

The classroom text is built around an activity devoted to considering the benefits of nuclear power, and more specifically a nuclear power station in the Australian city of Darwin. The total programme of work was developed over

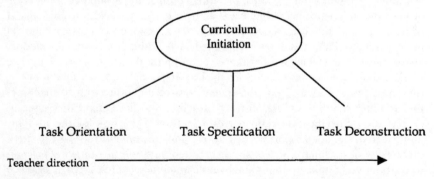

Figure 4.3 Simplified model of the Curriculum Initiation in Text 4.2

three weeks, and five of the seven lessons were recorded. The students undertook research of various kinds between the lessons.

The Task Orientation (having several distinct phases within it, not considered here) was initiated in teacher talk and, mainly because the class group constituted about half the normal class (the other half had gone with a specialist ESL teacher), a great deal of the first few minutes of talk was devoted to establishing seating arrangements preparatory to later work. In Chapter 2, I remarked the manner in which, as one aspect of the regulative register, a great deal of explicit direction to acceptable patterns of behaviour is realized in early childhood classrooms, and I also noted the fact that such talk disappears as the patterns are understood: the regulative register still operates of course but at a tacit level. Explicit directions regarding behaviour, seating arrangements and related matters can of course appear at any time, perhaps where students' behaviour has become unacceptable and is being corrected, or, as in this case, where some new aspect of the physical setting has emerged. Half the class has gone off with another teacher, so this teacher wants to re-arrange the group that is left. Above, I referred to issues of spatial arrangements as one aspect of the realization of the regulative register. Talk of physical arrangements did not appear at all in the Curriculum Initiation in Text 4.1, as we saw; the teacher in that case was working with a class whose members had taken up familiar, because well-established, positions in order to proceed. The Task Orientation here begins by focusing on physical dispositions, and, for reasons discussed beneath, I have marked the very frequent uses of modality in the teacher's talk:

Text 4.2 (extract only)

T: (*moving in between student desks as she groups students*) *The way [[to work]] might be [[to sit around this group]]. All right? Because perhaps people will be [inaudible] and less wriggling if they're seated. Now a lot of work [[that you may have to do]] may be with a partner. Some you'll do by yourself. So you're probably best to sit next to somebody [[that you will work with]]. OK? Now, two, four, six, eight... [turns to one table] there's one person away today so maybe it might be a group of three. All right? It's up to you. But could you find yourself a seat around the desks and be sitting next to someone that you will identify to work with please? If you two are going to work together... there'll have to be one odd person sitting there... ok? So move down one please.*

Richard: *Face to face.*

T: *No, side by side I think will be easier to work. Side by side will probably be a lot easier actually [Considerable noise and movement as students settle themselves] And... um right quick! Two, four, five, the people on the end might be able to turn your chair around a little bit. All right. You really do need something to write with so if you don't have your own pens and pencils would you collect those please? And there are a couple of organizational things [[to do]] before we get started.*

Capacity to work cooperatively with other students is highly prized in many curriculum guidelines produced in Australia, because a value attaches to being cooperative and willing to collaborate as part of the educative process. It is part of the ideal pedagogic subject position to be constructed. This partly explains the teacher's attention to such matters. It is notable that in pursuing her directions regarding seating the teacher makes such frequent use of modality, either modal verbs or modal adjuncts. Clearly the teacher is intent upon having her way in achieving seating arrangements and patterns for working for the whole period of activity. In one sense the whole passage is an interpersonal metaphor, where the congruent realization would be a command such as: *you must sit like this in these groups.* As it is, the teacher appears to offer information (*the way to sit might be to sit around this group*), instead of offering a command, and she makes use essentially of low modality (*may, might, perhaps.*) In this she is in contrast with the early childhood teacher in Chapter 2, and with the teacher cited above in the extract from Text 4. The early childhood teacher made little use of modality, though she used two instances of interpersonal metaphor (*I want you to listen* said twice) which, since they *meant you must listen*, indicated that high modality was involved. The teacher in Text 4.1 had a great range of linguistic resources, some of which made overt used of modality (*we've got to do a lot of concentrating*), and others of which were expressed in more metaphorical ways (*the main requirement is for various things to be done*); whether congruent or metaphorical, his expressions also expressed high modality. In the case of Text 4.2, where the uses of modality are either low or median, the result is that the teacher appears to be negotiating with the students what she wants, though negotiation is not for the most part an issue at all. This is apparent when, one student having suggested that they sit *face to face,* the teacher responds: *No, side by side I think will be easier to work.* This (apart from a reference to what happens *if you don't have your own pens and pencils*) is the only instance of a negative polarity in the opening. Positive polarity, as I noted earlier, is a feature of teacher talk, especially in openings of activities. It is part of the general disposition of the teacher to point directions forward in a positive manner.

The talk proceeds to an examination of an advertisement the teacher claims has appeared in the press calling for expression of opinion about the wisdom of introducing a nuclear power station to Darwin (this is in fact a fiction, though it certainly attracts the students' attention). Considerable talk of this advertisement follows, and since the students have previously read a story about an imagined nuclear war, they already have some sense of the instructional field issues. At one point the following exchange occurs:

> T: *But say there was an accident with the nuclear power station, what could maybe one of the problems be?*
> Ashley: *Radiation leaking and affecting everybody.*

Already technical language relevant to the instructional field is appearing in the discourse, while some general talk of the need to take action about a possible nuclear power station emerges.

The teacher signals the start of the Task Specification thus:

T: *Ok, well what are we going to do? Are we going to read this ad and let it go?*
     What are we going to do?

Initial responses from students to do with writing *personal opinion* against the
nuclear power station or collecting a *petition* are accepted by the teacher in
part though she also reveals that she wants rather more:

T: *All right. We could do that (i.e. arrange for a petition). But go back to the point*
     I was trying to push Layla with and go back to the thing that Richard said.
     Richard said our personal opinion. Layla said that we could get a petition but I
     said think about the research. Is there something better we can do? Your ideas are
     great but let's see if we can put all those ideas together.

Here the regulative register is clearly to the fore as the teacher works to
guide the students towards a different intellectual position. Her opening use of
a median modal verb here: *we could do that*, draws attention to the fact that
other possibilities are available. This is reinforced by a subsequent series of
clauses in which the teacher alludes to what has been suggested, while she also
contrives through the uses of the contrastive conjunction (*but* used three
times) to imply more might be sought. All this serves to dispose the students to
take up another option. Shortly, one student suggests they might write a
discussion genre (revealing incidentally, some familiarity of the class with this
technical term) involving research into the relevant facts about nuclear
power, and then preparing the discussion, setting out arguments for and
against, and ending with an expression of their own view.

The teacher's response here is revealing for several reasons, for it is an
interesting expression of the regulative register:

T: *Do you make your mind up now? (Several students say 'no') See, when we*
     first started talking, that's [[what I felt [[you had done]]]]. All right,
     because maybe... because of the story we read (i.e. about nuclear war). I felt
     that maybe you'd made your mind up and it's really good [[to see [[that
     people actually haven't made their mind up [[and that they're prepared to look
     at both sides]]]]]]. And it's that evidence [[that'll tell us]]. And I think
     writing a discussion is an excellent idea. It's probably the best idea. Because
     ≪ when we send that in ≫ * it means we've been fair. We've looked at it
     properly, we've looked at both sides and we've thought about it before we've
     made the decision.

(* a reference to the projected activity of sending off letters containing discussion
genres in response to the advertisement)

The teacher might have started her Curriculum Initiation with a
statement to the effect 'we are going to research whether it would be a

good thing to have a nuclear power station and then write discussion genres in which we set out the arguments and give our opinions'. Such a statement, or something like it, would be not that far removed from the example of the opening of the Task Orientation of the teacher above in the extract from Text 4.1. The differences in the openings of the two teachers no doubt reflect something of their quite different personalities. Yet I am not convinced that is the complete explanation here. In Text 4.2 the means by which the teacher has guided the students towards the decision to research matters and write a discussion tells us a great deal of the manner of operation of the regulative register here. There is a time-honoured convention in English-speaking societies to do with the values of dispassionate research into an issue and of arriving at a balanced decision on the evidence. Such values, among other matters, are very centrally involved in the operation of the regulative register in this curriculum macrogenre, and they have consequences for the way in which the teacher positions the students to commence their task. She would have missed some important pedagogic opportunities had she simply advised the students of the task, rather than disposed them to move through possible alternative courses of action before hitting on the one chosen. The same opportunities were not so obviously available in the very different context of Text 4.1, where the objects, activities and eventual target genre were so different. Here, what was at issue for teaching and learning was a Newtonian principle, very familiar in western science, and the object was that the students be apprenticed into an understanding of it.

The fragment of teacher talk is extraordinarily rich in its uses of linguistic resources to shape the relevant pedagogic subject position. Note, interpersonally, first of all, the fact that the teacher selects the interrogative: *do you make your mind up now?* By eliciting information of the students, the teacher obliges them initially to offer her a response. With this she can proceed, and for the rest of this fragment, she selects the declarative, with a gradually amplifying set of linguistic resources which build her general appreciation of the decision to research and write discussion genres. A mental process allows her to intrude her attitude into matters, where this is extended in the projected clause that follows:

I	*felt*	
Senser	*Process: affect*	
that maybe you	*'d made your mind up*	
	Senser	*Process: cognition*

Note the way from here on that transitivity, mood and modality are all implicated in the expanding sense of the teacher's appreciation (a modal adjunct is underlined):

and	it	's	really good [[to see [[that people <u>actually</u> haven't made their mind up and [[that they're prepared to look at both sides]]]]]]
Carrier	Pro: intensive		Attribute

The expression *it's really good* in itself carries evaluation, though its expression is a little more forceful, because a little more abstract, than if the teacher had said, *I am pleased to see that people haven't made their minds up*. Note in addition the significance of the modulation in the expression *they're prepared to look at both sides*: this means 'they are willing to look at both sides'.

Note the way relational processes, both attributive and identifying, become involved in building increasingly categorical statements about what is to be done, and hence increasingly powerful directions to the students:

and	it	's	that evidence [[that'll tell us]]
	Carrier	pro: intensive	Attribute

and I think	writing a discussion	is	an excellent idea
Modal adjunct*	Carrier	Pro: int.	Attribute

it	's probably	the best idea
Token	Pro: intensive	Value

* The mental process here is treated as a modal adjunct. Halliday (1994: 354–5) argues that the measure of the status of such a mental process as a modal adjunct lies in the use of the *tag question: I think writing a discussion is an excellent idea, isn't it?*, not *don't I?*

At this point in the discourse, a use of a causal conjunction (*because*) and a hypotactic clause placed in theme position serve to take the talk into a slightly different direction: *Because* ≪ *when we send that in* ≫ *it means we've been fair*.

because	it	means	[[we've been fair]]
	Carrier	Pro: intensive	Attribute

when	we	send	that	in
	Actor	Pro-	Goal	-cess: material

In the remaining clauses, note the following: the persistent use of *we* in the opening participant role, building solidarity in a joint enterprise; the consistent use of positive polarity, building a sense of asserting direction; the absence of modality, which would have suggested some possible qualification;[4] and the significance of the lexical choice in the adverb *properly*, carrying a strong sense of judgement:

we	*'ve looked at*	*it*	*properly*
Senser	process: cognition	Phenomenon	Circumstance: Manner
we	*'ve looked at*	*both sides*	
Senser	Process: cognition	Phenomenon	
and we	*'ve thought about*	*it*	
Senser	process: cognition	Phenomenon	
before	*we*	*'ve made the decision.*	
	Senser	Process: cognition	

In Martin's terms (see discussions in Martin, in Christie and Martin, 1997: 4–39; and in Eggins and Slade 1997: 116–68) at issue here are the linguistic resources involved in interpersonal assessment – an area to which he gives the name 'Appraisal'. Specifically, the resources for appraising involved here are those of appreciation (as in *an excellent idea*) and judgement (as in *we've looked at it properly*). By drawing on these and other interpersonal resources, the teacher has built a very positive sense of the values of proceeding towards the course of action identified.

The Task Deconstruction commences shortly after the above and this is a lengthy genre, taking part of the opening lesson and the second one. Here the students examine two examples of discussion genres on fields other than nuclear power and under teacher guidance they explore the functions of the elements of structure: *Topic* ∧ *Preview of Issue* ∧ *Arguments* π ∧ *Recommendation*. They also explore features of the grammatical choices in which the discussion genre is constructed, including most notably tense choices (often tricky in writing even for native speakers, because of the need to shift from present to past tense at different stages in the genre), and the various conjunction choices (temporal, causal and contrastive in particular) relevant to the discussion genre. They also discuss uses of certain textual theme choices such as 'on the other hand', of a kind that are used to signal the start of a new step in the discussion.

Overall, the Curriculum Initiation has served to establish directions and methods of working for the students, on the one hand to do with working collaboratively, and on the other hand, to do with researching information and writing discussion genres that will review the issues relevant to the instructional field. It has also established the strong value to be attached to behaving in such ways, and we have seen how significant is the teacher's role in this. Moreover, and because it has established these things, it has also defined the principles for evaluation to apply for the whole educational endeavour. Technical language relevant to both the regulative and instructional registers has been used, and a shared understanding of the issues to be explored has been created. A process of logogenesis has been commenced in at least two senses. Firstly, it has commenced with the introduction into the classroom text of technical language relevant to both the instructional and regulative fields. Secondly, it has commenced in that opportunities for pedagogic action have been explored and some rejected (e.g., preparing a *petition*) while others have been opened up (researching and then writing a *discussion genre*): as logogensis unfolds, one of its effects will be the closing down of some registerial choices, while others are opened up and expanded upon.

The Curriculum Collaboration and the Curriculum Closure

I have already noted that it is the 'middle' genre that shows the greatest variation in curriculum macrogenres. It is also normally the longest and will typically last for several lessons, since this is where the work initiated in the first genre is actively pursued. In the case of Text 4.1, the Curriculum Collaboration consists of some recursive phases in which the students work in groups making their simple machines. For very long sequences of time the teacher, while present in the room, is actually silent, for it is the students who work in animated ways, talking among themselves. In the case of Text 4.2, I term the middle genre a 'Curriculum Negotiation', since the teacher takes a more actively shared role with the students in their learning than is the case in the Task Collaboration in Text 4.1. She works alongside the students as they share the results of research (in books brought from home or from the school library), and, using a grid suggested by the teacher, they construct tables of information in which they amass data about the uses and dangers of nuclear power.

In both cases, as I noted earlier, the Curriculum Closure involves a culminating activity. It extends upon the work of the Curriculum Collaboration/Negotiation, and it involves the completion of the task or tasks which were very audibly foretold in the Curriculum Initiation. In the case of Text 4.1, the Closure involves the production in groups of oral recounts of what was done in making the machines, and the display of procedural genres showing how to make the machines.

In the case of Text 4.2. the Curriculum Closure involves the completion by each individual of a discussion genre, typed up on the class computers in a final form for reasonably permanent keeping.

In both cases, logogenesis has occurred, for, as the curriculum macrogenre has unfolded and gained momentum, the students have been enabled to use and understand patterns of language in new ways: their completed written work, and their capacity to talk about it, are measures of this. A few extracts

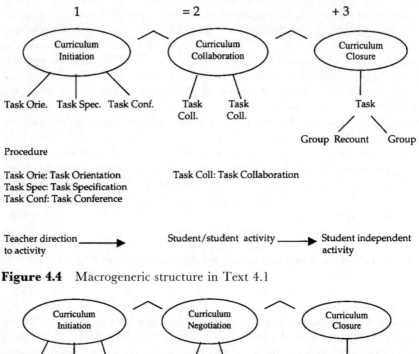

Figure 4.4 Macrogeneric structure in Text 4.1

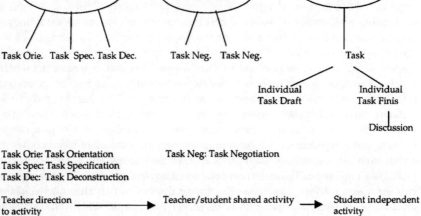

Figure 4.5 Macrogeneric structure in Text 4.2

from the two classroom texts will serve to demonstrate some of their features.

In Text 4.1, in one of the Task Collaboration phases, the students work in groups for several lessons while they make their machines. Here is an extract from the discussion in which one group is working on making a windlass, in which, it will be noted, much use is made of exophoric reference to implements in use in working on the model. The students have a set of written instructions which they take some time reading and talking about:

(Student starts to do something)

Naomi: *No, I don't think you do it that way. You've got to follow the instructions.*

Yvonne: *What instructions? There weren't no instructions. (looks around)*

Naomi: *Read the instructions. (points to the sheet)*

Aranthi: *Where's the... is there another one? Is there a cork? (a reference to some pieces of equipment needed)*

Naomi: *Oh well, do that later (i.e. find equipment), first we'll figure this (starts to read the instructions).*

Several minutes later, the students having got clearer what they are to do, they start to collect cutting implements, using pliers, scissors and a very sharp knife at one point.

Chanoa: *I've already cut that. We have done that right. What do you need? (Naomi picks up the knife, and Chanoa is concerned at the potential danger to her) Careful.*
           Later she says again: Careful please. Please be careful.

Yvonne: *Now what have we got to do?*

Katrina: *Can I have the other one?*

Naomi: *Let me have a try.*

Several minutes later.

Chanoa: *Give us the wire.*

Katrina: *This one (passes over an implement and the wire)*

Chaona: *I'll try it.*

Katrina: *In here. (points to a part of the windlass) Yeah yeah we got it, we got it!!*

The language here is quite unlike that in any other genres within the whole macrogenre, and that is not only because of the extensive use of exophoric references. The students are working on the task, and at this stage the two registers have effectively merged. That is because, on the one hand, the students follow the oral and written directions given them as an aspect of the working of the regulative register, and in so doing they also direct each other in a thoroughly collaborative way. On the other hand, they also learn about the principles that appear to determine the working of the windlass, making it a successful example of a machine. The talk is dialogic yet in a number of ways quite different from the dialogic phases earlier in the text. While the teacher is present in the room at all times, he is not an active participant in the talk, but available to give assistance when needed. In this stretch of language it is the students who shape the directions of the talk and in the process they negotiate and control both relationship and activity. To do this, they draw on the complete range of mood choices and speech functions available in the language, so that they: give information, *I've already cut that*; seek information, *now what do we have to do?*; issue commands, *please be careful*; offer a service, *let me have a try*. The linguistic evidence supports the view that learning is occurring of a kind different from that anywhere else in the macrogenre.

Capacity of students to talk and work thus in small groups in the classroom has often been extolled as a virtue, with the suggestion sometimes made that such talk is to be more highly valued than the pattern of teacher-directed talk that is a feature, say, of the IRE pattern. Yet, as I have earlier indicated, the issues are more complex than such claims often acknowledge. I would make two observations here. Firstly, in that the group talk in the text examined was successful, that in itself depended upon the teacher's having provided very explicit and clear directions in the former curriculum genre: without that, the students' talk and work would have foundered, as I have seen happen with many small groups. Secondly, the only reliable measure of the value of either small group talk or the IRE (or indeed any other pattern of language use) must lie in an examination of the role and significance of the particular pattern of talk in the total body of language that marks the macrogenre. This is why we need large-scale collections and analyses of classroom talk, the better to understand and interpret what actually happens. As it is, in this classroom text, the sequences involving the patterns of talk as indicated, extended over several lessons, marked by productive talk as the students made their models.

Evidence for subsequent further changes in the language of the text and hence in logogenesis is marked in the students' developing control of the technical language of the instructional field, and thus in their grasp of the uncommonsense knowledge encoded in that language. The group whose talk we have examined, present the following oral recount (elements indicated, though not of course introduced by the students) while displaying their machine to a school assembly.

Orientation

Naomi: *Hi, my name is Naomi (points to the others in the group): Aranthi, Yvonne, Katrina and Chanoa. Our project was to make a um, a lift using a windlass. We needed a cork, bendable wire and about 35cm of string, a cork, a match box, a heavy nut and, and 8 pins and a coil (points to the next person)*

Record of Events

Aranthi: *Um, we cut the coil and stuck the bendable wire in and we bent it like that (demonstrates) and we put a cork in the wire and wrapped the string around a couple of times and attached the string to a match box and a heavy nut and um, and then turn the handle and (demonstrates) it should go up and down.*

Significance

The mechanical advantage of this is um when you wrap it around, um it's easier to um. . . .

Yvonne: *Turn the cork.*

Aranthi: *Yeah.*

Yvonne: *And the windlass is the wire and the cork and it helps it lift*
(demonstrates)
The group finishes and sits down.

Their written procedure, accompanied by diagrams and displayed on a large poster in the school assembly room is as follows, where the elements of structure have been provided by the students, who in turn drew upon prior learning about scientific procedural genres:

Apparatus

A cork, bendable wire, about 35 cm of strong string, a matchbox, a heavy bolt, 8 pins, a plastic drink container (Coke bottle)

Objective

To find the mechanical advantages (of) using the windlass.

Procedure

- *Get a medium-sized bottle (approx 30 cm in height)*
- *Cut the bottle about 6 cm down from the top.*
- *Cut a doorway about 6 cm.*
- *Make two holes opposite each other around 5 cm from the base of the bottle.*
- *Get the piece of wire, e.g. a coat hanger.*
- *Thread wire a quarter through one of the holes in the bottle.*
- *Make a hole going through the centre of the cork.*
- *Holding the cork inside the bottle, push the wire through the other hole in the cork. Put the remaining wire through the other hole in the bottle.*
- *On one end of the wire leave 3–4 cm protruding from the bottle and on the other end leave around 11 cm.*
- *Bend 3–4 cm wire at a right-angle turn. Then get the other end of the wire, leave 3 cm, then bend down at a right angle. Then leave 4 cm of wire and bend at a right angle sideways. Refer to diagram.*
- *Get the matchbox, take the inner part of the box out, put a hole in the side of it and thread the string 35 cm. Tie a knot so the string does not slip out. Re-assemble matchbox.*
- *Take the heavy bolt and tie it on the other end of the string.*
- *Wind one end of the string around the cork a couple of times so both the matchbox and bolt are dangling downwards.*
- *Rotate the handle and the matchbox should go up and down.*

Result

Problems were encountered because the string had unstable balance, therefore it was consistently sliding off when the handle was turned. To fix this problem pins were pushed in the cork to make a pathway for the string to follow. See diagram 4 below.

Conclusions

This concludes the experiment of the lift. The model that has been made shows one of the uses of mechanical advantage – the windlass. It changes the direction of force to help lift things.

Applications

The lift may be used in a tall or large building, in the office, home or school. Variations of the lift can be used almost everywhere.

I shall make no detailed comments on either of these two genres, other than to note two matters. Firstly, both genres in their way capture some principles of scientific method. The recount retells what was done (using temporal sequence material processes and past tense); it then moves to a statement of significance where an identifying process and the present tense are employed (*the mechanical advantage of this is um it's easier to um turn the cork*). The procedure deliberately labels its various elements, where these in themselves signal scientific method; it draws heavily on material processes and the imperative mood to construct its meanings, at least in the Procedure element; in the later elements, while the process types remain mainly material, there are shifts to the present tense and the declarative mood choice, as well as some modality (*the lift may be used*). Collectively, these mark a shift in meaning. The scientific method involved is canonical in western cultures, and Newtonian in character (see Halliday in Halliday and Martin, 1993: 57–62, who has analysed aspects of the history and development of scientific language).

The second observation I shall make about the two genres here is that the oral recount involves (with one exception) largely congruent expression of the meanings involved, while the written procedure is less congruent; the latter has the lexical density of written language, and this is realized in part in its uses of grammatical metaphor. Capacity to move freely between speech and written language is an important aspect of learning, for meaning construction in the one mode is different from, but complementary to, the other. I have already remarked the fact that the term *mechanical advantage* is itself an instance of grammatical metaphor: note how the nominal group structure is expanded here in the expression, *the mechanical advantages (of) using the windlass*. Note other expressions such *as the experiment of the lift*, or *variations of the lift*. And note as well the abstractions involved in the expression: *Problems were encountered because the string had unstable balance*. Another aspect of the manner in which the procedure draws on the resources of written grammar is its absence of items that involve human agency (e.g., *we*) and its tendency, through its theme choices, to foreground such matters as *problems* in *Problems were encountered*. . . . The effect is to create a level of abstraction in the written text.

Overall, the differences in the language of the two texts, as well as the significant shifts in language use by teacher and students throughout the whole macrogenre provide persuasive evidence that some useful teaching and learning have taken place. Moreover, the principles for evaluation, established in the opening Curriculum Initiation, though developed as the fortnight's work proceeded, have been made clearly available. Evaluation for the purposes of this macrogenre and its activities, seeks to examine both how successfully the students have understood the instructional field, and how successfully they can represent it.

To turn to the other macrogenre involved in Text 4.2, I shall draw on just a little of the discourse, towards the end of the Task Negotiation phase, where the students consider how they will use the data they have amassed about nuclear power to shape their discussion genres. The teacher guides a long sequence of talk about the *main ideas* the students have researched for the writing of their discussions:

> T: *OK, Richard, what main ideas have you identified?*
> Richard: *(Reads from his notes) 'Nuclear power stations do not produce pollution but the radioactive fuel they use is very dangerous if it escapes into the air, water or soil.'*

Further talk leads Richard, a few minutes later, to go on and say of the book he is consulting:

> Richard: *It talks about how some waste are dumped into the ocean and when the metal corrodes it leaks into the sea which could get into the food chain.*
> T: *Good example. So it's making the ocean not clean. Now what would happen, Penny, if radioactivity leaked. . . they buried it in the ocean and it leaked into the food chain? What do they mean by the food chain? Yes, Penny?*
> Penny: *The food chain's all the fish and everything that lives at sea and if we like swallow a mouthful of contaminated water we'll get contaminated even having to*
> *] overlap*
> T: *Ok, yes. That's right.*
> Penny: *And if it leaks into the fish and one fish is very highly contaminated and say a pregnant woman had had it, her baby could be deformed or cause her cancer.*

The particular lesson in which this extract was recorded continues with lengthy discussion of the findings of the students from their reading, including further clarification of the food chain.

At this point, the students are wholly engaged with the instructional field, and one notes the apparent ease with which they use such technical terms as *nuclear power stations, radioactive fuel, food chain, contaminated water*.

The subsequent lesson recorded – part of the Curriculum Closure – where students have early drafts of their discussion genres before them, involves teacher-directed discussion of:

ways to introduce the issues: e.g. *Some people believe that nuclear power should be built;*
ways to signal the element of structure that introduces an alternative point of view :
e.g. *On the other hand; On the opposite side; On the other side...*
ways to summarize, e.g. *Thus, in summary...; In summary...*
ways to recommend: *Therefore, after examining all the arguments...; In conclusion...*

Through this process several students discover they have some elements
missing in their genres, and they amend them. They go on to write their
discussion genres. Here is one by a girl called Layla, in which the elements of
structure have been noted:

Topic

Should a nuclear power plant be built in Darwin?

Preview

*Some people believe that a nuclear power plant should be built because it is cheap and does
not pollute the environment as much as fossil-fuelled power plants. However, other people
believe that a nuclear power plant should not be built because they feel it is unsafe due to
accidents involving nuclear waste.*

Argument 1

*On one hand, some people agree that a nuclear power plant is a good idea. In Western
countries nuclear power stations have three main barriers to prevent leakage of radiation.
At Chernobyl, where a major accident occurred, there was no third barrier to prevent
radiation leaking in to the environment. Nuclear power plants are clean because they put
nowhere as much radiation into the environment as fossil-fuelled power plants. France has
one of the cheapest electricity costs in the world compared with the other industrialized
countries that use fossil fuel.*

Argument 2

*On the other side of the argument, just as many people believe that the power plant should
not go ahead. It is well known that nuclear waste stays radioactive for thousands of years.
Because of this, it is a problem disposing of nuclear waste, and even deep burial cannot be
100% guaranteed. Nuclear power plants only have a life span of 30 to 40 years. But after
this they have to be decommissioned and this can cost between 30 million to 4 billion
dollars. One of the ways of disposing of nuclear waste is dumping it into the sea. But this
can cause problems because the container can corrode and leak into the sea causing
contamination of the food chain.*

Summary and Recommendation

Thus in summary it would seem that there would be just as many advantages as there are disadvantages to having a nuclear power station. Therefore, after examining all the arguments, I believe that the risks far outweigh the advantages of building a nuclear power station. I strongly recommend that a nuclear power stations not be built in Darwin.

Incidentally, while most students were not in favour of the nuclear power station, a minority did support it, and the teacher had sought to encourage divergence of opinion, partly by avoiding indicating her own view. One student, Richard, stated that after reading the books he had consulted, he had actually changed his mind about the issue.

At the point of the writing of discussion genres such as the one cited, it will be apparent that it is the instructional register that is foregrounded, though the regulative register operates at an implicit level, for this has shaped all the decisions made with respect to the organization of the target genre. The goals for the overall macrogenre have been realized, and we can claim that a process of logogenesis has occurred.[5]

Conclusion: principles of evaluation as a feature of the two macrogenres

As in earlier chapters, some judgement needs to be made concerning the principles of evaluation that apply because it is evaluation which defines what counts as the knowledge learned by the students. The two macrogenres I have examined – the one devoted to upper primary school science, the other to upper primary social science – were both undertaken over sustained periods of time, and both employed a genre-based pedagogy. Because of this, so I have already suggested, their goals for teaching and learning were articulated reasonably clearly from the start, and both provided advice regarding the fields of knowledge to be explored and the genres to be eventually written with respect to those fields of knowledge. The one required mastery of the Newtonian principle of a mechanical advantage, production of a simple machine to illustrate it, an oral recount of how the machine was made and a written procedure to tell others how to make it. The other required research into the issue of nuclear power and the eventual writing of a discussion genre devoted to exploring arguments for and against its uses before making a recommendation about it.

The explicit advice given students in each case regarding goals and target genres was a part of a curriculum activity which was both strongly classified and strongly framed. Each macrogenre used a technical language relevant to both the regulative and instructional fields. Each was marked by logogenesis, evident in the manner in which the classroom language changed, moving through several distinct phases in which the experiential information dealt with was enlarged upon and/or amended, and in which teacher and students assumed different responsibilities vis-à-vis each other and towards the tasks at hand. Each macrogenre ended with completion of a culminating task, though, as I have noted, this is not a necessary feature of all curriculum macrogenres. Each saw students apprenticed into some forms of uncommonsense knowledge, and this was achieved in sustained, often effortful activity over time. The macrogeneric structure, with its deliberately paced sequence of activities in each case, their ordering signalled very clearly in teacher talk, brought about the successful learning that occurred.

Notes

1. I should also make clear here that I don't argue there is no place for discrete or 'one-off' genres: sometimes a teacher will legitimately decide that an activity is worth introducing, devoting no more than a lesson or two to it, and thereby generating interest and learning. However, I do suggest that this should not be the norm.
2. I should note that I earlier have tended to argue that the final genre stood in a relationship of 'projection' to the initiating genre, but that I have abandoned this on the grounds that the notion doesn't best represent what is involved, just as it doesn't do justice to the notion of projection in Halliday's grammar.
3. I hope it is evident that the apparent oddity of saying 'the main requirement is for various things to be done' is a commonplace feature of speech. The children had no difficulty understanding what the teacher meant.
4. Halliday, 1994: 362, has remarked the paradox that we only use modality when the matter talked about is in some way not certain: certainty is expressed in simple adoption of polarity in grammar, for it admits of no alternatives. Modality necessarily admits alternatives.
5. One matter I should perhaps address here, since it is sometimes raised as part of a criticism of genre-based pedagogies. It is the concern that such pedagogies are 'formulaic', encouraging students to adopt a particular model for writing, where they are often rather similar in any given classroom, and where the capacity for self-expression is denied. The concern is in my view misplaced for two reasons. Firstly, the pedagogy undoubtedly offers a clear structure to follow in writing, though that structure is not one the genre theorists invented: they found it in English-speaking communities, and its learning is an important feature of apprenticeship into such communities. Secondly, the argument re self-expression begs the question: wherein is this achieved, other than in successful mastery of the resources available in a linguistic systems? Once mastered, the evidence is that the genre in question is adapted, played with and amended with increasing maturity and experience.

5 Pedagogic discourse in an orbital curriculum macrogenre

Introduction

In this chapter we turn to some consideration of a macrogenre whose structure is 'orbital'. As I have already noted in Chapter 4, the curriculum macrogenres considered in that chapter and the curriculum genres considered in Chapters 2 and 3 were all linear in character. Their tendency was to move through a series of stages which unfolded in real time, ending with a final element (in the case of a genre) or a genre (in the case of a macrogenre), in which a culminating task or tasks were completed. The pacing and sequencing of activity, which was realized in the regulative register, was such that, especially in the two macrogenres in Chapter 4, a kind of momentum developed as the students moved to completion of their tasks. Evaluation rested quite fundamentally on completion of the task(s), and the tendency of the regulative register, among other things, was to dispose the students to understand the nature of the culminating task(s) as well as to understand the measures to be used to evaluate their performance. Mastery of the culminating task, at least in the two macrogenres, involved learning some kind of 'uncommonsense knowledge': a knowledge, that is, requiring some sustained effort to achieve its mastery, and some guided assistance in that mastery provided by a mentor. The disposition of these two curriculum macrogenres was quite overtly to apprentice the students into using new forms of knowledge, where the object was to learn both *how to approach and handle the knowledge* (as realized primarily in the regulative register) and *the knowledge itself* (as realized primarily in the instructional register). Strictly, as Bernstein argued, the two are but manifestations of the same discourse: the same *pedagogic discourse*.

The linear pattern involved in the manner of unfolding of a curriculum macrogenre offers but one way to represent the organization of such curriculum activity and, at least for the purposes of some curriculum macrogenres, it is not always the best one to use. That is because, as I hope to demonstrate in this chapter, the linear model indicates only one way of organizing and communicating knowledge, when in fact other models are available and often used. Such models do not build the initiation of the learners through a series of incremental stages which move towards a culminating task, as was true in those in Chapter 4. Instead, they build the initiation through sets of interrelated steps, some undertaken in parallel phases, and all of them creating a growth in understanding which is 'accretive' rather than incremental. A growth in learning which is accretive, I shall suggest here, involves expansion of understanding by the phasing in of new knowledge and skills at selected points, when other knowledge and skills are still in development, and when other tasks are still to be completed; the effect is that learning is enlarged in interconnected and overlapping ways, creating a conceptually unified body of knowledge. In such a process, the students are engaged in working on activities, often in parallel, where engagement with the one can enhance and enrich engagement with the other. A growth that is 'incremental', on the other hand, involves expansion by learning knowledge and skills in singular movements, progressing from one step to another: where it succeeds, it also facilitates expansion of understanding (as for example in the instances examined in Chapter 4), though by different means. Crucially, models of macrogenres which are accretive in character do not have a clearly defined culminating genre and/or task, though they will of course have a closure of some kind. Various tasks, normally of equal significance in the teaching and learning, are initiated in such macrogenres at several points in their development, and such tasks will achieve equal significance for evaluation purposes. The principles of evaluation in such a macrogenre are thus quite other than those that apply in macrogenres whose organization is incremental and which lead to a culminating stage.

In order to deal adequately with the character of macrogenres that are not linear, the metaphor of an 'orbital' structure is chosen, and this owes most to Martin (1996), Iedema (1994; 1997) and White (1997; 1998) alluded to earlier in Chapter 4. They in turn owed much to earlier work by Thompson, Mann and Matthiessen on rhetorical structure (cited by Iedema, 1994: 31), in which notions of a nucleus and associated satellites were used to account for the links between ideas in texts. The metaphor of the orbital structure is built on the idea of planetary activity, such that satellites revolve around a larger body which is the nucleus. The example of a curriculum macrogenre with an orbital structure to be examined in this chapter is drawn from secondary school geography. As I shall argue below, the structure of this macrogenre might well be shown in linear fashion, but the orbital structure provides for a much richer interpretation, illuminating in particular the manner in which the pedagogy works and how the pedagogic subject position is constructed. Before we proceed to a discussion of the geography macrogenre concerned, I shall outline some of the background theory with respect to orbital structures on which this discussion is drawn.

The notion of an orbital structure

I have already intimated that the interest in orbital structures emerged from a research project in Sydney in which Martin, Iedema and White were all involved in the early 1990s.[1] Examination of 'hard news' stories in White's case, and of administrative and bureaucratic memos in Iedema's case led them and Martin to argue that the conventional, essentially linear, way of modelling genres, by then well-established in much SF genre theory, did not necessarily adequately reflect the organization of a number of text types or genres. They all suggested that the classic linear model used, for example, in identifying many genres of schooling, such as the discussion genre cited in Chapter 4 (*Topic* ∧ *Preview of Issues* ∧ Arguments π ∧ Recommendation), tended to favour the experiential meanings of the genre, at the expense of the other meanings.[2] There were often, they argued, other principles at work having consequences for the ways in which genres were ordered, some of them to do with the particular interpersonal meanings the writer might intend, others to do with the textual meanings that might be selected.

Iedema (1997) demonstrated the point by reference to several 'directive genres' chosen from several work sites. He was able to argue that in any such genre there must be at least one Command element. In those instances of a directive that had one Command, Iedema argued that this was the 'nucleus', for it was this that was the *raison d'être* for the directive. The other elements, displayed in rather different generic ordering (and in greater and lesser numbers) in a range of directives, functioned like satellites to the Command element: hence the term an 'orbital structure'. Such satellite elements might include, for example, an 'Orientation' which positioned the reader with respect to the matter addressed in the Command, or a 'Legitimation' so-called because it provided information to legitimate the Command, or a 'Facilitation' which sought to facilitate the implementation of the Command, or a 'Background' which provided some relevant background information to the Command. These elements might, and indeed, did, fall in different places in the overall organization of the directive, and their different placements, as well as their frequency, had interesting effects. For example, Iedema argued, directives that make considerable use of Legitimation elements, sometimes strategically placed at several points throughout the text, tend to suggest that the writer is doing a great deal of 'work' to ensure that the Command is understood and acted upon: this may in turn suggest that the writer holds a rather equivocal position vis-à-vis the reader, and tries to compensate for that. Commands thus have considerable significance in an interpersonal sense. On the other hand, at least one of the directives Iedema examined contained no Legitimation elements at all: instead, it offered a sequence of Command elements, leading Iedema to call it 'serial' rather than orbital in structure. Such a directive, he noted, is also interpersonally interesting though in a different sense, for here the writer feels no reservations about his or her position vis-à-vis the readers, and hence has no need to offer legitimating or facilitating elements.

The structure of the 'hard news' story studied by White (1997, 1998) is of course very different from that of the directive, though the principle of the orbital structure can nonetheless be shown to apply. In such a story, so White has argued, the nucleus is captured, often in the Headline, sometimes in the Headline and first sentence, where a summary and/or abstract of what is to follow is provided; subsequent elements in the text are variously dependent upon the nucleus, their function to reiterate, expand upon and/or exemplify the nucleus in a number of ways. The relationship of the satellites is such that, though they unfold on the page in an apparently linear way, they are capable of being reordered, without significant loss of meaning. Indeed, according to White (1997: 116), the fact that the elements of structure apart from the nucleus are capable of considerable reordering is one important measure of the presence of an overall schematic structure that is orbital, rather than linear. A coherent meaningful text, he demonstrates, can be created by various forms of reordering, though of course the meanings of the text overall will therefore change in some ways.

For the purposes of the present discussion, a decision has been made to adopt the principle of an orbital structure in examining a curriculum macrogenre. However, while the discussion will draw on the work of Iedema, White and Martin in looking at orbital structures, it will depart from their work in several ways. They all examined written texts, which were, moreover, reasonably short, and they were all instances of genres. My discussion examines a curriculum macrogenre developed over the better part of a school term, involving both spoken and written language, and making use of textbooks, diagrams, maps, and a CD ROM. With two small exceptions to be explained below, I hold the complete transcript of the classroom talk as well as copies of written texts and resources used in the classroom. I shall make only selective use of aspects of the text however, because for reasons already discussed in Chapter 4, it is not possible to discuss the complete classroom text.

The reason for adopting the model of an orbital structure in examining the curriculum macrogenre in question is that this particular instance of classroom activity, unlike either of the two activities reviewed in Chapter 4, does not present as linear or serial in character. Instead, the activity is accretive in the manner I have suggested earlier, and in this it marks a sharp departure from the manner of unfolding activity as discussed in Texts 4.1 and 4.2 in Chapter 4. The structure will be shown to possess a Curriculum Initiation genre – really the nucleus, in which the students engage with the issues to be learned – and a subsequent series of orbital curriculum genres, phased in at select points in the total unfolding of the classroom text, all of them intimately connected to the Curriculum Initiation, and all of them contributing to the building of knowledge in ways that cross over and parallel each other.

Geography as a strongly classified subject

As a general principle, one of the characteristics of the strongly classified curriculum is that it attaches importance to a technical discourse, for it is in this that the disciplines or subjects at issue in the curriculum are understood as distinctive, and operating with a strong 'degree of boundary maintenance' (Bernstein, 1974: 205). Teachers attach particular importance to the technical discourse of their subject in the strongly classified curriculum, and they regard development of mastery of it as a critically important aspect of apprenticeship into the subject. A technical discourse serves to give definition to what a subject is about, what problems and/or questions the subject seeks to address, what methods of analysis and interpretation of phenomena it proposes, and hence what principles for reasoning it encodes. Finally, and because the technical discourse defines the subject in this manner, it also provides strong principles for evaluation: students will be evaluated in terms of how successfully they have mastered the technical discourse and its associated patterns of working and representing information. In the case of the geography curriculum used in the Australian state of Victoria (Victorian Curriculum and Standards Framework, 1995), and used in the classroom macrogenre to be examined in this chapter, this identified 10 Key Geographic Ideas (KGIs) all realized in a particular technical language: 'Location, Distribution, Scale, Region, Movement, Power, Spatial Association, Spatial Interaction, Spatial Interdependence, and Spatial Change over Time'. As we shall see in later sections of this chapter, the teacher was at some pains to see that the students used at least some of the terms (those relevant to the unit of study in hand) 'frequently, accurately, correctly'.

Subject geography has changed markedly over the last fifty years or so, and as a university discipline it has been subject to as much debate as other university studies, so that its principles of classification have changed over the years as geographers have sought to redefine their field. At the school level too, partly in response to shifts at the tertiary level, but also in response to changing curriculum priorities as expressed in the various curriculum guidelines, geography has been variously defined and classified. In Australia, at least since the early 1990s, it seems that, where geography is taught, it is strongly classified, and one manifestation of this is its insistence on a discourse distinctive to the study which students must learn to use if they are to be deemed successful.[3] Geography is thus in marked contrast with other subject disciplines such as English (see Christie, 1999 for a discussion of a curriculum macrogenre in secondary school subject English).

As for curriculum framing in geography, I should note that strong framing is not a necessary feature of the classroom in which a strongly classified curriculum applies. However, in practice, such a classroom is often strongly framed. That is because, in such a context, the act of working with a school subject which is clearly defined in discourse terms, and 'insulated' from other school subjects, will dispose the teacher to frame the activities in fairly exacting ways in order to ensure that the students are appropriately apprenticed into the relevant pedagogic subject position. Thus, the teacher generally exercises tight control over the selection of what is to be taught and learned, the pace at which it is to be taught and learned, the principles used for evaluating success in learning, the methods and procedures for communication of information among class participants, and the organization of the behaviours and dispositions of the students. Just as the geography curriculum is often strongly classified, in practice one finds that the geography teacher establishes strong framing principles.

Out of sometimes heated debates in Australia (which have, however, had their parallels in other countries such as England, with its adoption of its National Curriculum) there emerged in the 1990s a number of Key Learning Areas (KLAs), of which one is Studies of Society and the Environment (SOSE). This embraces a range of areas including geography and history, but also sociology, religion, anthropology, ecology, economics, business studies among others. Along with the other KLAs, SOSE must be taught to all students for all the compulsory years of schooling up to year 10. Some form of SOSE – normally a form of social studies of the kind involved in Text 4.2 in Chapter 4 – is taught in all primary schools in Australian states without much overt debate. It is in the secondary years that issues of SOSE, its definition and its focus of attention – tend to become more controversial. Schools are left discretion to teach SOSE in one of several ways: they may for example, adopt an integrated approach, drawing on some or all of the subjects listed above, and for the most part creating a curriculum which is weakly classified; they may choose to teach some of the subjects in bands of time in different school years; or they may opt to teach one only of the subject disciplines involved. Schools which opt to teach geography and/or history as distinct disciplines have in practice signalled their commitment to a strongly classified curriculum; they have rejected the claims of various integrated and 'banded' approaches in favour of an approach that proposes the values of retaining the 'integrity' of the particular discipline concerned (Geography Teachers' Association of Victoria, 1995). The geography curriculum macrogenre discussed here was taught in a school that had chosen the course of teaching geography and history as separate discipline areas.[4]

The secondary geography macrogenre to be examined here was recorded in a Year 9 class in an inner-city coeducational state high school in a major Australian city. The school was by Australian standards relatively old, dating from the earliest years of the twentieth century, and it had once been a fully selective high school, drawing in students on the basis of academic performance and IQ tests at the end of their primary schooling. By the last decade of the twentieth century, the old principles of selectivity had been abandoned. However, such was the reputation of the school, it still attracted gifted students, many of them the children of former students. The majority of the students were children of middle-class and professional parents, some of whom were academics at the nearby university. However, since the school lay in an urban district whose catchment areas included some reasonably poor parts of the inner city, at least some of the students came from poorer, non-professional and working-class families, including some for whom English was a second language. The class of year 9 students whose geography lessons I followed included a few who were of non-English speaking background, though none was a recent arrival, and none presented as having significant language learning problems.

The orbital structure of the geography curriculum macrogenre

The curriculum macrogenre involving seventeen 50-minute lessons was taught over six weeks – the better part of the usual 10-week term. The focus was the study of World Heritage. Two of the seventeen lessons taught were not recorded. One of the two involved an activity (working on an assignment) very like another that was recorded, and the teacher suggested it was not necessary to record. The other lesson not recorded was the final one, in which the students did a written examination on aspects of what they had learned, and since this was largely a silent affair the teacher again suggested it not be recorded, though copies of the written examination papers were collected.

Figure 5.1 represents the structure of the macrogenre in linear fashion, indicating something of the experiential nature of the macrogenre as well as its interpersonal meanings, and suggesting its unfolding in time. For reasons to be discussed below, the figure does not do particular justice to the textual organization of the macrogenre and, in that it fails to do this, it also to some extent distorts one's sense of the manner in which the experiential meanings are introduced and learned.

The Curriculum Orientation establishes goals for the whole unit of work and, as we shall see below, a great deal of attention is devoted to introducing technical terms and their meanings so that a strong sense of definition is constructed, having consequences for the directions to be followed. The later curriculum genres all involve activities in which students do research, read textbooks, CD ROMs and maps, and create posters and notes in which they exemplify aspects of World Heritage, as established in the Curriculum Initiation. It is because of this strong sense of exemplifying what was established in the first genre that I have termed these genres instances of Curriculum Exemplifications. Some such Exemplifications involve the students in identifying local World Heritage sites, others in identifying international sites. More than one manner of ordering the introduction of these Exemplification activities would have been possible, and it is because of this that I shall argue that the orbital structure more accurately represents the nature of this macrogenre than does the linear structure.

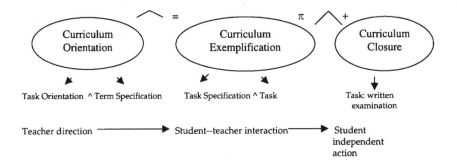

Figure 5.1   A linear representation of a geography curriculum macrogenre

As the figure seeks to indicate, Curriculum Exemplification (which is recursive) follows the Curriculum Orientation, while there is a Closure which is realized in the students writing answers to examination questions. The Curriculum Exemplifications stand in a relation of elaboration (=) to the Curriculum Orientation, and the Curriculum Closure stands in a relation of addition (+) to the Curriculum Exemplifications. Teacher direction is marked in the opening of the macrogenre and, while the subsequent genres involve teacher–student interaction, the teacher's presence remains a powerful one, for he is explicit about the principles to be followed by the students in all their work, though very open to answering questions and to explaining and exploring what is to be done. The Closure, while it requires student independent effort in the writing of answers to examination questions, is a relatively low-key affair, for it carries only partial significance in the overall assessment of student performance.

Figure 5.2 provides the alternative interpretation in its modelling of an orbital structure. It is most marked in its difference from the linear representation in terms of what it suggests of the overall textual organization of the macrogenre.

Each of the Curriculum Exemplifications has status and significance primarily because of its relationship to the Curriculum Orientation, and not because of their relationships to each other, and it is this in particular which the orbital analysis allows us to expose. As the figure seeks to suggest, it is the Curriculum Initiation in which goals are established and significant terms are

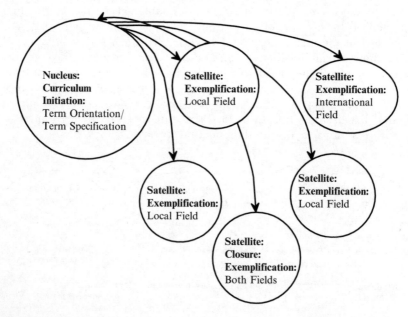

Figure 5.2 A geography curriculum macrogenre represented with an orbital structure

defined with respect to World Heritage: the subsequent Curriculum Exemplifications, each involving some activity or task which takes and exemplifies aspects of World Heritage, are linked primarily to the Curriculum Initiation, not to each other. Participation in the activities involved – often started before an earlier activity is completed – leads to the development of knowledge which is accretive. It is the relationship of the Curriculum Exemplifications to the Curriculum Initiation that is primary, in a manner analogous to the way in which White (1997) argues that in the news story the various orbital elements stand in relation to the Headline/Nucleus. The Headline/ Nucleus establishes what the story is about, while later elements of structure – all capable of what White terms 'radical editability' (White, 1998) – elaborate upon, justify, motivate or contextualize what is in the Headline. In the macrogenre here, I shall argue, the particular manner of ordering the Curriculum Exemplifications was no doubt chosen by the teacher for good reasons, though, in principle, they could have been ordered differently.

As already stated, the Curriculum Orientation defines terms and establishes goals in considerable detail. These terms and goals lead to a series of research tasks given the students at different points in the subsequent genres throughout the macrogenre, all of them counting towards the final assessment. All tasks are intended to contribute equally to the steady development of capacities in two senses. On the one hand, capacities are to be developed in recognizing and using the key geographical terms of concern alluded to earlier. On the other hand, capacities are to be developed in identifying instances of World Heritage sites by employing the key geographical terms. Both sets of overlapping capacities are of importance to the apprenticeship into the pedagogic subject position of school geographer. Table 5.1 provides an overview of the Curriculum Exemplifications, the lessons in which these are initiated and then sustained till their completion, and the broad topics covered in each case.

The first Curriculum Exemplification (introduced towards the end of the third lesson) involves the students in researching one Australian 'case study' of a World Heritage site – namely the Kakadu National Park in the 'top end' of Australia. The second genre, initiated in the fourth lesson, and before the first is completed, involves research into selected international World Heritage sites, using a CD-ROM, such as the palace of Versailles, Stonehenge or Quebec City. The third Curriculum Exemplification, commenced in the fifth lesson, involves research into another Australian World Heritage 'case study': namely the site at Lord Howe Island (which is off the east coast of Australia). The fourth Curriculum Exemplification, initiated in the twelfth lesson, is an Australian 'case study' of a different sort: namely investigating the proposals being made for nomination of a new site, the Great Ocean Road. This is a scenic road on the coast of Victoria and, if it were to be declared a site, it would be the first road so declared in Australia, and perhaps in the world. The final Curriculum Exemplification, occupying only the last lesson, involves a written test on selected aspects of World Heritage. All tasks associated with the Curriculum Exemplifications, apart from the last, are

Table 5.1 An overview of Curriculum Genres, topics introduced and covered in each and lessons devoted to each in the geography macrogenre

Curriculum genre	Lessons involved	Topic
Curriculum Initiation	1, 2 and part of 3	World Heritage: its definition and significance
Curriculum Exemplification	3 → 7	An Australian World Heritage site: Kakadu National Park
Curriculum Exemplification	4 → 8	International World Heritage sites: selections from Encarta CD-ROM
Curriculum Exemplification	5 → 12	An Australian World Heritage site: Lord Howe Island
Curriculum Exemplification	12 → 16	An Australian World Heritage site under investigation: the Great Ocean Road
Curriculum Exemplification	17	World Heritage, local and international: an examination

intended to take more than one lesson, and the work on them proceeds in several of the lessons, sometimes in overlapping ways, and at least some of it also undertaken as homework.[5]

Both in the patterns of classroom interaction about the issues involved, and in the assessable tasks given the students, illustrations, sketches and maps are revealed as very important aspects of the modes of making geographical meanings. Written texts always accompany illustrations, sketches or maps. In addition the written texts are normally constructed making use of frequent headings and subheadings, whose function is to give the text its overall structure and sequence of generic elements. These are matters to which I shall return as the discussion below proceeds, for they mark some of the most distinctive aspects of the modes of meaning making of geography as a school discipline.

The Curriculum Orientation

The Curriculum Orientation, which extends into three lessons, involves four phases or elements of structure, as revealed in Figure 5.3, though these might well be represented showing greater levels of delicacy in each case.

It will be apparent that the whole Curriculum Initiation is devoted to definition, classification and identification. The definitions relate both to the general study of geography and to the particular study of World Heritage; the classification refers to creating categories of World Heritage sites; and the identification refers to locating World Heritage sites in Australia. The work of establishing these matters defines the directions for the whole unit of six

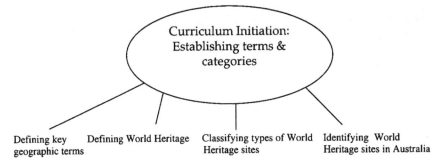

Figure 5.3   The Curriculum Initiation of the geography macrogenre

weeks' work, and it also indicates, at least in general terms, the principles of evaluation that will apply throughout.

Text 5.1 (which is cut in some places to save space) provides much, but not all, of the first two elements of structure, devoted to Definition, firstly definition of *Key Geographic Ideas*, and then definition of World Heritage. As in earlier chapters I shall develop this discussion making selective use of the text, and also drawing attention to those aspects of the metafunctions and their realization which are most salient to an interpretation of what is going on.

Definition: key geographic ideas

Looking to the opening, it is notable that, with no preliminary remarks, the teacher plunges the students into the activity by writing the principal instructional field items on the board, and asking the students to write these down. A number of his expectations, to do with appropriate behaviour in the classroom are realized without his needing to make comment: for example, the students are in their places, and they are sitting with notebooks open and pens ready, aware that this is a geography lesson. Spatial relationships are thus established without comment, though they remain important for the general patterns of work. The use of teacher monologue accompanied by much use of board summaries sets much of the mode of presentation of information that will apply throughout the whole macrogenre.

The regulative register is audible in the use of teacher monologue. Teacher textual Themes help to point directions (*and, okay, now*). Interpersonally, the teacher makes use of the resources of first, second and third person, variously indicating that he is directing behaviour or identifying with the students as a group:

> *Ah, I'll just give you a quick introduction.'*... and
> *but we'll come back to that in a moment*

His declarative mood choice indicates that in speech function terms he is giving information, while examples of high modality, some expressed metaphorically, reveal the importance the teacher attaches to certain matters:

Text 5.1

Curriculum Orientation

Task Orientation

Board heading, prepared before the lesson, reads: UNIT TWO: WORLD HERITAGE. Key Geographic Ideas: location, distribution, spatial inter-action (all written in different colours).

Ah, I'll just give you a quick introduction. Could you jot quickly down [[what I've put on the board]] and then we'll ah, we'll make a start. (There is a pause as students write the information down) Ooh! Try the spelling! (a comment on his own spelling error which T corrects) Ah, it's about a six-week unit more or less. Um, with a broad title of World Heritage. It's a fairly big title, but we'll come back to that in a moment. Um, we really need to get into these key geographic ideas and the two things [[I want [[you to do]]] is [[to remember the three [[that we are using: location, distribution and a fairly big one, fairly new one [[we call spatial interaction]]. There are nine ideas and I've got three here. (Note: the T means the 10 referred to earlier in this chapter though he has apparently forgotten one.) Um, and the second thing [[I want [[you to be able to do [[as you go through]]]]]] is [[to use those words um, frequently, accurately, correctly]].

Gordon: What's that third word...

T: I'll go through each of those. OK, first thing [[we'll look at]] is simply location of the location of different heritage sites: S-I-T-E-S, places. (Spells this out as he is writing on the board; his writing is often hard to read) Next to location, writes: 'of heritage sites'. Now, the sum total of all that location is [[what we call distribution]]. So we'll look at the distribution of sites within um, particular countries. Next to 'distribution' adds: 'of sites within a country'. Some are spread all over the place, some are concentrated. We'll look at where and why. And the third one, spatial interaction: S-P-A-T-I-A-L I-N-T-E-R-A-C-T-I-O-N. (Spelt out loud by T) And here, because of the nature of [[what World Heritage means]], we have to look at the interaction between people and the effect [[that they have on sites]]. And often that effect, unfortunately, is a fairly negative one. And because of that we come back to the idea of control. Next to spatial interaction T writes: 'between people and sites (negative - > control)'. We'll see how that works ah, as we go through. So, hopefully you're following the pattern of, I've used already three colours, you should have used at least three. *(colours – for taking notes.)* Ah, now we've only got a fairly ah, small, little screen (the white board is less than about a square metre in size) here so ah, 'cos there's a bit of writing I'll be rubbing it off at fairly frequent intervals, so the moral of the story, Mario, is keep up!

(Text is left out and T moves to define the word 'Heritage')

T: OK. Um,... Heritage. Give us an idea of [[what you understand by the word]]. Heritage, start off.

Regulatory register realized:

Interpersonally in:
(i) use of first person singular to direct: *I'll just give you...;*
(ii) use of first person plural to stress solidarity in shared task: *we'll make a start...;*
(iii) interpersonal metaphor: *Could you jot quickly down [[what I've put on the board]]*

Experientially in:
(i) material and behavioural processes to realize activities students and T are to engage in: *I'll give you...; could you jot quickly down; we'll make a start;*
(ii) attributive processes to define the task broadly: *it's about a six-week unit...; it's a fairly big title;*
(iii) identifying processes to identify specific tasks and point directions: *the two things [[I want [[you to do]]]] is [[to remember the three [[that we are using: location, distribution and a fairly big one, a fairly new one [[we call spatial inter[[action]]; and the second thing [[I want [[you to be able to do [[as you go through]]]]]]]] is [[to use those words um, frequently, accurately, correctly]]*

Textually in:
T textual Themes to guide: *and the two things...: so we'll look at...; so, hopefully, you're following...*

Instructional register realized:
Experientially in:
(i) key lexical items: *World Heritage, key geographic ideas; location, distribution, spatial interaction, heritage sites,* mostly found in Participant roles in processes that realize the regulative register
(ii) an identifying process to build definition relevant to the field: *the sum total of all that location is [[what we call distribution]].*

Regulative register realized:
interpersonally in: (i) T imperative mood choices *(Give us an idea...; C'mon, we had plenty of ideas; Let's put that in)* and interrogatives to provoke talk: *what else is involved with the word 'heritage'?*
(ii) student responses: *I don't know; people; cultures.*

text continues

Text 5.1 – *continued*

Catherine: I don't know.

T: Don't know. Away you go. (T turns to another student)

Kathy: No. I don't know either.

T: C'mon, we had plenty of ideas.

Student: Do you just write...

T: No, don't write anything at the moment. Just, I just want some ideas of what the word...

Catherine: Like a history of a place.

T: It's a history of something. OK, let's put that in. (writes 'history' and 'stories' on board) So it certainly needs something [[that is old generally, and often very old]]. What else is involved with the word 'heritage'?

Kathy: People.

T: People. Yeah?

Thomas: Cultures.

T: Culture.

Sandra: Identity.

T: Yeah.

Kathy: What does it say after history?

T: It doesn't say anything. (looks at the board) It says 'culture' but you don't need to worry about it yet. Don't write any of the words down because we're going to leave a lot of them out. Any others we've got? We've actually got the two key elements that I want on the board. So, let's go back to it. The first important one is it's certainly to do with something that is fairly old. Right. It may be in terms of a few months, it's more likely, as far as an old family goes, to be years. In terms of world heritage it could well be centuries. But there's something old, and it ties up with this word 'identity'. In other words, there is something that identifies you (writes: YOU),... or the place (writes: PLACE), if we're talking about a world heritage site,... that is very special. (writes: special) And what do we want to do with that? (pause)

Ken: Preserve it.

T: Sorry?

Ken: Preserve it. (Text is left out, and then T summarizes)

T: Alright, that's [[what we mean by heritage]]. Something that is very valuable to you, as a person, or you as a family, as a collective group, retained at the moment somewhere in your family home, or within a person, you know, the ethos that makes up a person, and will then be transmitted on.

---

experientially in: (i) behavioural and material processes: *do you just write?;* *we've got the two key elements*

textually in: (i) topical Themes that identify T or class members: *I don't know; I just want...,* (ii) interpersonal Themes: *do you just write...?; what else is involved...?;* (iii) textual Themes in T talk: *it says 'culture'... but you don't need to worry...; so let's go back...; but there's something old...*

Instructional register realized:
experientially in: (i) *key lexis: a history of some place; culture; identity;*
(ii) identifying processes: (a) *the first important one (i.e., thing on the board) is [[it's certainly to do with something that is fairly old]]; (b) all right, that's [[what we mean by heritage]]. (implicit, i.e.) Something that is very valuable to you, as a person...*

we really need to get into these key geographic ideas..
the two things [[I want [[you to do]]]...

Like most teachers, he uses positive polarity in the opening, part of the building of a strongly assertive sense of what is to be done.

Experientially, the teacher uses several resources, some of them to do with establishing the nature of the task, where the processes are attributive and the participant roles are built in reasonably general nominal groups to establish both the timescale for the unit of study (*six weeks*), and the magnitude of the task (*a fairly big title*):

it	's	*about a six-week unit more or less*
Carrier	Pro: attributive	Attribute
it	's	*a fairly big title*
Carrier	Pro: attributive	Attribute

As in other examples of classroom activity examined in this book, time is revealed as an issue in the manner in which the teacher defines tasks and gets the working principles established. Other process types, which are used to build aspects of intended student behaviours, include one process of cognition, which is, however, realized metaphorically in a material process:

we	*really need to get*	*into these ideas*
Actor	Pro: material	Circumstance: Location: Place
(Senser	Pro: cognition	Phenomenon)

Such metaphorical processes to do with thinking are very common in teacher talk: the relatively 'concrete' or material notion of 'getting into' something presumably appeals as a means of giving substance to the mental activity involved.

Sometimes a behavioural process is used:

we	*'ll look at*	*the distribution of sites*
Behaver	Pro: behavioural	Range

Two important identifying processes establish major tasks for the unit, where in both cases the embeddings also realize aspects of the second order or instructional field, and where, as so often occurs, the Token and Value roles involve considerable uses of embeddings to compress the relevant information:

---

the two things *[[I want [[you to do]] is*   *[[to remember the three [[that we are using: location, distribution and a fairly big one, a fairly new one [[we call spatial interaction]]]]]]*

Value   *Pro: int.*   *Token*

the second thing *[[I want*   is   *[[to use those words um,*
            [[you to be able to do   *frequently, accurately, correctly]]*
            [[as you go through]]]]]]
                        Pro: int.   *Token*

The instructional register is realized in transitivity, either in participant roles or within circumstances. Other examples are found in:

And here, <u>because of the nature of [[what World Heritage means]]</u>, (a Circumstance) *we have to look at <u>the interaction between people and the effect [[that they have on sites]]</u>.* (a Range)

It will be noted that, when introducing his three key terms, the teacher says at one point tha*t there are nine ideas and I've got three here.* He intends to refer to the 10 geographic ideas mentioned earlier, all of which are displayed on a chart in the classroom. As the unit of work unfolds, the teacher and student will also use two other terms involved: *scale* and *region.* These are apparently familiar to the class, so they merit no particular attention at this point.

Each of the three key geographic ideas is spelt out on the board: *location (of World Heritage sites); distribution (of these sites), and spatial interaction (between people and sites).* Their presence on the board, as well as the teacher admonition to use these *frequently, accurately, correctly,* serves to reinforce the very forceful manner in which the teacher directs the students towards the broad instructional field of geography. These matters having been attended to, the teacher directs the students towards the next element, involving definition of World Heritage.

Definition: World Heritage

A long passage of talk (most of it not reproduced here) ensues as the term 'World Heritage' is discussed and, at the end of this, the teacher offers a definition, using another identifying process, this time realizing an aspect of the instructional field:

alright	that	's	[[what we mean by heritage]]
	Value	Pro: int.	Token
(implicit, i.e.)			
(Heritage is)		something	[[that is very valuable to you, as a person, or you as a family, as a collective group, [[retained at the moment somewhere in your family home, or within a person, you know, the ethos [[that makes up a person, [[and will then be transmitted on]]]]]]
Token	Pro: int.	Value	

As I have remarked elsewhere, teachers use identifying processes sparingly and, whenever they do, they carry some categorical significance, either because they establish a desired behaviour (an aspect of the regulative field), or, as is the case here, they establish a definition, normally of a technical term relevant to the instructional field.

Classification: types of World Heritage sites

The teacher initiates the talk of what he terms *broad headings of things that are valuable within a nation* and, to sharpen the discussion, he directs the students to consult their textbooks, reading the sections in which these matters are considered. The talk leads to many suggestions about things valued as part of the heritage of countries, such as *flags, anthems, a food type, governments* and *how they run, traditions* and cultures, *flora and fauna, buildings* of many kinds. A blackboard summary is constructed by the teacher, and it emerges that a broad taxonomy of World Heritage sites may be created, recognizing those sites made by humans and those that are natural. Figure 5.4 sets the details out.

The broad distinction into those sites made by humans and those that are natural allows teacher and students to group and hence classify the rather disparate sets of items the classroom discussion has revealed.

Identification: World Heritage sites in Australia

The last of the elements in the Curriculum Orientation involves a task – that of mapping some Australian World Heritage sites – though the teacher indicates that this task carries no assessment significance: doing the task is just one aspect of setting the broad directions for the total unit of work. The task is

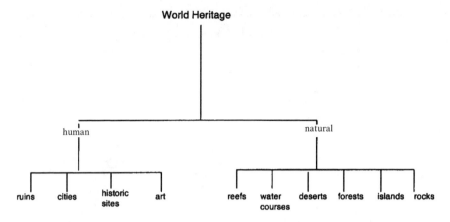

Figure 5.4   A taxonomy of World Heritage sites established in the Classification element

initiated towards the end of the first lesson and becomes the main focus in the second lesson. The teacher directs the students to their textbooks where there is a section on World Heritage sites in Australia, and initially the students name and identify the sites by reference to a map there. I shall reproduce only a short passage of talk, chosen for what it reveals of the teacher's preoccupations regarding what constitutes a suitable pedagogic subject position for geography. After the sites have all been named he advises the students to create maps of their own, identify five sites and also provide certain information about them:

> *Ok, um, we'll start with the final job for today. Um, you'll get a map of Australia. I want you to put it in the middle of a large page. If you've only got a small um, thing like this (holds up a student's book) then put it in... yeah, you use a double space, put the map here, and [[what I want you to do]] is [[to go around that map with the size and location and summary of the special features of any five, any five of those nine, um, World Heritage sites]]. But space them properly, OK. So, start off with the Great Barrier Reef, mark it in, write those comments down next to it, and then work around so you've got five, 'cos we really need to improve our map techniquing. Don't we Mark?(said in jocular tone and as a good-humoured way to attract his attention) Good. Right.*

Here the regulative register is foregrounded in particular in the process types (e.g., *we'll start; you'll get a map; start off with the Great Barrier Reef*), though the instructional field is also very much involved because in the teacher's terms what is at issue is the need to present information as a geographer should. In this sense, as elsewhere in this curriculum macrogenre, the two registers are very intimately associated. Hence also, the details about the disposition of the map on the page, and hence too, the specific advice regarding the need to identify the *size, location* and *summary of special features* of the selected sites, as well as the advice that *we really need to improve our map techniquing*.

A few minutes later Mark asks:

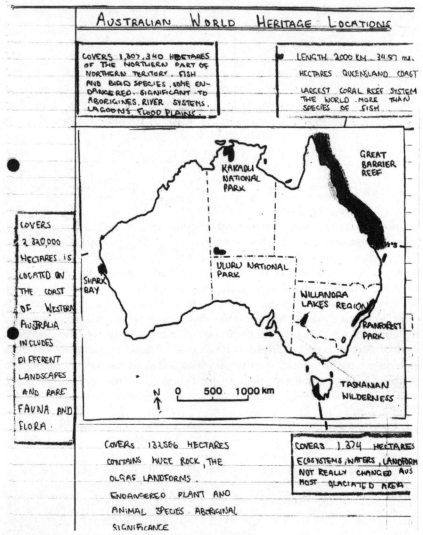

Figure 5.5 Map of Australia's heritage sites

Sir, do you have to print it? (a reference to what is to be written on the map),

and this leads to the following exchange:

> T: *I would always print it. Never write on a map.*
>
> Mark: *Well, I've written on a map.*
>
> T: *Well, you haven't (said jocularly). That's great (directed to a student). (Turns to the class) Ah, can you go back to some basic things. You must always print on a map, never write, and in this case, your printing should be fairly small and you should try as a final*

point, aim for uniformity. That is, if you've got a certain style, stay with it.

One of the most distinctive of the features of the discourse throughout this geography macrogenre is the teacher's insistence upon particular uses of terminology and particular modes of representing information as a geographer. In his terms the apprenticeship into being a geographer is of primary significance, and it colours all areas of his directions and advice about ways to proceed and work in his classroom.

Figure 5.5 reproduces one map with Australian Heritage sites prepared by a student called Kay.

As I noted earlier in this discussion, geography makes its meanings in quite distinctive ways. Here, as in other instances of work in this classroom, the association of map and written text (printed, as the teacher had asked) is very close. The teacher is to say later in the curriculum macrogenre that in order to master geography the students must make *links* between map, diagram or illustration and written text: this is in fact one of the principal measures he uses for evaluating students' success. Geography is multi-modal in its manner of constructing its meanings and, as a general principle, while it is clear that written language has an important role in its construction, there is a sense in which it often has a secondary significance to the image, map, table or sketch that is used.

There are too many instances of Curriculum Exemplifications to consider them all. I shall therefore deal with features of just two of these, though even then an enormous amount will need to be omitted. The two are to do with Kakadu National Park and Lord Howe Island.

Curriculum Exemplification: the 'case study' of Kakadu National Park[6]

Introduced in the third lesson, the Curriculum Exemplification devoted to the Kakadu National Park involves research and discussion of the site, examination of the reasons for declaring it a World Heritage site, and the challenges – environmental and otherwise – to its continued relatively pristine state. The structure of all the Curriculum Exemplifications, apart from the Curriculum Closure is similar, as displayed in Figure 5.6.

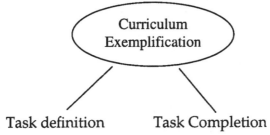

Figure 5.6 A Curriculum Exemplification in the geography macrogenre

Text 5.2

T: Alright, job for today, and... for a little while. (*writes the heading: Kakadu World Heritage Site on board*) Again, we'll just use the... the work because it's in your book and it's fairly accessible for you. Um, alright. We'll just have a look at it for a moment, what material is available from the book and we'll see what we need to do.

Student: What page is it?

T: Um, let's try page one fifty-four. (*pause*) Now, remember the three key [[ideas that we're going back to]], uh... that I want you to keep concentrating on for each of um, the countries, or, if it's a big site, for the particular site we're looking at. The first key idea [[we're looking at]] is, Alison? (doesn't reply)

Mark: Location. (writes on board)

T: Location, thank-you, good. Right, where it is terribly important. That's going to be important for a number of reasons (text left out) One of them particularly is the question of conservation. It's going to be much easier for us to protect Kakadu, if Kakadu happens to be out in the back blocks than if Kakadu happened to be stuck close to Melbourne. So the location is very important from that point of view. The second key geographic idea, Sally, was?

Sally: Ah, it was um,... distribution. (writes on board)

T: Good, distribution, a bit slow, but anyway, got there. I want the distribution within a country, but then for Kakadu, the distribution of the features within Kakadu. OK. Um, in other words, Kakadu is not, or no World Heritage Site in Australia is, given a status because of one feature. When we... when you went through that exercise last week you found at least three for all of them, alright. And the third... key geographic idea was?

Student: Spatial... (overlap)

T: Interaction, right. (writes on board) In other words, how um, it interacts with, um, or how people interact with this particular, um, site. Now just, diverting you for one moment, Kakadu has been in the news for the last two weeks – um, what sort of interaction may occur there that is causing some concern? (pause) Plum in the middle of Kakadu is what? (several students put up their hands)

Catherine: Um, Uranium. (writes on board)

T: Uranium mines. (Text omitted)

Regulatory register realized:
Interpersonally in:

(i) T use of first person plural to signal solidarity in the task: *we'll just have a look at it...*)

(ii) occasional T imperatives to direct behaviour: *now remember the three key ideas...*

(iii) T use of positive polarity to indicate positive commitment to directions take

(iv) T interrogatives to elicit information, some expressed metaphorically: *The first key idea we're looking at is, Alison?*

Experientially in:

(i) process types that realize students' behaviours: *remember* (cognition); *I want you to keep concentrating* (behavioural); *we're looking at...* (behavioural)

Textually in:

(i) T textual Themes to carry the discourse forward: *alright; now; so.*

Instructional register realized:
experientially in:

(i) key lexical items realizing participant roles in transitivity: *the first key idea; location; distribution; Kakadu.*

(ii) attributive processes to identify aspects of the field: *one of them (i.e., reasons location is important) is the question of conservation; the location is very important.*

textually in:

(i) topical Themes to identify aspects of the field: *one of them; the location; Kakadu.*

Text 5.2 displays an extract from the opening of the Curriculum Exemplification, in which it will be clear that three key geographic ideas are invoked as a necessary point of departure, using identifying processes, where students provide the Token in each case:

the first idea [[we're looking at]] is		location
Value	Pro: intensive	Token
the second key geographic idea was		distribution
Value	Pro: intensive	Token
the third key geographic idea was		spatial interaction
Value	Pro: intensive	Token

Subsequent relational processes (both attributive and identifying) articulate their significance more fully:

it (location)	is	terribly important
Carrier	Pro: intensive	Attribute
one of them (the reasons for its importance) is		the question of conservation
Value		Pro: Token intensive

Note the interesting way the teacher asks each of his questions to elicit the key geographic ideas:

> The _first key idea_ we're looking at is, Alison?
> The _second key idea_, Sally, was?
> And _the third geographic idea_ was?

Each is grammatically in the declarative mood, and each functions as a question because of the tone pattern adopted, and the uses of the vocatives towards the end. The effect is that the teacher is able to place the items of significance in topical theme position, an option which would not have been available to him had he chosen the orthodox grammatical way of asking a question:

> What is the first key geographic idea we're looking at, Alison?

The fundamental ideas associated with geography are thus foregrounded.

As the text proceeds, the teacher advises the students that they are to create a *poster on a case study of Kakadu,* using *the key geographic ideas.* The term *poster* is not one the teacher likes much (perhaps because it has overtones of primary school activities) but it becomes clear the term is found in the official geography curriculum statements he is following. The poster is to be presented on a large (A3 size) sheet of blank paper, and its production, involving both map, sketches and writing, is clearly seen as a part of apprenticeship into the meaning making processes of a geographer. I can reproduce only a fragment of the talk here. The teacher says the following as he writes on the board, allowing students to write down notes:

> *Right, okay. Using pages 154 to 162* (a reference to the textbook*), right, ah, prepare a... well, we'll use the word 'poster', but I don't like it but if you can think of a better word use it (writes 'prepare a poster' on the board). In other words you will be preparing it on that sheet (holds up A3 sheet). Um, about Kakadu World Heritage site, which will include: one, the location of Kakadu... um, put in brackets, 'map plus writing' (writes on board). Two the distribution of... World Heritage attractions... map plus writing (again writes on board). Three, um... problems of protection and conservation. Sketch plus, or sketches plus writing (Writes on board).*

Here, as I commented earlier, the two registers are revealed as very closely associated. In a sense that Bernstein would have argued, the regulative register has actually appropriated the instructional register, and it speaks through the latter, creating the text: the *pedagogic discourse.* (See for example, discussions in Bernstein, 1990: 165–218, and Bernstein, 2000: 25–39.) While the same general principle of appropriation would apply, according to Bernstein, in any instance of pedagogic activity, the classroom text in this particular geography macrogenre is nonetheless remarkable for the very close identification of the regulative and instructional registers that it reveals. Teacher direction to definitions of terms, to tasks that apply those terms, to the overall pace of work and to the principles of evaluation that will be invoked, are all explicit and overt, giving a very forcible expression to the regulative register. Yet that in turn is itself consistently expressed through the instructional field. This is a matter to which I shall return below.

Figure 5.7 displays the poster produced by one student. What are we to make of this poster and what it reveals of the meaning making associated with geography? In the past, systemic theorists (e.g., Hasan, 1980, 1984) have, from time to time, written of language as either 'constitutive of the activity,' as for example, in a commonplace passage of writing, or 'ancillary to' activity as on the football field, or in a written text with picture or illustration. Kress (2000) has challenged such a distinction because he argues it is based on linguistic theories which privilege language at the expense of other aspects of semiosis that are actually involved when language is used, such as gesture and facial expression in speech, or illustration or diagram in writing. All language uses, he concludes, are multi-modal, and really powerful models of semiotic behaviour, including language behaviour, will acknowledge this. I

KAKADU NATIONAL PARK

YEAR 9B1

Kakadu National Park is one of the best known and most popular of Australia's national parks. The park has an area of just under 20,000 square kilometers, and is about a quarter of the size of Tasmania.

LOCATION

Kakadu National Park is a remote area. The park is far away from all the capital cities except for Darwin. This isolation has allowed the park to be so huge.

The location of the park is shown on Figure 1.1. Kakadu is 230 km east of Darwin, the capital of Northern Territory. The park stretches over 200 km from north to south and over 100 km from east to west. Kakadu is bounded in the north by Van Diemen Gulf and to the east of the park lies Arnhem Land Aboriginal Reserve. Pastoral leases adjoin the southern and western boundaries of Kakadu National Park.

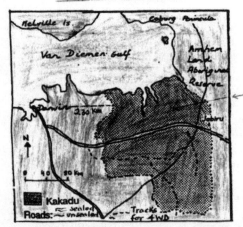

Figure 1.1 Kakadu: Location and access

DISTRIBUTION OF WORLD HERITAGE ATTRACTIONS

The main reason for Kakadu National Park's achievement of World Heritage status is its beautiful attractions of cultural and natural significance. The distribution of the attractions is scattered around the whole park.

Landscape Features

Plateaus The plateaus are a distinctive feature because of the 1400 to 1800 million years old beds of sedimentary rocks. The plateaus cover nearly all of the southern and eastern parts of Kakadu.(See Fig.1.2)

Flood Plains The flood present on the plains. The and near the East Alligate

Billabongs The billabong This is why people are so fauna life in the billabong billabong in Kakadu is no

Aboriginal Art

Aboriginal art is a huge at the unique cultural legacy rock art paintings show st Aboriginal sites record th There are two main Abor is near Obiri Rock and ar

Birds

Kakadu National Park has bird population represents renowned bird-breeding a of birds attract huge numb species habitat in billabon

PROBLEMS OF PI

Kakadu National Park fa to the environment of Ka plants.

Buffalos An introduced Their great weight and h as river banks. They con which bind the soil prote taken to a far away desti

Uranium Mining Uran have tried to dig out ura have on the environmen the water used in the mi downstream. I think that such as uranium mining

Tourism Tourism in Ka good for Kakadu in tern environment. Tourists d the primeval character o They destroy unique pla of erosion by leaving ca by minimising the touri

Figure 5.7 Student poster for Kakadu National Park

od plains attract people because of the variety types of vegetation
The flood plains are found basically around South Alligator River
gator River.(See Fig.1.2)

ongs are a habitat for different types of animals in dry seasons.
· so attracted to the billabongs. There is variety types and so much
ongs. There are many billabongs in Kakadu. The most popular
s near the Nourlangie Rock.(See Fig.1.2)

e attraction in Kakadu National Park. People are fascinated with
acy left behind by past generations of Aborigines in Kakadu. The
v structures and bones within plants and animals. Numerous
l the development of Aboriginal spiritual and religious values.
boriginal art sites distributed in Kakadu National Park. One art site
l another art site is near Nourlangie Rock (See Fig.1.2)

has many different species of birds, 273 species to be exact. This
nts a third of all the bird species of Australia. Kakadu is a world-
g area and a stopover for many migratory birds. The different types
imber of people. The birds provide a spectacular scenery. Most bird
bongs, rivers and/or wetlands.(See Fig.1.3)

PROTECTION AND CONSERVATION

c faces many problems which have, so far, led to unforeseen damage
· Kakadu. Such problems are either caused by introduced animals or

iced animal, buffalos are a disaster for the environment of Kakadu.
d hard hoofs damage habitats and can break down fragile areas such
compact the soil, reducing infiltration of rain, and destroy grasses
rotecting it from erosion. I think that it is better if buffalos were
estination where they can't destroy and environment

ranium mining has been a controversial issue. Mining companies
uranium and other minerals, but they don't realise the effect it will
nent of Kakadu. Mining produces changes to the landscape, poisons
mining process , and can damage the extensive wetlands
that it is best for the park to be left alone, free of any interferences
ing.(See Fig.1.2)

i Kakadu has been increasing a lot, recently. Although tourism is
erms of financial business, tourism can be a big threat to the
ts disturb the ecological balances that are vital for the preservation of
er of the park. Tourists disturb isolated areas where animals habitat.
plants by touching them. They cause an acceleration of the process
g car tracks. I think that the best way to solve this tourism problem is
ourist impact.

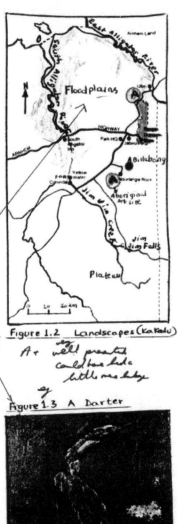

Figure 1.2   Landscapes (Kakadu)

A + very well presented
could have had a
little more labels

Figure 1.3   A Darter

concede the general point he is making and agree that all language uses are multi-modal in many senses. Writing has always been multi-modal (see Christie, 2000a for a discussion of this), while it is true that the spoken mode is always understood along with other semiotic behaviours creating important meanings.

Yet I would also argue that the distinction between matters that are ancillary to, or constitutive of, language, even though it may appear to over-simplify, seems to me to have some continuing value, particularly for pedagogic purposes. That is because, depending upon the analyses and descriptions one is attempting, one will always need to make choices about which aspects of semiosis will be the major focus of attention: whatever ones does, it will always be a selection, and one can never describe the lot. That said, it also follows that where, as in this book, the patterns of language are the major focus of attention, it is possible to draw attention to situations where the language is sometimes more ancillary to action than otherwise, and elsewhere, where it is largely constitutive of activity. For example, in Chapter 2 of this book, the child Susy produced two genres in her morning news, one of which (the show and tell) involved her in using language ancillary to the display of her toys, while the other (an anecdote about activities with her family) clearly was constituted in language, albeit with a great deal of use of her body, her intonation and so on. (See a discussion in Christie, 2000b in which the distinction is used in looking at other aspects of classroom work.) In some situations the distinction between matters ancillary to, or constitutive of, language, is often insufficient to explain what is going on in meaning-making because it is just too simple. In the case of Figure 5.7 it is, for example, insufficient to see the verbal text as 'ancillary' to the maps and sketches, or vice versa. Quite a different relationship is involved, such that the meanings are constructed collectively in the abstraction which is the map, in the sketches and in the written text. The relationships between these might be said to be one of 'synergy', for the various elements of the poster are intended to work in harmony in creating the meanings of the complete text. It is this kind of synergy that the teacher appears to strive for when he enjoins the students in this classroom to build the *links* between map and/or image or sketch and written text. In fact, a careful reading of the total classroom text I am discussing here leads me to say that the teacher was not very clear about what he meant about how to constructed the 'links' he valued so much. I take this as evidence that he lacked a language for talking about the multi-modal nature of geographical representation. About this I am not altogether surprised because the scholarly work to be done in teasing out and describing the relationships of written texts and diagrams, maps and illustrations, at least for pedagogic purposes, has only just commenced. Kress, already referred to, is one of those involved in researching in this area. See discussions in Cope and Kalantzis, 2000, in which Kress and others consider at least some of these issues, though the papers here do not directly address issues of pedagogic practices. Unsworth (2001) seeks in particular to address questions of pedagogy.

Curriculum Exemplification: the 'case study' of Lord Howe Island

The lesson in which this Curriculum Exemplification is initiated commences with advice from the teacher alluding to what work has been done hitherto, and what is to be done. His remarks are illuminating for what they reveal of his expectations of the students:

> *You should have already handed in one piece of work on Kakadu, if not it's getting. . . fairly late. Um, um, those [[that I have had handed]] in have ranged from great down to very good. We've had no duds yet. Um, but we probably haven't had enough, you know, really good quality. The two things [[I'm looking for here]] are excellent map and sketch work, excellent writing [[and then linking the two [[in whatever way you can]]]]. That's been the defect part, although some have come a little bit along. There are a number of ways of linking the two and you should certainly be working at that.*

As a general principle, this teacher often offers praise, sometimes as here tempered with advice about how things might be better. On occasion as we shall see below, he offers criticism, though in a manner that does not invite negative reaction from the students. The most notable feature of the advice just cited is that it is part of a consistent pattern by which he frequently indicates the principles for evaluation that will apply in responding to students' work. As elsewhere, he uses an identifying process to reiterate what is required:

The two things [[I'm looking for here]]	are	excellent map and sketch work, excellent writing [[and then linking the two [[in whatever way you can]]]]
Value	Pro: intensive	Token

Authority and its expression are important features of the operation of the regulative register at any time. Here two matters are at issue: in the immediate and most overt sense, the criteria for evaluation of performance are articulated; in the more profound sense, what is at issue is the regulation of the students' behaviour as pedagogic subjects. Regulation is strongly expressed, as we have seen in an identifying process, since its effect is categorical. Yet the issues over which the regulation finds its expression are drawn from the instructional field of geography. Thus, as I indicated earlier, the second order or instructional field provides the voice through which the regulative register does its work.

The Curriculum Exemplification devoted to the case study of Lord Howe involves use of maps, both interpreting those available in the textbook, and drawing maps in notebooks, as well as considerable researching of features of the island. This curriculum genre begins in extensive classroom talk constructed about the map provided in the textbook, though students are also given a task. The object here is to take the blank map and provide answers to the various questions provided, some of which involve working directly on the map.

Classroom talk develops about Lord Howe and the associated questions; the teacher moves about the room, chatting to individual students about their work, while also occasionally returning to the board to write directions there. Here, because the talk is very long, I can do no more than cite some fragments from the talk to capture something of the ways the teacher and students interact, and the ways in which teacher authority continues to be expressed:

> T: *(to a student who has just finished the exercise in response to question 2) You've finished? Aren't you brilliant?*
> Daniel: *No. I wouldn't go that far, but ah, what do you call the cross-section?*
> T: *Surprisingly you call it a cross-section.*
>   ] overlap
> Caroline: *Cross-section!* (said in tones of surprise, as the question seems so obvious)

Some time later:

> Sandra: *Um, for number 3, is it 80 per cent forest?*
> T: *Whatever you like, whatever you think. I want you to tell me what you think is green as the percentage of the whole, the whole island.*
> Sandra: *So, I would say about 90 per cent.*
> T: *I'm quite happy about that.*
> Catherine: I said 85.
> T: *I'm quite happy with that too. (Looks at Andrea's work) I'm certainly not happy with that!*
> Andrea: *I haven't started yet.*
> T: *Oh, right.*

Within the limits imposed by the requirement to get on with dealing with the questions, the teacher tolerates – even invites – a degree of ironical or humorous comment (*Aren't you brilliant? No, I wouldn't go that far...*), asks of the students that they *think* about their work (*whatever you think*), and also indicates when something is inadequate (*I'm certainly not happy with that*).

The activity of working with the map and associated questions having been completed, in the next lesson (still a part of the same genre) the teacher works through the responses required to each of the questions, allowing the students opportunity to amend and/or develop what they have done. Here again I shall select only a fragment from the talk to indicate the ways in which the students are directed to proceed. Looking at the fourth question on

Lord Howe Island, to do with the distribution of fishing sites, the teacher says among other things:

> T: *Briefly, what's distribution ... mean, John?*
> John: *Um, like, like ah ... distributed, like how it's spread out around.*
> T: *OK. In other words it's ... in a sense, combined with the word location which is where things are, (writes location on board) and it's the sum total of all the locations (writes sum total on board) which produces a pattern, or of course it may produce no pattern at all. (writes pattern/no pattern on board) However, you're required to say something about it, and ≪ what I insist on, whether you like it or not, it's tough ≫ you must use these words (writes even/uneven and widespread/ concentrated on board) somewhere. The only reason [[that I get people to do this]], is [[it then gives a structure to an answer on distribution]], otherwise we tend to find that answers sort of go off in all directions, and people miss the point. For distribution, the first thing to comment is the overall pattern, and then you come down to the detail. (writes overall –> detail on board)*

The same general pattern in the expression of both registers has emerged here as in earlier examples cited. The two registers are both realized in the discourse, it is the regulative register that is foregrounded, and yet this is in turn expressed through the instructional register. Thus, the extract begins with definition of a key geographic term, realizing the instructional field in transitivity:

distribution	is	the sum total of all the locations
Value	Pro: intensive	Token

and this leads to some elaboration:

(the sum total of the locations)	produces	a pattern
Token	Pro: causative	Value
or of course it	may produce	no pattern at all
Token	Pro: causative	Value

Both identifying and causative processes express meanings that are categorical, and they are thus authoritative. In addition, interpersonally, the teacher invokes a strong sense of authority, using high modality:

you're required to say something about it
you must use these words,

and, found in the enclosed clauses, another verbal group that expresses modality:

what I insist on...

All this is reinforced by the other enclosed clauses:

whether you like it or not
it's tough

A further identifying process establishes a reason for the requirement:

The only reason		
[[that I get people to do this]]	is	[[it then gives a structure to an answer on distribution]]
Value		Pro: Token
		intensive

The process and its Value and Token realize the regulative register, though the instructional field is expressed within the Token: *distribution*. Thus, while the regulative register is foregrounded, it is clear that the instructional field is also involved: it is in fact appropriated by the regulative register, which in turn gives it authority.

One student, Anna, whose completed task was judged a good one by the teacher writes the following answer to the final question:

The island has quite a lot of creeks and lakes, none of which actually reach the sea. The creeks and rivers all start on high land and flow down to lower land where they drain into lakes or just stop. I'm not sure why they stop but I think it might be that before the coast line there is quite a lot of flat land and so when the rivers and creeks enter the flat land they lose momentum and stop before they reach the coast. There are also a couple of marshes on the island.

The answer involves some reading of the written information in the textbook, but it primarily rests on capacity to interpret the physical significance of the island, as deduced from the available maps. This student's work was awarded an A grade, though the teacher attached no comment to it.

Hopefully, enough has been said to give something of the character of at least two of the Curriculum Exemplifications genres. Each involved a task which constituted the focus of the genre, and all tasks were held to contribute to the overall evaluation of the students' performance for the six weeks of work. The Curriculum Closure involving a written test on aspects of what had been studied, as I noted much earlier, brought the total unit of classroom activity to a conclusion, though the test made only partial contribution to the marks awarded for the total unit of work. The written test involved distribution of a sheet of information, setting out the World Heritage logo, a map of Australia, two photos from Lord Howe Island, and a range of questions on World Heritage, most of which required short written answers. Two will suffice, though no discussion of the students' responses can be provided here in the interests of saving space:

1) Refer to all data shown (on the sheet) and to your own knowledge and explain why Lord Howe Island was nominated for World Heritage.

2) World Heritage sites outside Australia are often human-made constructions linked to some important event/time period. Select two that would fit this description. Describe their location.

A retrospective look at the unfolding of the macrogenre in secondary geography

Now that my selective sampling of the text of the macrogenre covering six weeks of schooling has been completed, what can be argued of its structure and its goals? To recapitulate a little of what has been said, it will be recalled that I argued the structure here was better represented as an orbital rather than a linear structure. That was because an opening Curriculum Orientation (the 'nucleus') essentially established definitions relevant to the instructional field, while the subsequent genres involved the students in work that exemplified the terms introduced in the first place: hence they were 'orbital' in character, and termed Curriculum Exemplifications. Each of these and their associated tasks related primarily to the Curriculum Orientation and, with the exception of the Curriculum Closure, they could have been introduced at different points in the overall cycle of work. Thus, for example, the Curriculum Exemplification devoted to Lord Howe Island could have been introduced before that devoted to Kakadu National Park, while that involving international World Heritage sites might well have come at any point. As it happened, once the various genres and their associated tasks were introduced, they led to work – some of it done as homework – which was still in progress when the students commenced work on other genres and tasks: this was certainly true, for example of the work on both Kakadu and the international sites, some of which was still being completed by some students when the genre devoted to Lord Howe Island was initiated. In that these – and others not discussed – were initiated when they were, there is evidence both that a body of experiential information to do with the instructional field of World Heritage was covered in the macrogenre, and that in principle its ordering might have been other than it was.

Martin, Iedema and White, referred to much earlier in this chapter, argued that attention to the various potential means of ordering and re-ordering genres with orbital structures allowed one to see how particular configurations of elements were possible and, how, on occasions, the meanings

– interpersonal, textual or experiential – were more or less privileged. In the case of the macrogenre analysed in this chapter, I would suggest that identification of the orbital structure has allowed us to expose, firstly, the particularly privileged role of the experiential meanings and, secondly, the functioning of the textual meanings in facilitating their privileged status. I would add that the interpersonal meanings to do with the relationship of the teacher and students are profoundly important to the successful operation of the macrogenre, though it is doubtful that the orbital structure exposes these any more clearly than might a linear structure analysis.

The experiential meanings are privileged both because they are so forcibly established in the Curriculum Orientation, and because those meanings are so consistently elaborated upon, revisited and reinforced in the subsequent Curriculum Exemplifications. These experiential meanings, it will be noted, are of the instructional register, to do with the *key geographic ideas* and their application with respect to *World Heritage*; yet as we have also noticed, they are given status and power for pedagogic purposes because they are appropriated by the regulative register, whose function is to nurture and shape pedagogic subject positions. In other words, the regulative register regulates by speaking through the voice of the instructional register.

The experiential meanings to do with geography are built upon deliberately orchestrated redundancies in the manner in which terms – all to do with the instructional field of geography generally, and World Heritage in particular – are dealt with in the discourse of the classroom. Thus, certain essential terms – to do with the *location and distribution of World Heritage sites*, and with the issues of *spatial interaction of phenomena within those sites* are frequently revisited throughout the macrogenre. Redundancy – or repetition, at least – is to some extent a feature of most classroom discourse, though its operation in this classroom macrogenre is remarkable for its thoroughness and consistency. What is important to note is that (with the exception of the written test at the end of the macrogenre, in which some recall of matters learned is required) the teacher does not involve the students in 'doing the same thing' or 'learning the same thing' each time, which would be pedagogically unproductive. Instead, the redundancy is pedagogically very useful because it allows revisiting the terms and their meanings by reference to several contexts, thereby extending the understanding of those meanings. Lemke (1995: 166–75) draws attention to the importance of redundancy in all semiotic activity, noting the folly of the lay view that redundancy is not useful. 'Since events', he writes, 'including spoken and written words, do not have intrinsic meanings, but only the meanings we make for them by fitting them into various contexts, regular or predictable ways of combining events and contexts are necessary' (Lemke, 1995: 169). Hence, for pedagogical purposes, deliberately orchestrated redundancy is an important feature of the success with which the regulative register does its work.

As for the textual meanings in the macrogenre, as already noted, the orbital structure exposes the non-linear manner by which the orbital genres are introduced, demonstrating that, though the ordering of the genres is not arbitrary, it is capable of flexibility and change. What seems to have shaped the teacher's decisions in organizing matters as he has done is the principle of redundancy to which Lemke alludes; the frequent revisiting of the *key geographic ideas* by reference to different *World Heritage sites* has proved to be the principle that overwhelmingly guided the ordering of curriculum genres and associated tasks, and their phasing in at times in parallel and overlapping fashion. The learning afforded the students in such classroom organization is one that is accretive in character, to return to a term I introduced quite early in this chapter; it involves learning about the basic terms and what they represent by reference to several sites, often in parallel, so that the conceptual under-standings to do with geography are expanded, strengthened and reinforced.

A question arises from all this: what accounts for the presence of an orbital structure in the geography macrogenre I have been discussing in this chapter? Such a structure is not a feature in those examples of secondary classroom texts I have collected in English (Christie, 1999), or secondary physics (Christie, 1998) at least, nor is it a feature of the curriculum macrogenres I have examined in primary schools generally. Is there evidence here that geography is organized differently? The issue is itself one that requires further empirical investigation, though my sense is that this is not a feature distinct to geography, but rather to the pedagogical decisions made by the teacher. What does seem to be important, as already noted, is the insistence upon a strongly classified and strongly framed curriculum – one in which the technical language, in this case characteristic of the discipline of geography, is so explicitly stated and so explicitly valued. It is this, as we have seen, which causes the very intimate association of the regulative and instructional registers. Such an insistence and association could in principle generate a linearly structured macrogenre. Having said that, it is also notable that the non-linear structure adopted allows a very rich interplay and overlapping of learning activities.

To turn to another matter, what of the issue of logogenesis in a classroom macrogenre of the kind examined here? It will be recalled that, in Chapter 4, I claimed that one measure of the successful unfolding and completion of a curriculum macrogenre would be the presence of logogenesis: a process by which the language changes as students move to control of new language and hence of new understandings. The shift in logogenesis often involves some uses of grammatical metaphor, for it will be in this that many new technical terms and/or abstractions are realized. Several of the Key Geographic Ideas used in the geography macrogenre were instances of grammatical metaphor: *spatial interaction, spatial interdependence* or *spatial change over time* are all examples of grammatical metaphor. These and the rest of the Key Geographic Ideas represent abstractions of various kinds, some more than others directly constructed in grammatical metaphor. As we saw, the critical terms were introduced as part of the work of the opening curriculum genre – the Curriculum Orientation – and the work of the rest of the rest of the macrogenre involved learning to apply them by reference to different examples of World Heritage. It was in the redundant processes of application and re-application of these terms that logogenesis occurred.

Finally, before this discussion concludes, I should comment on the evaluation principles that apply in a curriculum macrogenre of the kind I have discussed. It will be apparent that the principles of evaluation involved are intimately part of the total curriculum experience. As we have seen, advice about the need to use the technical language appropriately, as well as directions for the development and creation of posters, notes and maps is explicit, shaping a great deal of the pedagogic behaviour of the class participants. A curriculum that is strongly classified and strongly framed will normally adopt reasonably explicit principles of evaluation.

Notes

1. The project was known by the rather unhappy name of the 'Write It Right Project' (not the choice of the participants), and it sought to investigate literacy in a number of work sites and in the range of secondary school subjects. Several of the discussions in Christie and Martin, 1997, draw on the work of the project.
2. There are, I would argue, very valid pedagogical reasons for selecting the model of the discussion genre displayed in Chapter 4, and this discussion is not intended to suggest otherwise. Rather, the object is to open up and acknowledge the fact that much genre identification and description tends to foreground the experiential meanings, while the other meanings achieve a much reduced significance. The point is an important one for linguistic theory, for as Martin (1996) argues, a great deal of linguistic theory, not only SF theory, has unconsciously tended to privilege experiential over other meanings.
3. The issues over what should constitute geographical knowledge and pedagogic practices for its teaching remain controversial. See, for example, discussions by Gilbert, 1989; Singh, 1990; Lee 1996, all of whom variously argue for a more 'socially critical' orientation (Singh's term). The effect of their critiques would be to expand and change the classification principles of geography. On the other hand, writers such as Crabb, 1995, Slater, 1995 and McDonald, 1995, appear to be concerned about what they see as a disturbing lack of rigour in the manner in which geography changes, as it absorbs some of the concerns of such studies as environmental science, though Slater and McDonald appear more sanguine about the possibilities than Crabb.
4. I should perhaps note that I did not approach the school involved to study there because it had adopted such a view of the curriculum. Rather I approached it requesting opportunity to study the implementation of their SOSE programme, and I was advised that this was the choice the school had made.
5. One other task is introduced towards the end of the cycle, to do with the status of the Victoria Falls in Africa as World Heritage, though the teacher does not appear to regard this as assessable, and its significance in the overall scheme seems to fade. This is probably explained by the fact that the teacher found the students were fully occupied with the other tasks, all of which (apart from the last) were intended to take time over the course of the several lessons involved.
6. Kakadu National Park lies in the northern part of Australia and is remarkable both for its extensive Aboriginal wall paintings and other artefacts, and for its flora and fauna. It was one of the first World Heritage sites listed in Australia.

6 Pedagogic discourse and the claims of knowledge

Introduction

Central to the arguments in this book has been a model of classroom discourse and its analysis based on a use of the systemic functional grammar and associated notions of genre – in this case notions of curriculum genres and macrogenres. Classroom activity, it has been argued, is like other socially constructed and negotiated activity, in that it may be analysed in terms of genres – staged, purposive, goal-driven activities in which teachers and students structure and organize teaching–learning processes of various kinds. Where the teaching–learning activity is large enough, so I have suggested, the result may be a curriculum macrogenre: a set of related genres that together create a larger unity. The latter will typically be found in relatively long sequences of classroom work of the kind we saw in Chapters 4 and 5. A characteristic of a curriculum genre, or of a curriculum macrogenre, I have argued, is that it will unfold through the operation of a first order or regulative register and a second order, or instructional, register, where the latter terms are adapted from Bernstein's discussions of pedagogic discourse. Bernstein's proposals with respect to the operation of the pedagogic discourse are part of an ambitious sociological theory to do with describing and explaining cultural production, reproduction and change. (See Solomon's interview with Bernstein (1999, 2000) for some discussion of the sweep of the theory.) I have made selective use of the theory, to inform what is essentially a linguistic model of classroom discourse. In this final chapter I aim to summarize much of what I have sought to argue with respect to the operation of curriculum genres and macrogenres, and with respect to the claims made for a view of pedagogy in terms of apprenticeship. In developing the discussion, I shall make reference again to some aspects of Bernstein's work, where such references are relevant to the proposals developed here.

It will be recalled that in Chapter 1, where I outlined aspects of Bernstein's work, I noted that for him it consisted of a 'regulative discourse' and an 'instructional discourse', where the latter was said to be 'embedded' within the former. For reasons already discussed, in doing what is essentially a linguistic analysis, I have used the notion of two registers and the metaphor of 'projection' rather than of embedding in explaining the relationship of the two registers. In analysing classroom discourse in long passages of curriculum activity I have sought, among other things, to provide linguistic evidence for the operation of the two registers. I have sought to show how the regulative register is instrumental in bringing the classroom text into being, and in determining the directions, sequencing, pacing and evaluation of activity; how the latter realizes the 'content' or the specialist experiential information that constitutes the substance of the teaching–learning activity; and how the regulative register actually appropriates and speaks through the instructional register. In addition, in undertaking to demonstrate these matters, I have also sought to demonstrate how a particular kind of relationship – a pedagogic relationship – is constructed, as a necessary enabling feature of a successful instance of pedagogic activity.

The pedagogic relationship of schooling is only one of a very large range of pedagogic relationships recognized in Bernstein's theory (see Bernstein, 1990: 134–41), and the school is only one of the agencies of 'symbolic control' he recognizes. Among other fields of symbolic control and their agents, schools and their agents – teachers – work to achieve a symbolic control of pedagogic subjects, such that certain forms of consciousness are shaped and given specialist expression.

I would argue that the notion of the pedagogic relationship developed in the discussions of this book is helpful in at least four related senses. Firstly, it draws attention to the discourses – and their specialist technical language –. that are intended to be imparted in the pedagogic relationship. Secondly, it draws attention to the privileged and privileging status of such discourses, and the power that possession of them potentially confers. Thirdly, it suggests the authority ideally carried by the teacher in initiating, facilitating and structuring the pedagogic relationship. Fourthly, it suggests a great deal of the ideal pedagogic subject position of the 'clients' in the pedagogic relationship, namely the students; it is they whose consciousness is shaped and who acquire various ways of behaving, responding, reasoning and articulating experience of many kinds.

At issue in the model of classroom discourse discussed, among other matters, is a particular model of the pedagogic subject as apprentice: one who is initiated into ways of behaving, of knowing and of thinking, ways of identifying and responding to issues, ways of addressing problems and ways of valuing. In that schools play such a powerful role in the contemporary world in apprenticing the young, their methods and procedures in achieving their particular kinds of symbolic control deserve our closest scrutiny. Schooling in fact constitutes one of the most important agencies of symbolic control in the modern world. In order to explore more fully some aspects of the symbolic control in the pedagogic relationships of schooling, I want now to turn more directly to the nature of the authority that operates in the discourses of schooling, and to the associated notion of the 'moral regulation' said to operate in such a discourses.

Authority and the moral regulation of schooling

In Chapter 3, I have referred already to the claim that a pedagogic discourse involves a 'moral regulation' of pedagogic subjects. The notion is itself linked to the related idea of the 'recontextualization' of forms of specialist knowledge which are said to be transmitted in pedagogic activity. Writing of what is involved in effecting the successful transmission of such specialist discourses, Bernstein states:

> It is of course obvious that all pedagogic discourse creates a moral
> regulation of the social relations of transmission/acquisition, that
> is, rules of order, relation, and identity, and that such a moral order
> is prior to, and a condition for, the transmission of competences.
> (Bernstein, 1990: 184)

I suggest that such a 'moral regulation' in the terms of schooling has at least two dimensions, both of which are important, though one can be shown to be the more significant over time. One dimension has to do with establishing what constitute acceptable patterns of behaviour interpersonally, where these involve behaving within the terms, both spatial and temporal, that apply within the classroom and the wider school context and its community. The other has to do with establishing behavioural patterns of another sort: those to do with the patterns and methods of handling information, reasoning, thinking, arguing, describing and explaining particular to the instructional fields that are taken from elsewhere and relocated within the school as part of the operation of the pedagogic discourse. Successful regulation in the former dimension is itself instrumental to achievement of regulation in the latter dimension.

Of the two, the former dimension tends to be more audibly and consistently apparent in the earlier years of schooling, for it is in those years that many of the acceptable behavioural patterns are established in matters as various as: learning the principle that the day is broken into various activities, defined partly in terms of the time allocated to them, as well as the physical spaces devoted to them; learning to move about the classroom in accepted ways, taking up different physical dispositions at different times of the school day; eating and drinking at acceptable times; and expressing willingness to participate in classroom talk by putting up a hand to respond to teacher questions. Such matters, often explicitly foregrounded in teacher talk in the early years, frequently cease to find explicit expression as children grow older, or alternatively, as they establish familiar understandings of those behavioural routines that are acceptable in a particular teacher's classroom and school. It is for this reason that they become less noticeable over time, though their very continuing implicit expression is a measure of their importance in the totality of what constitutes acceptable pedagogic behaviour. As for the latter dimension of the operation of the regulative discourse, this is the more significant over time, for it is in and through this that pedagogic subjects are inducted into patterns of reasoning, methods of addressing questions and ways of reasoning and valuing, all of which are said in some way to mark the educated person, conferring a degree of power on those pedagogic subjects who master these. These matters may be illustrated by reference to some of the classroom texts examined in earlier chapters.

Thus, for example, in Chapter 2, which examined an early childhood classroom text devoted to morning news, two goals of the activity were that the children learn to position themselves vis-à-vis each in acceptable ways and that they practise 'good manners', in the sense that they address each other quite formally (as well, of course, as learning to tell about experience in a sustained way):

> Student: *Good morning, boys and girls!*
> Chorus: *Good morning, Susy!*

and in that they pay polite attention to each other, while also offering comments deemed by the teacher at least to be acceptably polite. It will be recalled that one child offered a negative comment on an item displayed by the news giver, and the teacher immediately made clear her displeasure:

> *Shh! Right, that's enough, don't forget your manners!*

It will also be recalled that in Chapter 2 it was noted the activity of morning news typically involves a news giver placed in a significant position at the front of the class, while the rest of the students are grouped at her feet. The physical dispositions of both news giver and class are important, symbolizing the relative status of both, and underscoring the acceptable behaviours required of the interlocutors involved.

In the case of Chapter 3, devoted to an early literacy learning activity, the teacher was also concerned with acceptable behaviour, partly as that was defined by reference to what might acceptably be done at different times of the day, and partly by correction of inattentiveness and an associated requirement to participate appropriately as a member of the class group. Thus, in the manner of many teachers, she invoked some consideration of time in initiating the activity, thereby providing some definition to the time and task to be commenced, and distinguishing it from what had gone before:

> *Well, now these people are back, I want you to listen to this little tiny short story like the one we had yesterday.*

As the lesson proceeded, she corrected one student who was playing with a pocket comb, and did so by establishing a principle to do with the time at which use of a comb was acceptable:

> *Frankie, put the comb away. The time to do your hair is at play time.*

As for the student who was inattentive, it will be recalled that the teacher invoked some sense of a moral value attaching to good behaviour as a feature of being a good participant in his 'grade' or class, when she chided a child who was not listening to her:

Joseph, you're spoiling the grade. Now wriggle up please and start listening. You'll get back to your place and you won't know what to do.

While it would not be true to say that such overt directions to use of 'good manners' and acceptably attentive behaviour are not a feature of the later years, it does seem to be the case both that such directions are often less frequent as students grow older and that, where they occur, they are realized linguistically rather differently. Thus, if we recall the second of the two teachers whose classroom text was discussed in Chapter 4, I drew attention to the amount of trouble she devoted to establishing acceptable behaviours for the students – all of them in year 6, and thus considerably older than those in Chapters 2 and 3. I shall not reproduce here all that she said, though I shall display a little, reminding the reader of the extensive uses of low and median modality the teacher employed to construct with the students acceptable ways to sit together preparatory to working together on the tasks she proposed:

The way [[to work]] might be [[to sit around this group]]. All right? Because perhaps people will be (inaudible) and less wriggling if they're seated. Now a lot of work [[that you may have to do]] may be with a partner. Some you'll do by yourself. So you're probably best to sit next to somebody [[that you will work with]]. OK? Now, two, four, six, eight ... (turns to one table) there's one person away today so maybe it might be a group of three. All right? It's up to you. But could you find yourself a seat around the desks and be sitting next to someone that you will identify to work with please? If you two are going to work together ... there'll have to be one odd person sitting there ... ok? So move down one please.

The teacher's authority in directing the students' behaviour was not really in doubt but the reasonably oblique means she sought to establish acceptable behaviours was in contrast to the more frequent uses of imperatives in the talk of early childhood teachers, and their more frequent tendency to invoke considerations of morally unacceptable behaviours such as *spoiling the grade*. As for the other teacher, also of year 6, considered in Chapter 4, he also invoked considerations of time to help definition to the task:

Right, OK now we are going to start our theme next week, but we are actually starting a bit earlier because of it...

while as for the authority with which he established goals and directions, he used several linguistic resources, including high modality:

so we've got to do a lot of concentrating.

Notably, however, he employed abstractions such as *the main requirement* or *the main one*, as in:

> *the main requirement is for various things to be done*
> *the main one is on science day...*

Authority is at its most powerful when it expresses itself in abstractions of this kind, because the human agency involved (in this case, the teacher's) is rendered invisible in favour of the more abstract principle that is expressed. Such expressions are much less commonly a feature of the language of teacher talk in early childhood classrooms.

The teacher of year 9 in Chapter 5 was dealing with students aged 15. Like many other teachers, he did, in initiating the curriculum macrogenre, define the task partly by reference to time:

> *Ah, I'll just give you a quick introduction. Could you jot quickly down what I've put on the board and then we'll ah, we'll make a start.... Ah, it's about a six-week unit more or less.*

Otherwise, uses of language overtly devoted to directing and/or correcting student behaviour were infrequent in the teacher's talk. Where they occurred they sometimes used interpersonal metaphor, as for example when he looked towards a student who apparently was inattentive, and said of the need to take notes at some speed from the board he was using:

> *'cos there's a bit of writing I'll be rubbing it off at fairly frequent intervals, so the moral of the story Mario is keep up!*

Expressed more congruently this might read: 'Mario, you must keep up!' Irony was sometimes used, as in a congratulatory remark made to a student later in the macrogenre:

> *You've finished? Aren't you brilliant?*

As a general principle, however, of all the teachers whose curriculum activities have been discussed in this book, it was the geography teacher who made least use of language in what I have identified as the first of the dimensions involved in the operation of the regulative register: namely, that to do with overt advice and direction concerning desirable behaviours for the classroom. This was because he assumed an understanding of acceptable behaviours in the students, and on the evidence the assumption was justified. Of course, in other ways, the teacher provided quite overt and explicit advice regarding student behaviours, though these were often, as we saw in Chapter 5, expressed through an appropriation of the instructional register. This brings us to some consideration of the second of the dimensions of the functioning of the regulative register.

The instructional register and its appropriation by the regulative register

It is in the second sense I have identified that the most important work of the regulative register is done, although for reasons already argued, it must be stressed that the first of the two senses is nonetheless of great significance. This is because the learning of the acceptably 'good' behaviours that characterize the first sense is instrumental to establishing the predispositions that make possible the learning of the behaviours that characterize the second sense: that of developing the methods of reasoning and thinking encoded within the instructional register. Thus it is that, though the 'moral regulation' associated with the 'delocation', 'relocation' and transmission of the instructional field is in one way of a different order from the regulation to do with acceptable 'good' behaviour, in another way the two are merely manifestations of the same process at work: that of shaping pedagogic subjects as they learn methods and manners of functioning in the classroom, where these are valued for their relevance for participation in the wider world beyond school. It is this process that lies at the heart of the functioning of the pedagogic discourse, and at the heart of the pedagogic relationship.

In Chapter 5, the very close identification of the instructional field of geography with the articulation of acceptable behaviours as a feature of the regulative register, was very marked in the teacher's discourse throughout the whole macrogenre, while the principles he articulated for behaving acceptably as 'geographic pedagogic subjects' were evident in the various texts the students produced. Recall for the moment the following:

- the teacher's admonition to use the Key Geographic Ideas *frequently, accurately, correctly*
- the advice to create maps showing Australian World Heritage sites which identified *size, location and summary of special features* of the sites
- the advice that *we really need to improve our map techniquing*

as well as exchanges such as the following in which the instances of modality (underlined) and of instances of negative polarity (with double underlining) are pronounced:

Student: *Sir, do you have to print it?*
     T: *I would always print it. Never write on a map.*
Student: *Well, I've written on a map.*
     T: *Well, you haven't.*

and a few seconds later the advice to the whole class:

     T: *Ah, can you go back to some basic things? You must always print on a map, never write, and in this case, your printing should be fairly small and you should try as a final point, aim for uniformity. That is, if you've got a certain style, stay with it.*

In the last teacher exchanges, it will be clear that the voice of teacher authority was strong. Moreover, it is probably significant that the authority is not expressed metaphorically. Metaphorical expressions were often chosen by this teacher on those relatively few occasions when he either corrected unacceptable behaviours or directed acceptable 'good' behaviours. In this case, the teacher authority was expressed wholly through congruent realizations, as he made very clear some principles for producing maps – principles worth observing in the process of becoming a satisfactory pedagogic subject for the purposes of geography. This instance of teacher direction, like many others found in the geography macrogenre, is very clearly an instance of 'moral regulation' in the sense that Bernstein intended.

As already indicated in Chapter 5, the geography macrogenre we have analysed was marked by strong classification and strong framing. As we saw, the strong classification meant that the discipline was taught as having a distinctive technical language (much of it expressed through the resource of grammatical metaphor), while a function of the macogenre as it unfolded was that students learn to recognize and use that technical language, applying and re-applying it in several activities. The class activity was strongly framed, in that as the teacher initiated and developed the macrogenre with the students, he set significant constraints upon the principles that applied for interaction and hence for learning. Yet the framing principles were very intimately related to the principles of classification, and the sum effect was that the students operated within well-defined guidelines in working with him. What happened in the geography macrogenre was of course to some extent, a condition of the personality of the teacher though, having said that, it is also notable that secondary teachers in some other disciplines, at least in the mid to upper secondary years of schooling, often adopt similarly strong principles of classification and framing.

Thus, for example, two teachers (in different Australian states) whose classroom activities were observed, on the one hand, in Year 11 physics (Christie, 1997), and on the other hand, in Year 11 chemistry (discussed briefly in Christie, 2000b), taught their disciplines in ways that made clear they saw what they were doing as involving initiation into traditions of reasoning, where the language in which those traditions were encoded was of primary importance. Both attached an importance to following what might be termed 'received traditions' in the teaching and learning of their subjects, the chemistry teacher specifically advising the students both that *the object when we do an experiment is to write it up carefully so we can do it again,* and that the experiment they were doing was *very old.* Both macrogenres operated very much on the principle that what was involved was an initiation into established practices and established language for dealing with those practices. In both cases, the voice of the regulative register spoke most directly through that of the instructional register.

To return for the moment to the two classroom texts considered in Chapter 4, and to which some reference has already been made above, it can be argued that in both cases, in rather different ways, the regulative register successfully appropriated and thus spoke through the instructional register. In the case of the macrogenre devoted to teaching and learning the Newtonian principle of the mechanical advantage conferred by machines, the sequence of activities was such that once beyond the Curriculum Initiation, the students increasingly adopted the language of the instructional field, even, by the time of the Curriculum Closure, being able to produce both oral recounts of what they had done in making machines, as well as writing procedural texts about how the machines were made. For the purposes of that activity, the students had become 'scientific pedagogic subjects'.

As for the second of the two macrogenres discussed in Chapter 4, it will be recalled that a great deal of teacher effort went into shaping the pedagogic subjects here as persons who would be willing to research and consider the issues before developing an opinion – in this case about the propriety of a nuclear power station:

> T: *Do you make your mind up now?*
> Students: *No.*

and in part the teacher went on, using several instances of modality, either median or high:

> *it's really good to see that people actually haven't made their mind up and they're prepared to look at both sides. And it's that evidence that'll tell us. And I think writing a discussion is an excellent idea. It's probably the best idea. Because when we send that in, it means we've been fair. We've looked at it properly, we've looked at both sides and we've thought about it before we've made the decision.*

One of the most powerful means by which teachers shape the process of 'moral regulation' that occurs in classrooms is through the ways in which they offer praise of particular courses of action. Here, apart from the uses of modality referred to, one notices as well the strong attitudinal expression in such items as: *an excellent idea*, or *the best idea*. All successful teachers seem to make effective use of language that builds a very positive sense of the 'good' of some course of action taken with respect to the instructional field. The geography teacher in Chapter 5, for example, said at one stage of pieces of work he had received on Kakadu National Park that:

> *those that I have handed in have ranged from great down to very good. We've had no duds yet,*

though, perhaps contradictorily, he went on a few seconds later to say:

> *but we probably haven't had enough, you know, really good quality.*

Thus far, I have addressed matters of the two registers – the regulative and instructional – by reference to classroom texts of the upper primary and secondary school years. I want now to turn to the realization of these in the early childhood years of schooling. I have already noted above that the regulative register is realized rather differently in the early childhood years from the later years of schooling with respect to its role in constructing acceptably 'good' behaviours for the purposes of schooling. What now can we say of the relationship of the two registers in the second of the two senses I have related – that to do with the 'delocation', 'relocation' and transmission of instructional fields?

In some ways the issues are different in the early years of schooling. This is partly because, as already noted, a great deal of effort goes into developing students who are socialized into some of the expected behavioural patterns of school life, and partly because young children simply know less than do older students, so that the manner of their being taught as well as what they learn, are rather different. Yet in other ways the general principles that apply should be seen as very similar. The goals with respect to the regulative register will be to do with transmission to the pedagogic subjects of skills, habits and ways of dealing with experience, where these must be selected and given substance through engagement with instructional fields of some kind. As I argued in Chapter 2, what has complicated the practices and procedures of early childhood education for some time has been the adoption of certain ideological positions which have had less than satisfactory results for education. Such ideological positions, on the one hand, have tended to place a particular premium on children's 'own experience' as a basis for school activity, and on the other hand, have tended to promote a model of the person developed in education in the 'competence' terms I alluded to in Chapter 2. In both senses, the issue of what constitutes a pedagogically productive instructional field has been given a diminished status.

To take the former of these, it is clear that children's experiences are a necessary, but in themselves insufficient, basis for teaching and learning. Whatever the principles that apply in selecting fields of knowledge for working with in schools for any age group, they will, I would argue, need to be selected for the potential they offer in developing students in both intellectual and imaginative senses: they will, in other words, provide opportunity to engage with significant knowledge. The educational practices of valorizing individual experiences in schools – sometimes also referred to as their 'personal voices' – are analogous to (and historically also related to) the practices of valorizing 'voice' in various approaches to the sociology of education critiqued by Moore and Muller (1999). They argue that those who promote the claims of various 'voices' in sociology of education, taking issue with what they see as certain dominant knowledge forms, often function in very anti-intellectual ways. This is because the very bases on which they launch their critiques of dominant forms of knowledge are primarily built on a position defined in terms of being marginalized and/ or subordinated to the dominant position (which is, in any case, often misrepresented). No substantial assessment of the knowledge claims of the dominant position tends to be offered, and this is explained, even justified, in terms of the values held to attach equally to all forms of knowledge and/

or all voices. Yet, as Moore and Muller also argue, not all forms of knowledge are of equal value:

> Although it is true that we do not know or agree about exactly how it is that some explanations are better than others or how we know this, the one thing we know beyond serious doubt is that all explanations are *not* equal. (Moore and Muller, 1999: 198; their italics)

A sociology of education which gives an apparent equality of status to all forms of knowledge, normally referred to as 'experience' (Moore and Muller, ibid: 201), regards all perspectives as privileged. Yet this is to trivialize, not least because such positions effectively escape the need to develop a rigorous language of their own in development of their theory. At best such positions can only describe and re-present the various persons and relationships they valorize: they have no language and no theoretical base with which to do more.

The arguments for personal voice and for expression of personal experience have had considerable impact in curriculum theory and educational practices in the Anglo-Australian traditions over the last forty years or so, though at the time of writing this book there was evidence that a challenge of sorts had been offered, at least through the emergence of such things as the National Curriculum in England; about this I shall have a little more to say below. Yet the challenge has been at best ambiguous, while the impact of 'personal voice' and 'self-expression' remains quite strong, at least in a great deal of educational theorizing. Such classroom practices as morning news are not unique in their significance as activities in which the personally self-expressive is apparently privileged, often in unhelpful ways.

It will be recalled that in Chapters 2 and 3 I argued of both the morning news activity and the early writing activity that in rather different ways these two left issues of the significance of 'content' or instructional field poorly articulated. This is an inevitable consequence of a curriculum theory that extols the virtues of children's selections of fields for talking or writing about. The justification for the morning news activity is that it is said to allow the news giver an opportunity to select and talk about an aspect of personal experience. While ostensibly the news giver enjoys a reasonably free hand in selecting the field, in practice some fields are more privileged than others. Moreover, since the field selection is to be made by the child, the teacher, who necessarily has normally not been part of an activity undertaken outside school time, is often handicapped in helping students who experience difficulty in either selecting a possible field or, on occasion, having chosen one, in sustaining its construction.

The issue of developing young children able to talk about experience is indeed an important one educationally. However, a more desirable and productive course of action will be one in which a field of activity is chosen both for its educative value and because it permits development of shared classroom work. Where this occurs, the teacher can draw students into joint participation in talking about and reconstructing class activities. Opportunity can also be made for individuals to talk about such experience, and also to embellish and extend it. Gray (2000), to whose work with Australian Aboriginal children I referred in Chapter 2, has demonstrated how shared experience of an instructional field can be used to model and practise talking about it, while also using the shared activity and talk to provide a basis for movement into new areas of activity and knowledge. Where such principles apply, it will be apparent that it is the teacher who exercises authority over selection of the instructional field, though this does not preclude consultation with the students about such selection. Moreover, where the selection of the field for talk is constrained or framed in this sense, it will normally have been chosen as part of a larger unity of field information or knowledge, constituting a more substantial part of the curriculum, and allowing more than the 'one-off' presentations that so much morning news work represents.

For example, one unit of work undertaken some years ago with young Aboriginal children at a school in Australia (Gray, 1985) involved a study of the post office and its role and functions.[1] A class visit to the post office (including going behind the scenes and meeting the postal workers) led to several subsequent classroom activities, some of which included such oral activities as talking about the functions of the post office as well as role playing running a post office. There were in addition reading activities about post offices and joint writing about the post office and its functions. The talk thus drew upon shared activity, was informed by reading about post offices in selected books, and led to some joint writing. In this sense the talk was embedded in an engagement with a broader instructional field than the average morning news session allows, one which permitted exploration of an important social institution and its role. The talk was also part of a unit of work – a curriculum macrogenre in fact – in which learning activities were developed, revisited and sustained over time (some weeks in fact), allowing the kind of development in learning which I have termed 'incremental'. This is to provide a very different educational experience from the kind provided in morning news, for example.

To turn to the matters raised in Chapter 3 regarding early writing, it will be recalled that I argued there the need for an approach to teaching writing which brings about a better alignment of regulative and instructional registers. In other words, the regulative register did not successfully appropriate the instructional register. As a result, the guidance to the students about *what to write* (the story genre required) and *what to write about* (the instructional field to do with one's lost lunch) was rather poorly focused. The regulative and instructional registers were brought together in teacher talk in ways that broadly alluded to *reading* or *thinking about* the task with respect to the instructional field:

> *. . .when we finish reading this story, something's going to happen to your lunch today, or we're going to pretend that it does,*

and later:

> *Now what I want you people <u>to think</u> about is something coming along and taking your lunch, or something happening to your lunch so that you couldn't eat it.*

Moreover, though some effort went into constructing possible sequences of events of the instructional field for writing:

> T: *What happened, Jodie, when you had no lunch to eat?*
> Jodie: *Mum didn't bring it up. She left it at home.*
> T: *Left your lunch at home on the bench, and her mum didn't bring it to school, and she had no lunch. And what happened?*
> Jodie: *Found no lunch.*

and later:

> T: *... Emily? What happened yesterday?*
> Emily: *My sister left hers on the dressing table...*
> T: *And what happened when she found that she had no lunch? Was she happy? What was happening to her?*
> Emily: *She was crying,*

the two registers were not brought together in the sense that the regulative register could appropriate or speak through the instructional register. Without such appropriation, as I have already suggested, students are left with insufficient direction and advice about the task of writing ahead.

Having stated this, I should acknowledge that the teacher in the classroom concerned was a conscientious person who would not have seen the matters in these terms. For her, given the general models of pedagogy and of curriculum design with which she worked, the fact of the children's writing at all was in itself sufficient. My interest – as I hope I have already made clear in Chapters 2 and 3 – is not gratuitously to criticize teachers who were generous enough to allow me into their classrooms. My object is, however, to consider and critique approaches of the kind adopted by the teacher in Chapter 3 (which were in no sense her own invention, by the way, but part of the pedagogical principles she had been offered in her own training), and, in the light of the theoretical position developed in this book, to examine the consequences of a pedagogy such as hers. I have used the notions of a pedagogic discourse and the two registers in order to uncover the sources of what I would claim are the limitations in the pedagogical approach. As I have argued at some length in this book, a successful instance of a classroom discourse will be one in which the regulative register appropriates and speaks through the instructional register, functioning in such a way that a form of 'regulation' occurs, in the sense that Bernstein intended. Such regulation, working through the authority which is invested in the regulative register, operates to position pedagogic subjects to address questions and/or to reason in particular ways, or to adopt certain values and/or habits of working. Had these matters been much clearer in the early childhood writing classroom we have considered, the students would have been positioned the better to understand the text structure for writing, while the field for writing about would have been more fully developed. Such an approach would produce a very different pedagogic discourse and a very different early childhood classroom activity from that which we have considered. One of the very important differences would have been that the classroom activity was not conceived as a 'one-off' activity, but part of some larger unity of the kind that characterizes a curriculum macrogenre. This brings me back to considerations of 'competence' in educational theorizing: I suggested above that promotion of 'competence' in the particular terms discussed by Bernstein was, together with notions of 'personal experience' involved in the ideologies of early childhood education which gave a limited status to selection of instructional fields of teaching and learning. 'Competence' models of the pedagogic subject are in marked contrast to what I shall term 'developmental' models of the pedagogic subject. As Bernstein discusses the matter, 'competence' models are in contrast with 'performance' models. While the developmental model I propose is not to be confused with the performance model, the two are nonetheless related, a matter to which I shall return below.

A developmental model of the pedagogic subject

In Chapters 2 and 3 I referred to notions of 'competence' in education, following discussions of Bernstein. Such notions, he suggested (2000: 41–66), achieved some power and significance in educational theorizing over the last 30 to 40 years of the twentieth century. They were associated with various progressivist models of education which had important influences on curriculum theory and its implementation in both England and Australia. It will be recalled that I discussed several characteristics of 'competence' models in education as Bernstein identified them, including the ideas: that 'competence' is in some sense available to all; that all operate creatively in constructing meanings and practices, where the latter seem to be held as equally valid, and that 'difference' rather than 'deficit' explains variation in acquisition of competence; that the individual achieving competence is self-regulating, and that formal instruction is given a reduced significance; relatedly, that hierarchical relations are viewed sceptically and that the function of the teacher is that of 'facilitation, accommodation and context management'; and finally that a perspective is adopted which focuses on the immediate or the present, such that 'the relevant time arises out of the point of realisation of the competence, for it is this point which reveals the past and adumbrates the future' (Bernstein, 2000: 43). (See Muller, 2000: 102–9 for a related discussion of Bernstein's notions of 'competence' and 'performance'.)

All these characteristics, I would argue, are features of the model of the young learner in curriculum genres of the kind discussed in Chapters 2 and 3, though it is clear that such models have had considerable impact in curriculum activity well beyond the early years, extending up into the secondary school years. One area of the curriculum particularly affected by competence models has been subject English. Here the Australian experience from the 1970s on is relevant, borrowing as it did quite extensively from theory and practices in England. Thus, for example, a review of all English curriculum documents from all states in Australia in the early 1970s (Christie and Rothery, 1979) revealed that they specifically proclaimed the virtues of fostering 'listening, speaking, reading and writing skills' (sometimes also referred to as 'modes') as ends in themselves, rather than as skills or abilities instrumental to more comprehensively defined ends. Yet the issue should always be: listening, speaking, reading and writing about what, to whom, and what for? The preoccupation with development of competence by promoting facility in the four language modes led to statements of English curriculum which were largely free of any considerations of 'content' or knowledge, for 'experience' was the focus of concern. This led Britton and Squires, for example, to write of the content' of English that it was nothing less than 'the sum total of the planned and unplanned experiences through language by means of which a child gains control of himself and of his relations with the surrounding world' (Britton and Squires, in Dixon, 1975: xviii) There can be few less helpful statements about the content of English than this. At the very least, it leaves the teacher without any guidance concerning goals and directions for teaching their subject. At its worst, such a view of English has denied the values of any teaching of knowledge about language, on the grounds that this somehow compromised or impeded the capacity of the young to express their opinions and ideas about life 'in their own way'. Notions of the values of 'self-expression' 'creativity' and 'authorship' have often led to very diffuse and unfocused activities in English teaching (see, for example, discussions in Gilbert, 1990, Cranny-Francis 1996, Rothery, 1996 and Christie, 1999), and an associated tendency to deny the value of teaching and learning any technical language about English as an important part of the instructional field of the subject.

At the time of writing this book, it was apparent that some reassessment of the teaching of English had begun to take place. In England, for example, in a remarkable manner, given what had been older historical precedent in that country, a *National English Curriculum* had been adopted, which went through a series of changes and amendments in the early 1990s; the last version of this at the time of writing this book, called *English: the National Curriculum for England*, was dated 1999. In Australia from the early 1990s there had also been a move towards adoption of a *Statement on English for Australian Schools* (1994) and an associated statement called *English: a Curriculum Profile for Australian Schools* (1994). The various Australian states all more or less adopted the National English curriculum, most, however, producing adaptations for their own jurisdictions, many of which were variously amended after 1994: this tendency to produce state variants reflects the federal structure by which education remains a state responsibility. In their rather different ways, both the English and the Australian curriculum statements attempt to define areas of knowledge for teaching and they represent a considerable advance on earlier curriculum statements. In the English context, the new curriculum has been implemented as part of a wider enterprise in national curriculum design which is committed to a regular testing regime that is excessive and in many senses anti-educational. As for Australia, it too has adopted a national testing regime. It may be that the testing regime is potentially less constraining in Australia than is true in England, because the tests are administered at the state rather than the federal level.

These developments noted, the body of knowledge that is English often remains poorly defined, at least as that is expressed in the curriculum statements, which are at best general, and often rather vague. What were once well-established concerns of rhetoric and of grammar still receive very limited expression, while the grammatical features of literacy, as distinct from those of speech, are poorly understood and rarely articulated in curriculum advice. (See Christie, 1993, for some discussion of these matters. Another work, Christie, forthcoming, will consider these matters in some detail.)

Other areas of the school curriculum apart from English which have felt the impact of various progressivist competence models have include the social science curriculum (Cope and Kalantzis, 1990) and the science curriculum (Martin, 1990). Reviewing developments in the curricula of the school social sciences, Cope and Kalantzis (ibid.) discussed the emergence of so-called 'inquiry methods' of learning social knowledge, whether in geography, history or the subject called 'social studies'. Such methods, they noted, were intended to move away from the 'facts' of earlier models of social curriculum and to concentrate instead on the 'processes' by which students engaged with and found out about social science. The arguments for such methods they said were at best superficially attractive and at worst harmful, for several reasons. Thus, the arguments denied the particular skills in researching and amassing information that are required in any of the social sciences. Furthermore, because they attached importance to 'self-discovery', inquiry methods failed to teach students the methods of analysis, argument and description that were encoded in language (literacy in particular) and which are characteristic of the various subjects. Finally, I would add, inquiry methods also failed because they denied the need for the presence of a mentor (the teacher) who can guide and teach for mastery of these matters. Wignell (1994) has considered the patterns of written language in a range of school subjects, including history as an example of the humanities and technical subjects such as metalwork, showing the specialist range of genres involved in each, and the need for some systematic teaching of these. Coffin (1997; 2000) has investigated the various patterns of literacy needed in order to achieve skill and facility in the study of school history. Coffin has documented how the earliest genres students need to write are historical recounts, encoding reasonably simple retelling of researched historical information. Subsequent developmental stages will – or should – take students through a series of steps, in which, with growing maturity, they learn other historical genres, each building in greater explanatory, causal, interpretive and argumentative power. These things are not 'discovered' by any individual, but rather learned as part of the developmental processes of becoming pedagogic subjects for the purposes of history.

In the case of school science, Martin (1990) some years ago wrote a critique of approaches to its teaching, examining the tendency in at least some school science curricula to favour the writing of narratives, 'personal reports', even science fiction, over the writing of the genres which more accurately and usefully express scientific knowledge: procedures, taxonomic reports, explanations and so on. Halliday and Martin (1993) have written a work devoted both to the emergence of scientific language and to a consideration of those kinds of reasoning which are realized in its discourse patterns. Scientific knowledge is not 'commonsense', but esoteric, and its learning involves entering into its ways of reasoning, analysis and description. Veel (1997) has documented the forms of literacy required for successful mastery of scientific knowledge.

Turning to another area of schooling, namely that of mathematics, Muller (2000: 57–74) offers a related discussion of what he identifies as 'constructivist' approaches to the teaching of mathematics, as these have been pursued in South Africa (though they have been influential in other parts of the English-speaking world). Such approaches, he states, have sought to identify a mathematics close to the lived experience of the poor and the disadvantaged, and have been intended to address the needs of students who often do very badly in school mathematics. But they often fail, he argues, because they are naive about the 'definite limit to the usefulness of everyday knowledge in inducting learners into school mathematics' (Muller, ibid: 71). Mathematical knowledge, like that of science, is esoteric in that it has a logic of its own, requiring effort in its learning

A serious attempt to engage with questions of what constitutes useful knowledge for school learning necessarily takes one into thinking about curriculum practice and pedagogy in 'non-competence' ways. Sustained learning that engages seriously with 'uncommonsense knowledge' requires the investment of effort over time. It requires what I have termed 'a developmental history', where that will be marked in the classroom discourse by any of a number of possible forms of logogenesis: that is to say, as the classroom text unfolds successfully over time, it will reveal shifts and some kind of developmental progress in the language uses where the instructional register is appropriated by the regulative register, and where the pedagogic subjects adopt the appropriate technical language and the patterns of reasoning encoded in it.

Schools are sites for initiation and induction into ways of knowing, ways of valuing, ways of reasoning. A fundamental responsibility of the teaching relationship is that the young are *taught*, so that they may enter with some confidence into the world beyond school, possessed of at least some sense of the major bodies of knowledge that shape their societies and the wider global community of which they are a part. I use the term the term 'major bodies of knowledge' deliberately, mindful that for some the notion of definitive areas of knowledge has an old-fashioned, even conservative ring. Over the years of working in faculties of education I have heard some colleagues adopt one of two possible positions in order to diminish the claims of any 'bodies of knowledge'. The first of the positions is of the kind I have discussed above, and which has been variously expressed in terms of the values of promoting 'competences' (in the decontextualized sense to which Bernstein alluded), or 'discovery' or 'inquiry' learning; in this view the desired learning of value focuses on what the child discovers himself/herself, and the notion of definitive areas of knowledge is anathema (the Plowden Report, referred to in Chapter 2 endorsed such a view). The other position sometimes proposed is that knowledge grows and changes so rapidly that it is out of date by the time the child leaves school; hence, rather than be too preoccupied with passing on knowledge that is potentially dated, so it is said, it is better to develop learners who have the skills to learn. This latter argument it turns out, is not very different from the former one, though it is expressed in different terms. It still proposes a notion of the decontextualized individual, acquiring skills or competences in ways incidental to material and social circumstances and the sets of issues they are to address as part of the educational process. Neither position is adequate, and in fact as Moore and Muller (1999) suggest, not only are such positions anti-intellectual, they are also dishonest.

They are anti-intellectual because, as I have now suggested more than once, they deny the ways in which significant areas of knowledge are built up, developing and pursuing their own logic, their own 'reflexivity' to use a term take from Muller (2000: 2). Both positions I have alluded to are dishonest because even though they deny the claims of established areas of knowledge, in the absence of any criteria for judging and evaluating students' performance, they fall back on criteria taken from the very knowledge they purport to reject. Thus, for example, the secondary English classrooms that follow the growth and 'self-expressive' proposals to which I alluded earlier, purport to reject what might be termed 'mainstream' argumentative essay genres. However, close inspection reveals that such classrooms actually reward those students who adopt fairly orthodox genres – argumentative essays in particular – rather than other 'self-expressive' genres (Christie, 1999; Rothery and Macken, 1991). Moreover, since the teachers in such classrooms neglect to teach the argumentative genres on the grounds that these 'constrain' individual self-expression, it is always the students of privilege – those who are equipped by life circumstance and opportunity – who deduce the desired essay genre, while it is the less privileged, without access to such circumstance and opportunity, who do not.

All bodies of knowledge – or instructional fields – are socially constructed, and they are therefore open to refutation and challenge. They certainly also change over time. However, the more explicitly any areas of knowledge in any period of intellectual history are stated, and the more the bases for their claims to truth laid bare, then the more they are potentially open to discussion and to challenge. These conditions are the most reliable we have in considering the quite awesome areas of knowledge now available. The practices of schooling seek to take at least some of the various bodies of knowledge and 'relocate' them for the purposes of teaching and learning. It is not helpful to require students to deduce some fundamental principles that lie behind the various areas of school knowledge by obliging them to engage in self-expressive and/or inquiry learning, or to rely on their own 'commonsense experience'. Better by far, as I have argued here, to be overt and as far as possible explicit about the various bodies of knowledge to be taught, their methods of constructing information, their procedures for representing what it is they have to say. Learning these matters will take some years of schooling, and some respect for the considerable challenges to learners in mastering what it is the bodies of knowledge have to offer, as well as mastering how to critique them. As Macken-Horarik (1998) among others, has shown, critique and critical capacity in general depend upon a very well-developed ability to comprehend and interpret the very positions that will become the foci of the critique.

In writing this book I have sought to demonstrate how a discourse analysis of the kind provided by the systemic functional grammar permits some analysis and interpretation of patterns of classroom language as they function variously to position both teacher (or agent of symbolic control) and student (or pedagogic subject). Through developing such an analysis, I have also sought to argue the values of a pedagogy that draws on principles of strong classification and strong framing. It may well be the case as Bernstein (1970) once wrote in a famous paper that 'education cannot compensate for society'. But that does not mean that education can do nothing. On the contrary, let us assert the claims of an education that values knowledge and that values the learner, by seeking to make available to learners as explicitly and unambiguously as possible significant and useful information and ideas. And let us recognize and accept that what constitutes significant and useful information or knowledge is itself a volatile and shifting matter which is quite properly open to constant debate and discussion. Indeed, the various sites – still mainly universities – in which new knowledge is generated, are by their nature unstable, leading to new areas of knowledge or at least to re-definitions of existing knowledge. What constitutes valid knowledge to 'relocate' for the purposes of school learning will always be a matter for discussion. Yet the broad steps for effecting a successful 'relocation' of knowledge should always apply: such knowledge should be comprehended and taught for its value in providing entry to a principled set of understandings, having a logic, a methodology and procedures which can be made known to, and be discussed by, the learners. And finally, in the twenty-first-century world of multi-literacies, let us value the patterns of language, both spoken and written, in which these things are realized.

Note

1. The children at the time lived in bush camps on the fringe of the Australian town of Alice Springs, and the post office was well outside their immediate community experience.

References

Adendorff, R. (1999), 'A critical microethnographic investigation of the role of news time in the acquisition of literacy in pre-democratic South Africa', unpub. PhD thesis, University of Natal, Durban.

Aidman, M. (1999), 'Biliteracy development through early and mid-primary years. A longitudinal case study of bilingual writing', unpub. PhD thesis, University of Melbourne.

Arkoudis, S. (2001), 'The epistemological authority of an ESL teacher in science education', unpub. PhD thesis, University of Melbourne.

'A Statement on English for Australian Schools' (1994), A Joint Project of the States, Territories and the Commonwealth of Australia initiated by the Australian Education Council. Melbourne: Curriculum Corporation.

Baker, P. and Perrott, C. (1988), 'The news session in the infants and primary school classroom', *British Journal of Sociology of Education*, 9(1), 18–37.

Barnes, D. (1978), 'The study of classroom communication in teacher education', in M. Gill and W.J. Crockers (eds), *English in Teacher Education*. Armidale, NSW: University of New England, 85–94.

Barnes, D., Britton, J. and Rosen, H. (rev. edn) (1971), *Language, the Learner and the School*. Harmondsworth: Penguin Books.

Barnes, D. and Todd, F. (1977), *Communication and Learning in Small Groups*. London: Routledge & Kegan Paul.

Bellack, A.A., Kliebard, H.M., Hyman, R.T. and Smith, F.L. (1966), *The Language of the Classroom*. New York: Teachers' College Press.

Benson, J.D. and Greaves, W.S. (1973), *The Language People Really Use*. Agincourt, Canada: The Book Society of Canada.

Bernstein, B. (1970), 'Education cannot compensate for society', *New Society*, 26 February, 344–7 (reprinted in A. Cashdan *et al.*, (eds), (1972), *Language in Education: A Source Book*. London and Boston, Routledge & Kegan Paul and the Open University Press, 213–18).

Bernstein, B. (1971), *Class, Codes and Control*, Vol. 1: *Theoretical Studies towards a Sociology of Language*. London: Routledge & Kegan Paul.

Bernstein, B. (ed.) (1973), *Class, Codes and Control*, Vol. 2: *Applied Studies towards a Sociology of Language*. London: Routledge & Kegan Paul.

Bernstein, B. (1974), *Class, Codes and Control: Theoretical Studies towards a Sociology of Language*, 2nd edn. London: Routledge & Kegan Paul.

Bernstein, B. (1990), *Class, Codes and Control*, Vol. 4: *The Structuring of Pedagogic Discourse*. London and New York: Routledge.

Bernstein, B. (1994), 'The Pedagogic Device', a paper delivered at the *21st International*

Systemic Functional Linguistics Association Congress, held at the University of Ghent, 1–5 August.

Bernstein, B. (1996), *Pedagogy, Symbolic Control, and Identity: Theory, Research, Critique* (*Critical Perspectives on Literacy and Education*, series editor: A. Luke). London and Bristol, PA: Taylor & Francis.

Bernstein, B. (1999), 'Pedagogy identity and the construction of a theory of symbolic control: Basil Bernstein interviewed by Joseph Solomon', *British Journal of Sociology of Education*, 20(2), 265–79 (also published in B. Bernstein (2000), *Pedagogy, Symbolic Control and Identity: Theory, Research*, rev. edn. London: Rowman & Littlefield.

Bernstein, B. (2000), *Pedagogy, Symbolic Control and Identity: Theory, Research, Critique*, rev. edn. London: Rowman & Littlefield Publishers.

Britton, J. and Squires, J. (1975), 'Foreword', in J. Dixon, *Growth through English*, 3rd edn. London: National Association for the Teaching of English and Oxford University Press, vii–xviii.

Brown, A. (1999), 'Parental participation, positioning and pedagogy: a sociological study of the IMPACT primary school mathematics project', unpub. PhD thesis, Institute of Education, University of London.

Bruner, J. (1983), *Child's Talk: Learning to Use Language*. Oxford: Oxford University Press.

Bruner, J. (1986), *Actual Minds, Possible Worlds*. Cambridge, MA, and London: Harvard University Press.

Bruner, J. (1990), *Acts of Meaning*. Cambridge, MA, and London: Harvard University Press.

Butt, D., Fahey, R., Feez, S., Spinks, S. and Yallop, C. (2000) *Using Functional Grammar: An Explorer's Guide*, 2nd edn. Sydney: National Centre for English Language Teaching and Research.

Cazden, C. (1986), 'Classroom discourse', in M.C. Wittrock (ed.), *Handbook of Research on Teaching: A Project of the American Educational Research Association*, 3rd edn. New York and London: Macmillan, 432–63.

Cazden, C. (1988), *Classroom Discourse: The Language of Teaching and Learning*. Portsmouth, NJ: Heinemann.

Chouliaraki, L. and Fairclough, N. (1999), *Discourse in Late Modernity: Rethinking Critical Discourse Analysis*. Edinburgh: Edinburgh University Press.

Christie, F. (1993), 'The "received tradition" of English teaching: the decline of rhetoric and the corruption of grammar', in B. Green (ed.), *The Insistence of the Letter: Literacy Studies and Curriculum Theorising* (Critical Perspectives on Literacy and Education, Series Editor: A. Luke). London and Washington, DC: Falmer Press, 75–106.

Christie, F. (1997), 'Curriculum macrogenres as forms of initiation into a culture', in F. Christie and J.R. Martin (eds), *Genre and Institutions: Social Processes in the Workplace and School*. London: Cassell Academic, 134–60.

Christie, F. (1998), 'Learning the literacies of primary and secondary schooling', in F. Christie and R. Misson, *Literacy and Schooling*. London and New York: Routledge, 47–73.

Christie, F. (1999a), 'The pedagogic device and the teaching of English', in F. Christie (ed.), *Pedagogy and the Shaping of Consciousness: Linguistic and Social Processes*. London and New York: Cassell, 156–84.

Christie, F. (ed.) (1999b), *Pedagogy and the Shaping of Consciousness: Linguistic and Social Processes*. London and New York: Cassell.

Christie, F. (2000a), 'The changing face(s) of literacy', in A. Brown (ed.), *English in*

South East Asia. Proceedings of the *Fourth English in Southeast Asia Conference*, held National Institute of Education, Singapore, 22–24 November 1999. Singapore: National Institute of Education, 1–20.

Christie, F. (2000b),'Pedagogic discourse in the post-compulsory years: pedagogic subject positioning', *Linguistics and Education*, 11(4), 313–32 (also published in J. Cumming and C. Wyatt-Smith (eds) (2001), *Literacy and the Curriculum: Success in Senior Secondary Schooling*. Melbourne: Australian Council for Educational Research, 94–103).

Christie, F. (2002), 'The development of abstraction in adolescence in subject English', in M. Schleppegrell and C. Colombi (eds), *Developing Advanced Literacy in First and Second Languages: Meaning with Power*. Hillsdale, NJ: Lawrence Erlbaum, 45–66.

Christie, F., Gray, P., Gray, B., Macken, M., Martin, J.R. and Rothery, J.
(1990a), *Exploring Procedures*, Student Books 1–4 and Teachers' Book.
(1990b), *Exploring Reports*, Student Books 1–4 and Teachers' Book.
(1990c), *Exploring Explanations*, Student Books 1–4 and Teachers' Book. Sydney: Harcourt Brace Jovanovich.

Christie, F. and Martin, J.R. (eds) (1997), *Genre and Institutions: Social Processes in the Workplace and School*. London and Washington, DC: Cassell.

Christie, F. and Misson, R. (1998), *Literacy and Schooling*. London and New York: Routledge.

Christie, F. and Rothery, J. (1979), 'English in Australia: an interpretation of role in the curriculum', in J. Maling-Keepes and B.D. Keeps (eds), *Language in Education: The Language Development Project Phase 1*. Canberra: Curriculum Development Centre, 208–42.

Christie, F. and Soosai, A. (2001), *Language and Meaning 2*. Melbourne: Macmillan Education.

Cope, B. and Kalantzis, M. (1990) 'Literacy in the social sciences', in F. Christie (ed.), *Literacy for a Changing World*. Melbourne: Australian Council for Educational Research, 118–42.

Cope, B. and Kalantzis, M. (eds) (1993), *The Powers of Literacy: A Genre Approach to Teaching Writing* (Critical Perspectives on Literacy and Education, Series Editor: Allan Luke). London: Falmer Press.

Cope, B. and Kalantzis, M. (eds) (2000), *Multiliteracies: Literacy Learning and the Design of Social Futures*. Melbourne, Victoria: Macmillan.

Crabb, P. (1995), ' "Les professeurs de géographie savent ou ils vont." Or do they?', *Geographical Education*, 8(3), 9–11.

Cranny-Francis, A. (1998), 'Technology and/or weapon: the discipline of reading in the secondary English classroom', in R. Hasan and G. Williams (eds), *Literacy in Society* (Applied Linguistics and Language Study series, Series Ed.: C. Candlin). London and New York: Addison Wesley Longman, 172–90.

D'Andrade, R. (1987), ' A folk model of the mind', in D. Holland and N. Quinn (eds), *Cultural Models in Language and Thought*. Cambridge: Cambridge University Press, 112–50.

Daniels, H. (1995), ' Pedagogic practices, tacit knowledge and discursive discrimination: Bernstein and post-Vygotskian research', *British Journal of Sociology of Education*, 16(4), 517–32.

Delpit, L. (1995), *Other People's Children: Cultural Conflict in the Classroom*. New York: The New Press.

Derewianka, B. (1990), *Exploring How Texts Work*. Sydney: Primary English Teachers' Association.

Derewianka, B. (1995), 'Language development in the transition from childhood to adolescence: the role of grammatical metaphor', unpub. PhD thesis, Macquarie University, 112–50.

Dixon, J. (1975) *Growth through English*, 3rd edn, London: National Association for the Teaching of English/Oxford University Press.

Edwards, A.D. and Westgate, D.P.G. (1994) *Investigating Classroom Talk*, rev. edn, London and Washington, DC: Falmer Press.

Eggins, S. (1994), *An Introduction to Systemic Functional Linguistics*. London: Pinter.

Eggins, S. and Slade, D. (1997), *Analysing Casual Conversation*. London and Washington, DC: Cassell.

'English: a Curriculum Profile for Australian Schools' (1994). A Joint Project of the States, Territories and the Commonwealth of Australia, initiated by the Australian Education Council. Melbourne: Curriculum Corporation.

'English. The National Curriculum for England. Key Stages 1–4' (1994). London: Department for Education and Employment and Qualifications and Curriculum Authority.

Fairclough, N. (1992a) *Discourse and Social Change*. Oxford: Polity Press.

Fairclough, N. (ed.) (1992b), *Critical Language Awareness* (Real Language Series, eds: J. Coates and J. Cheshire). London and New York: Longman.

Fawcett, R. (1980), *Cognitive Linguistics and Social Interaction: Towards an Integrated Model of Systemic Functional Grammar and the Other Components of an Interacting Mind*. Exeter: Exeter University Press.

Flanders, N.A. (1970), *Analysing Teaching Behaviour*. Reading, MA.: Addison-Wesley.

Freedman, A. and Medway, P. (1994), *Genre and the New Rhetoric* (Critical Perspectives on Literacy and Education, Series Editor: Allan Luke). London: Taylor & Francis.

Fries, P. and Gregory, M. (eds) (1995), *Discourse in Society. Systemic Functional Perspectives. Meaning and Choice in Language: Studies for Michael Halliday* (Volume 50 in the Advances in Discourse Processes Series. Editor: R.O. Freedle). Norwood, NJ: Ablex.

Gee, J.P. (1992), *The Social Mind: Language, Ideology and Social Practice* (Series in Language and Ideology, Series Editor: D. Macedo). New York: Bergin & Garvey.

Gee, J.P. (1999), *An Introduction to Discourse Analysis: Theory and Method*. London and New York: Routledge.

Gilbert, P. (1990), 'Authorising disadvantage: authorship and creativity in the language classroom', in F. Christie (ed.) (1990), *Literacy for a Changing World*. Melbourne: Australian Council for Educational Research, 54–78.

Gilbert, R. (1989), 'Language and ideology in geography teaching', in F. Slater (ed.), *Language and Learning in the Teaching of Geography*. London: Routledge, 151–61.

Goffman, E. (1981), *Forms of Talk*. Oxford: Blackwell.

Gray, B. (1985), 'Helping children to become language learners in the classroom', in M. Christie (ed.), *Aboriginal Perspectives on Experience and Learning: The Role of Language in Aboriginal Education*. Geelong, Victoria: Deakin University Press, 48–75.

Gray, B. (2000), 'Accessing the discourses of schooling. English language and literacy development with Aboriginal children in mainstream schools', unpub. PhD thesis, University of Melbourne.

Green, J. and Dixon, C. (eds) (1993), 'Special Issue: Santa Barbara Classroom Discourse Group', special edition of *Linguistics and Education*, 5, 3 & 4.

Green, J. and Kantor-Smith, R. M. (1988), 'Exploring the complexity of language and learning in the life of the classroom', a paper given at the Post World Reading Congress Symposium on Language in Learning. University of Queensland, Brisbane, 10–15 July 1988.

Green, J. and Wallat, C. (1981), *Ethnography and Language in Educational Settings*, Advances in Discourse Processes Series, Editor: R.O. Freedle). Norwood, NJ: Ablex.

Gregory, M. and Carroll, S. (1978), *Language and Situation: Language Varieties and Their Social Contexts*. London: Routledge & Kegan Paul.

Gumperz, J.J. and Hymes, D. (eds) (1972), *Directions in Sociolinguistics*. New York: Holt, Rinehart & Winston.

Halliday, M.A.K. (1961), 'Categories of the theory of grammar', *Word 17*, 241–92.

Halliday, M.A.K. (1974), 'Discussing language', in H. Parret (1974), *Discussing Language: Dialogues with Chafe, Chomsky, Greimas, Halliday, Hartmann, Lakoff, Lamb, Martinet, McCawley, Saumjan and Bouversse*. The Hague: Mouton, 81–120.

Halliday, M.A.K. (1976) (ed. G.R. Kress), *Halliday: System and Function in Language. Selected Papers*. London: Oxford University Press.

Halliday, M.A.K. (1978), *Language as Social Semiotic: The Social Interpretation of Language and Meaning*. London: Arnold.

Halliday, M.A.K. (1979), 'Models of meaning and modes of expression: types of grammatical structure, and their determination by different semantic functions', in D.J. Allerton, Edward Carney and David Holcroft (eds), *Function and Context in Linguistic Analysis: Essays Offered to William Haas*. Cambridge: Cambridge University Press, 57–79.

Halliday, M.A.K. (1982), 'How is a text like a clause?', in Sture Allen (ed.), *Text Processing: Text Analysis and Generation, Text Typology and Attribution*. Proceedings of Nobel Symposium, 91. Stockholm: Almqvist & Wiksell International, 209–47.

Halliday, M.A.K. (1985), *Spoken and Written Language*. Geelong, Victoria: Deakin University Press.

Halliday, M.A.K. (1994) *An Introduction to Functional Grammar*, 2nd edn. London: Arnold.

Halliday, M.A.K. and Hasan, R. (1985), *Language, Context and Text: Aspects of Language in a Social-Semiotic Perspective*. Geelong, Victoria: Deakin University Press.

Halliday, M.A.K. and Martin, J.R. (1993), *Writing Science: Literacy and Discursive Power* (Critical Perspectives on Literacy and Education, Series Editor: A. Luke). London and Washington, DC: Falmer Press.

Halliday, M.A.K. and Matthiessen, C.M.I.M. (1999), *Construing Experience through Meaning: A Language-based Approach to Cognition*. London and New York: Cassell Academic.

Hasan, R. (1980), 'What's going on? A dynamic view of language', in J.E. Copeland and P.W. Davis (eds), *The Seventh LACUS Forum*. Columbia, NY: Hornbeam Press, 106–21 (reprinted in C. Cloran, D. Butt and G. Williams (eds) (1996), *Ways of Saying: Ways of Meaning*. London: Cassell, 37–50).

Hasan, R. (1984), 'The nursery rhyme as a genre', in Nottingham Linguistics Circular 13, 71–102 (reprinted in a revised version in C. Cloran, D. Butt and G. Williams (eds) (1996), *Ways of Saying: Ways of Meaning*. London: Cassell, 51–72).

Hasan, R. (1989), 'Semantic variation and sociolinguistics', *Australian Journal of Linguistics*, 9, 221–75.

Hasan, R. (1995), 'The conception of context in text', in B. Fries and M. Gregory (eds) (1995), *Discourse in Society. Systemic Functional Perspectives. Meaning and Choice in Language: Studies for Michael Halliday*. (Advances in Discourse Processes Series, Editor: R.O. Freedle.) Norwood, NJ: Ablex, 183–283.

Hasan, R. (1996) (ed. C. Cloran, D.Butt and G. Williams), *Ways of Saying: Ways of Meaning*. London and New York: Cassell.

Hasan, R. and Martin, J.R. (1989), *Language Development: Learning Language, Learning Culture. Meaning and Choice in Language: Studies for Michael Halliday.* (Advances in Discourse Processes Series, Editor: R.O. Freedle). Norwood, NJ: Ablex.

Heath, S. Brice (1983), *Ways with Words.* New York: Cambridge University Press.

Hicks, D. (1995), 'Discourse, learning and teaching', *Review of Research in Education* 21, 1995/1996. Washington: American Educational Research Association, 49–95.

Hymes, D. (1977), *Foundations in Sociolinguistics: An Ethnographic Approach.* London: Tavistock.

Iedema, R. (1994), *The Language of Administration: A Detailed Description of the Literacy Demands of Administration and Bureaucracy,* a Report of the *Write It Right* Project. Sydney: Disadvantaged Schools Programme.

Iedema, R. (1997), 'The language of administration: organizing human activity in formal institutions', in F. Christie and J. R. Martin (eds), *Genre and Institutions: Social Processes in the Workplace and School.* London and Washington, DC: Cassell, 73–100.

Kress, G. (2000), 'Multimodality', in B. Cope and M. Kalantzis (eds), *Multiliteracies: Literacy Learning and the Design of Social Futures.* South Yarra, Australia: Macmillan, 182–202.

Labov, W. and Waletzky, J. (1967), 'Narrative analysis: oral versions of personal experience', in J. Helm (ed.), *Essays on the Verbal and Visual Arts: Proceedings of the 1966 Annual Spring Meeting of the Ethnological Society.* Seattle: University of Washington Press, 12–44.

Lee, A. (1996), *Gender, Literacy, Curriculum: Re-writing School Geography* (Critical Perspectives on Literacy and Education, Series Editor: A. Luke). London: Taylor & Francis.

Lemke, J. L. (1985), *Using Language in the Classroom.* Geelong, Victoria: Deakin University Press.

Lemke, J.L. (1995), *Textual Politics: Discourse and Social Dynamics* (Critical Perspectives on Literacy and Education, Series Editor: Allan Luke). London and Bristol, PA: Taylor & Francis.

Lemke, J. L. (1998), 'Analysing verbal data: principles, methods and problems', in K. Tobin and B. Fraser (eds), *International Handbook of Science Education.* London and Dordrecht: Academic Publishers, Part 2, 1175–90.

Love, K. (1999), 'The whole class text response discussion genre in secondary English: a case study', unpub. PhD thesis, University of Melbourne.

McDonald, G.T. (1995), 'Environment and society: future directions in geography', *Geographical Education,* 8 (3), 17–21.

Macken-Horarick, M. (1998), 'Exploring the requirements of critical school literacy: a view from two classrooms', in F. Christie and R. Misson (eds), *Literacy and Schooling.* London and New York: Routledge, 74–103.

Malinowski, B. (1923), 'The problem of meaning in primitive languages', Supplement 1 in C.K. Ogden and I.A. Richards (eds), *The Meaning of Meaning* (International Library of Philosophy, Psychology and Scientific Method). London: Kegan Paul.

Malinowski, B. (1935), *Coral Gardens and Their Magic,* Vol. 2. London: Allen & Unwin (reprinted as *The Language of Magic and Gardening.* Bloomington, IN: Indiana University Press in *The History and Theory of Linguistics* series).

Martin, J.R. (1985), *Factual Writing: Exploring and Challenging Social Reality.* Geelong, Victoria: Deakin University Press.

Martin, J. (1990), 'Literacy in science: learning to handle text as technology', in F. Christie (ed.), *Literacy for a Changing World.* Melbourne: Australian Council for Educational Research, 79–117.

Martin, J.R. (1992), *English Text: System and Structure*. Philadelphia, and Amsterdam: Benjamins.

Martin. J.R. (1994), 'Macrogenres: the ecology of the page', *Network*, 21, 21–52.

Martin, J.R. (1995), 'Text and clause: fractal resonance', *Text* 15.1, 5–42.

Martin, J.R. (1996), 'Types of structure: deconstructing notions of constituency in clause and text', in E. H. Hovy and D. R. Scott (eds), *Computational and Conversational Discourse: Burning Issues – an Interdisciplinary Account* (NATO Advanced Science Institute Series F – Computer and Systems Sciences, Vol. 151). Heidelberg: Springer, 39–66.

Martin, J.R. (1999), 'Mentoring semogenesis: 'genre-based' literacy pedagogy', in F. Christie (ed.), *Pedagogy and the Shaping of Consciousness: Linguistic and Social Processes*. London and New York: Cassell, 123–55.

Martin, J.R. and Rothery, J. (1980), *Writing Project Report, Number 1* (Working Papers in Linguistics, Number 1). Department of Linguistics, University of Sydney.

Martin, J.R. and Rothery, J. (1981), *Writing Project Report, Number 2*. (Working Papers in Linguistics, Number 2). Department of Linguistics, University of Sydney.

Matthiessen, C. (1988), 'Representational issues in systemic functional grammar', in J. Benson and W. Greaves (eds), *From Systemic Functional Approaches to Discourse: Selected Papers from the 12th International Systemic Workshop*. New York: Ablex, 136–75.

Matthiessen, C. (1992), 'Interpreting the textual metafunction', in M. Davis and L. Ravelli (eds), *Advances in Systemic Linguistics*. London and New York: Pinter Press, 37-81.

Matthiessen, C. (1995), *Lexicogrammatical Cartography: English Systems*. Tokyo: International Language Sciences Publishers.

Matthiessen, C. and Halliday, M.A.K. (1999), *Construing Experience through Meaning: A Language-based Approach to Cognition*. London and New York: Cassell.

Mehan, H. (1979), *Learning Lessons: Social Organization in the Classroom*. Cambridge, MA: Harvard University Press.

Mercer, N. (2000), 'Intermental zones and discourse zones: explaining how dialogue supports development', a plenary paper given at the Conference on *Scaffolding Language and Learning in Educational Contexts: Sociocultural Approaches to Theory and Practice*, held at the University of Technology, Sydney, 6–8 December 2000.

Michaels, S. (1986), 'Narrative presentations: an oral preparation for literacy with first graders', in J. Cook-Gumperz (ed.), *The Social Construction of Literacy*. Cambridge: Cambridge University Press, 95–116.

Moore, R. and Muller, J. (1999), 'The discourse of "voice" and the problem of knowledge and identity in the sociology of education', *British Journal of Sociology of Education*, 20(2), 189–206.

Muller, J. (2000), *Reclaiming Knowledge: Social Theory, Curriculum and Education Policy* (Knowledge, Identity and School Life Series, Series eds: P. Wexler and I. Goodson). London and New York: Routledge/Falmer.

Perera, K. (1984), *Children's Writing and Reading: Analysing Classroom Language*. Oxford: Blackwell.

Plowden Report (1967), *Children and Their Primary Schools*. London: Her Majesty's Stationery Office.

Plum, G. (1988), 'Text and contextual conditioning in spoken English', unpub. PhD thesis, University of Sydney.

Plum, G.A. (1998). *Text and Contextual Conditioning in Spoken English: A Genre-based Approach* (Monographs in Systemic Linguistics, no. 10). Nottingham: Department of English Studies, University of Nottingham.

Reid, I. (1987), *The Place of Genre in Learning: Current Debates*. Geelong, Victoria: Typereader Publications no. 1. Centre for Studies in Literary Education.

Rothery, J. (1990), ' "Story" writing in primary schools: assessing narrative type genres, unpub. PhD thesis, University of Sydney.

Rothery, J. (1991), ' "Story" writing in primary school: assessing narrative type genres', unpub. PhD thesis, University of Sydney.

Rothery, J. (1996), 'Making changes: developing an educational linguistics', in R. Hasan and G. Williams (eds), *Literacy in Society* (Applied Linguistics and Language Study Series, General Ed. C.N. Candlin). London and New York: Longman, 86–123.

Rothery, J. and Macken, M. R. (1991), 'Developing critical literacy through systemic functional linguistics: unpacking the "hidden curriculum" for writing in junior secondary English in New South Wales'. Monograph 1 in *Issues in Education for the Socially and Economically Disadvantaged*. Sydney: Metropolitan East Disadvantaged Schools Program.

Sacks, H. (1992), *Lectures on Conversation* (ed. Gail Jefferson, Introduction by E. Schegloff). London and Cambridge, MA: Blackwell.

Sinclair, J. McH. and Brazil, D. (1982), *Teacher Talk*. Oxford: Oxford University Press.

Sinclair, J. McH. and Coulthard, R. M. (1975), *Towards an Analysis of Discourse: The English Used by Teachers and Pupils*. London: Oxford University Press.

Singh, M. (1990), 'Mapping possibilities for a critical geography', *Geographical Education*, 6(2), 8–14.

Slater, F. (1995), 'Geography into the future', *Geographical Education*, 8(3), 4–6 and 63.

Stubbs, M. (1976), *Language, Schools and Classrooms* (Contemporary Sociology of the School series). London: Methuen.

Stubbs, M. (1986), *Educational Linguistics*. Oxford: Blackwell.

Unsworth, L. (ed.) (2000), *Researching Language in Schools and Communities: Functional Linguistic Perspectives*. London: Cassell Academic.

Unsworth, I. (2001), *Teaching Multiliteracies across the Curriculum: Changing Contexts of Text and Image*. Buckingham and Philadelphia: Open University Press.

Van Lier, L. (1996), *Interaction in the Language Curriculum: Awareness, Autonomy and Authenticity* (Applied Linguistics and Language Study Series, series editor: C. Candlin). London & New York: Longman.

Van Lier, L. (2000), 'An ecological perspective on scaffolding', a plenary paper given at the Conference on *Scaffolding Language and Learning in Educational Contexts: Sociocultural Approaches to Theory and Practice*, held at the University of Technology, Sydney, 6–8 December 2000.

Veel, R. (1997), 'Learning how to mean – scientifically speaking: apprenticeship into scientific discourse in the secondary school', in F. Christie and J. R. Martin (eds), *Genre and Institutions: Social Processes in the Workplace and School*. London and New York: Continuum, 161–95.

Wells, G. (1993), 'Reevaluating the IRF sequence: a proposal for the articulation of theories of activity and discourse for the analysis of teaching and learning in the classroom', *Linguistics and Education*, 5(1), 1–38.

Wells, G. (1999), *Dialogic Inquiry: Toward a Sociocultural Practice and Theory of Education*. Cambridge: Cambridge University Press.

Wertsch, J.V. (1985), *Vygotsky and the Social Formation of the Mind*. Cambridge: Cambridge University Press.

Wertsch, J.V. (1991), *Voices of the Mind: A Sociocultural Approach to Mediated Action*.

(Theoretical Imagination in Psychology Series). Hemel Hempstead: Harvester Wheatsheaf.

White, P. (1997) 'Death, disruption and the moral order: the narrative impulse in mass media: "hard news" reporting', in F. Christie and J.R. Martin (eds), *Genre and Institutions: Social Processes in the Workplace and School.* London and Washington, DC: Cassell, 101–33.

White, P. (1998), 'Peaks, troughs and rhythmic pulses – new approaches to modelling genre structure', a paper given at the 25th International Systemic Functional Linguistics Congress held at the University of Wales, Cardiff, July 1998.

Wignell, P. (1994), 'Genre across the curriculum', *Linguistics and Education,* 6(4), 355–72.

Williams, G. (1995), 'Joint book-reading and literacy pedagogy: a socio-semantic examination', unpub. PhD thesis, Macquarie University.

Williams, G. (2001), 'Literacy pedagogy prior to schooling: relations between social positioning and semantic variation', in A. Morais, H.Baillie and B.Thomas (eds), *Towards a Sociology of Pedagogy: The Contribution of Basil Bernstein to Research.* New York: Peter Lang.

Index

Page numbers in *italics* refer to figures.